TEMENOS

THE DESIGN AND EXPERIENCE OF
URBANISM AS SPIRITUAL PATH

WILL SELMAN

Copyright © 2023 by Will Selman
ISBN: 978-1-950186-49-5

All rights reserved. No part of this publication may be reproduced or transmitted in any form or by any means, mechanical or electronic, including photocopying and recording, or by any information storage and retrieval system, without permission in writing from the author and/or publisher.

All permissions for quotes and images are held by the author, who releases the publisher from all liability.

Cover Image "Spiral Transit" © 2023 Remedios Varo, Artists Rights Society (ARS), New York / VEGAP, Madrid
Temple of Canova photograph © can stock photo / perseomedusa

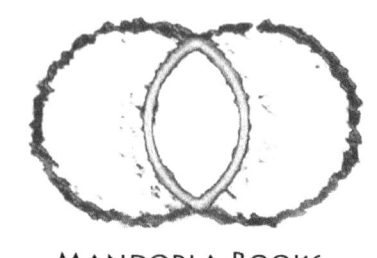

MANDORLA BOOKS
WWW.MANDORLABOOKS.COM

With thanks to many, and hope for all

TABLE OF CONTENTS

Author's Preface   1

Introduction   3
"Mind takes form in the city; and in turn, urban forms condition the mind."
– Louis Mumford

PART 1 – URBANISM AS INCARNATED SPIRITUALITY

I. Urbanism and the Spiritual Path   11
"It is good for the soul to nurture relationships with places as well as with people"
– Thomas Moore
    What is the Purpose of a City?
    What is a Spiritual Path?
    Consider the Transformer
    Incarnation

II. An Evolutionary Spirituality   23
"I have much more to say to you, but you are not ready to hear" – John 16: 12
    The Integral/ Evolutionary Movement
    The Trend to Greater Complexity and Connection
    Catafalque, the Apocalypse, and the Ages of Humanity
    Kintsugi and the Integration of Values

III. The Merging of Urbanism and Spirituality   35
"A fact is weak unless seen in light of some comprehensive truth" – *Coleridge*
    Incarnation on Earth: A Boarding School Experience
    Jane Jacobs, Meet Joseph Campbell
    The Bypass
    A Convergence of Changes
    The Story of Apsu and Tiamat

IV. Changes and Paradigm Shifts   49

"It is not the strongest of the species that survives, nor the most intelligent, but the one most responsive to change" – Charles Darwin

    Demographics
    Markets: Co-working, Co-housing, Cafés, and Dying Malls
    Climate Change
    The Increasing Pace of Change

PART 2 – THE DESIGN OF PLACE

V. A Brief History of Suburban Sprawl   57

"Everywhere is within walking distance, if you have enough time" – Steven Wright

    The Sources of Sprawl
    The Elements of Sprawl
    The Effects of Sprawl

VI. The Deeper Materialism of Michael Stone   67

"The biggest environmental disaster facing the world is the American middle-class lifestyle" – Andres Duany

    Accumulating Material Goods – And Letting Them Go
    Spiritual Materialism or Materialistic Possession
    Detachment and Connection – Two Types of Meditative Practice
    A Deeper Urbanism – A Spirituality of Embodied Connection

VII. How to Bake A City   73

"Eternity is in love with the productions of time" – William Blake

    The Ingredients of Community
    The Recipe for Community
    The Menu of Community
    The Cookbook of Community: Zoning Ordinances and Holy Scripture
    Counting Calories; or, A Few Words on Density
    The Charter of the New Urbanism

VIII. Money, Finance, Taxation: **99**
    The Practical Necessities of a Spiritual Urbanism
"Money is coined energy" – *C.G. Jung*
        Money as Stored Spiritual Potential
        A Matter of Scale
        Municipal Tax and Finance
        The Small-Scale Developer as Impresario
        Efficiency, Sustainability, or Something Else?

PART 3 – THE EXPERIENCE OF PLACE

IX. Embodiment and Place   **113**
"The real question is, can a 5-minute walk be a journey of discovery?" – *David Dixon*
        The Flaneur
        How to Walk Down the Street
        Café Life
        Living Car-free
        A Stage for the Senses
        The Night-Time Flaneur
        Bridges
        Dreaming and Waking in the Streets of Paris

X. Urbanism as Storytelling   **137**
"Frankly there isn't anyone you couldn't learn to love if you knew their story" – *Mr. Rogers*
        What Makes Us Distinctly Human
        Why Cities Exist
        Urbanism as Archetype and Dreamscape
        Urbanism and the Narrative Arc of Storytelling

XI. The Interplay of the Natural and Urban Worlds   **145**
"Man's course begins in the garden, and ends in the city" – *Alexander MacLaren*
        What is "Nature?"
        The Split
        "Green" Nature
        "Structural" Nature
        Urbanism as an Aspect of Natural Systems

PART 4 – A DEEPER URBANISM

XII. Sacred Urbanism   157
"The city is the solid exposition of the communal soul" – James Hillman
- A Human Instinct
- The Mandala: Urbanism as Cultural Shadow Work
- Chakras and the Transect
- The Begijnhof as a Spiritually Inspiring Urban Form
- Cities Built as Spiritual Metaphor
- The Importance of Nonexistent Places

XIII. The Search for New Metaphors   173
"Believe those who seek the truth. Doubt those who find it" – Andre Gide
- Conventional Paradigms
- Evolution
- Gaia
- Shamanism
- Integral Spirituality
- Jung's Alchemical Psychology
- The Urban Design of an Unknown Metaphor

XIV. L'Enfant and Washington, DC: 191
Designing the City of Metaphor
"The life of a city is rich in poetic and marvelous subjects. We are enveloped and steeped as though in an atmosphere of the marvelous; but we do not notice it." – Charles Baudelaire
- The Founding of the City
- The Story of L'Enfant
- L'Enfant's Design Process
- Conflict, Dismissal, and Ellicott's Revisions
- Calling in the Patron Goddess of Washington
- The Intentional Misalignment of the Washington Monument
- The Legacy and Opportunity
- Where is the Center?

XV. Sacred Geometry and Mythic Symbolism: 223
A New Foundation for Urban Design
"The task is to bring the ancient back to life in a new way" – C.G. Jung
- What is Sacred Geometry?
- The Creation Story

    Sacred Geometry in the Natural World
    Sacred Geometry in Art and Architecture
    Time and the Zodiac
    Symbols, Signs, and Myths
    The Alchemical City

XVI. The Principles and Practice of Symbolic Urbanism: 241
Myth and Meaning in the Design of Place

"He who moves with familiarity in this world of the street has as his god Hermes" – Károly Kerényi

    What is Symbolic Urbanism?
    Principles
    Process
    Implementation at Scale
    On Ritual as an Aspect of Placemaking
    The Task

XVII.   Sacred Redevelopment: 257
Testing Symbolic Urbanism

"The creation of the world did not take place once and for all time but takes place every day" – Samuel Beckett

    Park City Mall and Downtown Lancaster
    An Experiment in Redevelopment

XVIII. Back To School   267

"The future is already here, it's just not evenly distributed" – William Gibson

    The Inadequacy of Sustainability
    Love and Imagination as Practical Values
    Urbanism as a Tool for Expanding Spiritual Horizons
    Three Tasks of Life
    Faust and His City
    The Urbanist as Alchemist and Shaman

XIX. Attitudes and Actions   285

"A city must be a place where groups of women and men are seeking and developing the highest things they know." – Margaret Meade

    What You Can Do
    What Cities and Towns Can Do

Afterword	293
About the Author	297
Further Reading	299

AUTHOR'S PREFACE

Not until the writing was complete and the draft ready for publication, did I land on a straightforward explanation of what issue this book tries to address. As is so often the case, I found that someone else had already touched on the story and phrased it more succinctly.

An essential text for any urban planner is Camillo Sitte's work, *The Art of Building Cities*. Written in 1889, the consequential words for me appear on page 72, as follows: "At present there are severe limitations upon art in building cities. We can no longer create a superior, finished work of art like the Acropolis of Athens. Even if the tremendous cost were supportable, *we lack the basic art idea – a universally accepted explanation of reality throbbing in the daily life of the people – that could find expression in such a work...*" [emphasis mine].

What Sitte realized was that urbanism does not merely face a design problem, but an overwhelmingly larger spiritual crisis. In this, the weaknesses of our cities are merely aspects of the larger story of civilizational decay and loss of vision.

Remember that he was writing decades before the victory of the automobile and the suburban sprawl that we now suffer, a time when churches were still full and there was at least a semblance of a unified culture despite Nietzsche's misunderstood proclamation that "God is dead."

Sitte's response to this spiritual decline of western civilization was to outline an approach to urban design emphasizing a repair operation making use of artistic fundamentals for the design of civic squares and plazas amid the growing trend toward predictability and engineered problem-solving.

In retrospect, what I have been up to in my own thinking and writing is to go beyond that; to explore the reasons why we have lost that "universally accepted explanation of reality" and trace its source back to locate our culture in context and thus understand ourselves more clearly. While Sitte apparently simply accepted the slow demise of Christianity and 2,500 years of western civilization and sought to find a way to carry on as best as possible, what I have apparently been led to do is seek out a new way forward for the purposes of urban life – to experience the life of a city and make use of urbanism as a setting and tool for the advent and experience of some as-yet unrealized spiritual rebirth. What constitutes that new vision is of course unknown, but it will no doubt function as a continuation and expansion of what has gone before. So too will its urban expression.

Thus, there are two fundamental assumptions driving this book. First, the essential task of humanity, throughout all time and cultures, is spiritual quest and psychological development. This has both a personal and collective aspect and is evolutionary in nature; that is, over the centuries, humanity awakens to greater insight. This is a search to understand who and what we are; what the purpose is, if any, of our being here; and how to conduct ourselves. This psychological quest has been expressed over tens of thousands of years in the form of myth, ritual, poetry, mysticism, and religion.

The second assumption is that the built environment has a basic role in that process – that the shape and design of our cities and towns can and should support this quest. As spirits embodied in the physical realm, we are blessed with the opportunity to discover the eternal through our experience of the temporal.

In order to elevate the task of our urbanism, infusing the design and redevelopment of urban places with meaning and purpose is a critical need. Providing the right elements of community is no longer sufficient, but those elements in relation to one another in a *meaningful pattern*. Myth, symbol, and the geometry of metaphor can provide this. In his research and writing, the psychiatrist C.G. Jung described the context and need; Pierre L'Enfant provided us a method and an example in his design of Washington, DC.

As architectural critic Louis Mumford reminds us, "The task of city design involves the vaster task of rebuilding civilization."

INTRODUCTION

"Mind takes form in the city, and in turn, urban forms condition the mind"
– Louis Mumford

What place defines the center of the planet? There are as many options as there are people to identify it, but let's consider New York as a natural contender. It is said, after all, that eventually all the money on the planet (a questionable tool, I'll admit) passes through Wall Street in New York. But then, where is the heart of New York, physically? Central Park seems pretty obvious ... and the central feature of Central Park? Bethesda Fountain. Can we say then that the whole world revolves around Bethesda Fountain?

The story behind the Fountain lends some legitimacy to such an idea. Designed by Emma Stebbins and dedicated in 1873, it commemorates the opening of the Croton Aqueduct. The Aqueduct was enormously important as a source of clean water for a city perennially plagued by disease. The source of inspiration for the design was a story found in the Gospel of John. This story describes a fountain or pool named Bethesda in Jerusalem which had healing power for those suffering from illness or disease. If we ought to consider any place as a center, globally or locally, such a story of healing is as foundational as a story can be. Given the state of our civilization today, specifically that of our cities, an attitude of healing must take precedence.

We all define the center in our own way. Some places hold special cultural meaning for us, personally and privately, and in a shared cultural sense. For many years, my own private version of Bethesda Fountain was Dupont Circle in Washington, DC. For a shaman, a practitioner of the world's oldest spiritual heritage, a relationship is often formed with one special tree, representing the center of a personal universe, a portal or doorway into the larger spiritual realm. Such ancient relationships with place – to a memorable tree, or pond, rock formation, or other natural feature – have often formed the beginning of an urban settlement. As G.K. Chesterton has said, "Go back to the darkest roots of civilization and you will find them knotted around some sacred stone or encircling some sacred well. People first paid honor to a spot and later gained glory for it."

An intriguing question emerges from this: can such inspirational centers of passion and energy be created by intentional design as well as from the natural energy of the earth itself? The story of Bethesda Fountain tells us it can. The title of this book, *Temenos*, speaks to this. The term is Greek in origin, referring to the space fronting a temple, usually designed as a formal plaza, which had been designated as sacred space in its relation to a sacred temple. The temple itself may have been originally seen as sacred space by virtue of occupying some original sacred natural feature; the temenos expanded this to reach out to the wider city. The working assumption of this book is that now more than ever, the entirety of a city must be viewed as sacred space.

The recent renewed interest in urban living here in the United States has come about for many reasons, not least the mortgage and financial crisis of 2008. Shifting cultural values certainly play a major part as well; the desire for "experience" over acquiring "things" seems to have taken hold at about that time. My sense is that a larger global shift in spiritual need is also reflected here. All those aspects of civilization we hold dear – art and museums, education and universities, music and concert halls, laws and courts of justice – have always been brought together in memorable urban settings since we began building cities over 6,000 years ago. A city or town then is the metaphorical cup into which we pour all the lessons of life, all the aspirations of civilization. It is the manifestation of our collective spiritual journeys. As cultural values change, as indeed is required of us now, our more soulful sense of the purpose of cities must rise to the occasion. The time is right to rediscover an old, or perhaps add a new layer of understanding of the purpose of place-making – the creation of meaning and purpose.

A city provides this by operating as a classroom and laboratory for the development of soul. We find this in the everyday experience of simply walking down the street, observing the small, ordinary activities of normal life; our sense of connection and the circle of empathy is expanded in this way. At the same time, we may be confronted with a grander, though more subtle, even hidden, meaning of cultural significance. The urban writer Louis Mumford reminds us that among the chief functions of a city is to convert dead matter into living symbols of art.

INTRODUCTION

While our ancestors thought and acted in such terms, we no longer do, in our rational and agnostic fashion. For the past several decades, since we chose as a culture to abandon cities for suburbia, our public imagination has viewed cities as a collection of problems to be solved. But solutions aren't as much about finding the right technical fix, but reframing the way we think about urbanism. What is its purpose? Get that right, and new and unexpected solutions, technical and otherwise, begin to appear and fall into place. The city is not a problem to be solved so much as an opportunity to be taken.

Redefining and reimagining the city must include redefining ourselves. We are essentially spirits who are temporarily embodied physically, seeking to awaken into ever-increasing consciousness. The whole sweep of history, and thus of the city, is the story of (god/ creator/ spirit/ source ... choose your favored term) breaking into ever-greater conscious manifestation and relationship with humanity and all creation. Our role is to act as tools of that manifestation. Cities develop for reasons of politics, security, economics, and technology, of course, but they are also shaped by the larger aspirations and values of the soul.

We find ourselves at an epochal transition point in history. A break with the past has occurred, both culturally and urbanistically, and we must knit the pieces back together in a new, more comprehensive manner. This requires looking back to, respecting, and making use of our ancestors' intentions and knowledge, as well as looking forward with our own insights and technical skills. As the urbanist Kevin Lynch reminds us in his book *The Image of the City*, "We need an environment which is not simply well organized but poetic and symbolic as well." Poetry, symbol, myth, and metaphor come to us through dreams and visions. The material used by soul to speak to us in visions and dreams comes from the natural world. The natural world easily accommodates this process as a setting, providing all sorts of material for symbols – plants, animals, rocks, wind, and water, the whole of the natural landscape. We have been interacting with the natural world for thousands of generations, since our biological beginnings, so the images are deeply embedded in us.

The human environment, which we construct for ourselves, also has a history, though not nearly as long. Extending back 6,000 and perhaps as much as 8,000 years, our ancestors created a built environment of cities for their most significant places, with symbolic meaning designed into the physical layout – an immersive environment of their cultural aspirations and cosmological understanding. This continued perhaps as recently as the 1700s, through many different visions and philosophies. Starting in the 1700s, however, this came to a slow halt in the western world, so that our cities today reflect no spiritual meaning; efficient engineering and financial return are the only apparent goals now, leaving our cities, towns, and most obviously our suburbs, with the harsh look of mere infrastructure.

The city has traditionally been the highest manifestation of humanity's attempt to unite spirit and matter, to align physical matter with heavenly aspirations. Increasingly we spend our time disconnected from natural settings and interact primarily in and with the created/ built environment. In our ever more technocratic and engineering mindset, we are not designing places rich in symbolic meaning for the "creative spiritual forces" to use as tools of communication. Almost no urban source material exists for any creative "spiritual force" to use as a symbolic language to speak to us. There is almost no valuable symbolic material built into our cities that can act as a language between our ego and soul. As spiritual beings, a fundamental task of ours is to grow in consciousness; and as the psychiatrist C.G. Jung has said, "Formlessness seems to be practically the equivalent of unconsciousness." Giving form to our physical environment, and infusing it with meaning and purpose, is an aspect of coming to greater intentional consciousness.

We give form in such small acts as arranging flowers amidst the place settings at our dinner table, and we are quite adept at composing our homes into the comfortable retreats we crave. However, at the largest scale of physical form, that of city-making, we are failing miserably. If the forming of space is an aspect of coming to consciousness, the consciousness we are coming to seems quite neurotic, scrambled, and misdirected.

This book is heavy on anecdote and metaphor, and it is safe to say that little of it is original; it leans heavily on the thoughts of a lengthy list of other writers, spiritual teachers, and urbanists more capable than I. What I contribute is seeing links and connections, assembling the insights of others in new ways, and finding metaphors for viewing the world of urbanism through my own soulful lens.

I have structured the book in four parts, each including chapters on what might be seen as random subject matter. There is a good deal

INTRODUCTION

of bouncing around from one chapter to the next. This results from my attempt to bring together wildly divergent subject matter, from a discussion of mythological symbolism to the technical aspects of real estate finance. The reader must be willing to bounce along with patience, hopefully seeing my intent to reach an end goal in my own roundabout way. In these pages there are a dozen or more ideas than I can successfully explore. I sometimes skim very lightly over deep waters. Readers may find themselves frustrated by the thin discussion of topics; they are of course encouraged to go further than I have. There is material enough here to last a lifetime of discovery. This is also the result of my intention to introduce two separate communities to one another, which seem hardly aware of each other's presence, but I feel must be in deep discussion together. One of those communities, the realm of professional urbanism, may include professionals who seek to deepen their sources of insight and infuse their work with a greater depth of meaning. The other is that made up of spiritual seekers wishing to ground their quest more firmly in the everyday experience of their built surroundings. Both have much to say to one another.

Readers will note that I use the terms "psychological," "spiritual," and "psycho/spiritual" interchangeably. I do so for the sake of those who may not share any particular spiritual sensibility. In my personal view, the work involved is the same whether we think in terms more traditionally spiritual or religious, or more rational and psychological. In either case, my effort remains the same – to explore how to urbanistically support and symbolize the process of personal inner growth.

The question being explored here is this; how can the design and experience of urbanism, in all its various forms, support our personal and collective spiritual journeys? As Jung once remarked, "There is no coming to individuation without relationship to place." The places we build reflect the values we hold. Aristotle has said that the highest wisdom is that needed to design cities. Are we up to the task? A very different outlook is needed to achieve this today, to not only repair the damage we have inflicted on both the natural and built environments, but to equal, perhaps surpass, the best that our ancestors produced.

This book grew out of my attempt to weave together the two strands of life that have been with me since childhood: urbanism and spiritual quest. It is perhaps also an attempt to introduce two communities of readers to one another, each of whom needs the other in ways not commonly recognized. These pages grew almost on their own, turning into something much more than I anticipated. This is particularly evident in the chapters of Part 4. I was seemingly led purposefully from one insight to another. This came from research and conversation as well as meditation and a series of synchronicities that have directed my life over the last seven years. In my effort to "knit" the strands of my life together, I came to understand that cities can be reclaimed as sources of spiritual symbolism, expression, and experience. I am convinced that this is a vital necessity. These pages describe my experience of this vision and my attempt to make it manifest.

PART 1

URBANISM AS INCARNATED SPIRITUALITY

CHAPTER I

Urbanism and the Spiritual Path

"It is good for the soul to nurture relationships with places as well as with people" – Thomas Moore

As a young child, I was blessed with being raised in settings that could not be more different from one another. For three and a half years, my family lived in Saint-Germaine-en-Laye, on the western outskirts of Paris, France. The most sophisticated urban city in the world was my daily experience. Then for the following eight years, I was raised in a small beach cottage in Virginia, overlooking the Chesapeake Bay, surrounded by empty salt marshes. Like any boy might, I spent hours exploring the marshes filled with bayberry shrubs and loblolly pines. My strongest memory is of constructing a primitive hut from old driftwood found on the beach, weaving cattail rushes to form walls and roof. In both settings, the streets of Paris and the sandy marshes, I had a clear sense of place, that each contained something important. There was something important about being there, and doing that. I sensed the soul they each contained. How do these two fit together, the design of place and spiritual experience? That question is the object of this entire book. First, we must get a sense of what the two are, in and of themselves. So perhaps this first chapter is more about definitions.

What is Urbanism?

Why we build cities is a complicated question that others have explored deeply. There are of course many reasons, the most basic being defense, economics, mutual support, and religion. Humans have been building cities, towns, and villages for at least 6,000 years. We have plenty of experience to draw from; urbanism, or perhaps more generally, the shaping of place, can be considered an instinct of ours.

A good approach to defining my understanding of urbanism for a typical audience is to distinguish it from architecture. For me, architecture is the design and programming of buildings and structures. Urbanism, on the other hand, refers to the parts of a city, town, or neighborhood, how they are assembled, and how the parts work together to form a whole. Buildings (architecture) are a fundamental element of urbanism of course, along with streets, open and green spaces, commercial, civic, and residential components, and so on. Urbanism then is about providing choices and connections in the built environment.

A great many of my contemporaries will dispute my limited perspective on the nature of architectural work. Indeed, architecture as a profession once held primacy in the creation of urban places, but now is limited essentially to individual buildings, viewed far too often as merely sculptural objects in space, usually devoid of context or connection. I view the fall of architecture as symptomatic of the larger collapse of the values of western civilization. Art, architecture, and music as well once had an unspoken understanding and task to reflect and enhance the highest values of civilization. We no longer have such cultural aspirations or even much respect for our history, so it is no wonder that today's architecture is mediocre at best. With few inspirational and aspirational values for it to reflect, the best-known practitioners apparently seek nothing more than the expression of only their own unique and personal concepts. As members of a disintegrating society that loves nothing more than the entertainment of ego, this is hardly surprising. The practitioners of contemporary urban planning and development, as opposed to architects, have their own massive failures to answer for; Chapter V is devoted to this dilemma.

When I speak of urbanism, I envision more than simply the downtown of a large metropolitan city. Urbanism encompasses a full variety of human settlement patterns, including residential neighborhoods, small towns, villages, and hamlets – the whole of the built environment.

I generally include the term "sustainable" to describe my view of urbanism. Cities certainly are almost impossible to kill and can sometimes last thousands of years. While sustainability is a term and attitude currently fashionable (or is it passe already, replaced by some newer more enlightened term?), it speaks to a true need. The current trajectory of land use and development patterns set in the US for the past 75 years or so has emphasized separating each element of life into isolated pockets connected only by the automobile. This has caused enormous damage, not only environmentally but socially, culturally, fiscally, and spiritually. That pattern cannot be sustained.

A sustainable urbanism is one in which the physical pattern of development, including infrastructure, has a built-in versatility – the flexibility to respond to a full range of needs that may change over time, with as little energetic input as possible. This means not just the need for the practical functionality of streets and sewers but also, unexpectedly, the need for a place of beauty and grace and love. Just as in our personal relationships, we will not care for and maintain a place we do not respect and love.

In searching for a yet more satisfying description of urbanism, I cannot improve upon the words of architectural theoretician and mathematician Christopher Alexander. In the preface of his book *The Battle for the Life and Beauty of the Earth*, he describes his view on the purpose of architecture. I substitute the term urbanism for his use of architecture, but the words still ring true: "The purpose of all [urbanism], the purpose of its physical structure and organization, is to provide opportunities for life-giving situations. The central issue of [urbanism], and its central purpose, is to create those configurations and social situations which provide encouragement and support for life-giving comfort and profound satisfaction – sometimes excitement – so that one experiences life as worth living."

So, with all that background regarding how I understand urbanism, the question remains: why do we build these places? We clearly are attracted to urban living. Just like any other animal, humans will seek out the most advantageous places to live. If the total global population was spread out evenly, each person would have 5 acres of land for themselves; but actually, 50% of the human population inhabits just 1% of the land. I posit three reasons cities exist that help us understand why. First, urban living is practical. Urbanism gives us protection, efficiency, and ease of commerce. It is a way of wealth creation. In an article entitled "Why Cities Exist," Malcolm Gladwell shows that the three wealthiest nations on earth have the highest urban populations, all over 90% – Luxembourg with 91% of its population living in urban settings, Qatar at 99%, and Singapore with a completely urbanized population at 100%. The three poorest nations all have urban populations under 50%, including Congo at 43%,

Central African Republic at 40%, and Burundi at a mere 13%.

The second reason is that we are social creatures, a species that enjoys the company of others. We have been so forever, for millions of years, and long before we evolved into modern humans some 200,000 years ago or started building cities over 6,000 years ago.

Finally, I believe we build cities for reasons that we can term either religious, spiritual, or psychological. In its earliest forms, urban life provided a new and vastly enhanced setting for the expression of spiritual reflection and practice that had been our heritage for the previous 35,000 to 50,000 years. Urban life also in a very real sense required humans to discover new spiritual truths; the story of the Mesopotamian gods Apsu and Tiamat is a prime example that will be explored in Chapter III.

A succinct vision of this urge of ours to create cities comes from Louis Mumford: "The chief functions of the city are to convert power into form, energy into culture, dead matter into living symbols of art, biological reproduction into social creativity." Cities are, in other words, a means to transform us into something greater, our higher selves.

What is a Spiritual Path?

Well, this is no small subject to take on, is it?! But indulge me while I explore it in-depth for the rest of this chapter, as it's foundational for answering the question I posited in the introduction: how can the design and experience of urbanism, in all its various forms, support our personal and collective spiritual journeys? On spirituality, I have my own very eclectic perspective, but perhaps a good starting point is the well-known quote from Pierre Teilhard de Chardin: "We are not humans who might have a spiritual experience; we are spirits who are having a human experience." From this everything else flows.

A spiritual life consists of seeking a connection to "the other side," however that is conceived – eternity, reality, one's higher self, unity, God, the Universe, Source. More than that, such a quest seeks to discover how we (collectively and privately) are to live and conduct ourselves in the here and now. What then would a spiritual being intend for themselves out of life, of physical incarnation on earth? My sense is that our purposes, our intentions as incarnated spiritual beings, focus on two things: experience and growth – to become more than we currently are, or more simply put, to become more conscious.

URBANISM AND THE SPIRITUAL PATH

The work of C.G. Jung provides much insight in this; his concept of "individuation" is essentially this process of conscious and intentional awakening. Aniela Jaffé, a student, colleague, and editor of Jung's, explains the process thus: "Basically, individuation consists of constantly renewed, constantly needed attempts to amalgamate the inner images with outer experience. Or to put it differently, it is the endeavor to make what fate intends to do with us entirely our own intention." My own interpretation is hopefully a little clearer, if less precise. For me, individuation is the process of bringing my conscious intentions into alignment with what my unconscious – my soul, my higher self – envisions for my conscious life. Yet another approach; I am not truly the author of my life but an actor riffing or ad-libbing off a script that I can only partially see. Individuation – the process of psychological and spiritual growth – is the process of seeing the script, written by my soul, more clearly. This process is natural in one sense and takes place whether we intend it or not. Just as an acorn grows into an oak, a kitten into a cat, so do humans grow toward their intended higher self. It is the process of bringing elements of our unconscious lives into conscious awareness and aligning their purposes. While it happens as a normal aspect of growth, it is best accomplished with intentionality. Thus, we can say that a fundamental task of humanity is to discover the eternal through the experience of the temporal. That temporality is expressed most completely in human terms in the experience of urban life and form, of civilization in its fundamental, physical manifestation.

Consider the Christian story of Christ dying on the cross. From the view of individuation, Christ did not die on the cross so that we do not have to; we must. Rather, Christ gives us the example of how to die to unnecessary and unhelpful things before our body dies, so that we may live and focus instead on our true purpose.

Any approach, be it Zen meditation, monastic chant, psychological reflection, Catholic prayer, shamanic journeying, Bible study, or any of a thousand other methods, is merely the bridge; the goal remains the same no matter the bridge we choose. The role of urbanism in this process is to act as a stage upon which we can discover all those existing bridges and construct one for ourselves.

We are therefore not intended to seek ways to escape this life, through meditation or enlightenment or anything else, but to dive into it, to participate in both physical and psychological experiences. This involves pain and pleasure, joy and sadness. Meditation and similar spiritual disciplines are best understood not as tools for escape, but as ways to wake ourselves up and make us more open to and aware of the love available to us, the life in us and around us, and the lessons to be learned.

A distinction should be made here between what I understand as "religion" as opposed to "spirituality." Each is an aspect of the other. I distinguish them thus. Religion is a shared, socially sanctioned and collective effort to understand matters of a mystical or spiritual nature, and involves shared customs and rituals, intended to describe for its followers what lies on the other side of "the veil," in the spiritual realm. A spiritual quest, on the other hand, is the process of "lifting the veil" for oneself. Both use myth and metaphor in that revelatory process; both offer strengths and dangers. Religion provides stability and continuity, maintaining and passing on a culturally established pattern of collected knowledge and wisdom. As an organized cultural system, it is identified with a patriarchal vision. It operates best when in humble service to a private individual spirituality. Religion's partner, spirituality, is concerned with the new and creative, as part of and in service to the inner growth of the individual. The matriarchy, being nurturing yet chaotic, represents the more personal spiritual quest. Religion seeks to provide a comfortable security, while that private spiritual questing will involve uncertainty, confusion, and fear because it ventures into the unknown. Given our recent cultural history of seeking pleasure and convenience at the cost of cultural and planetary destruction, we now have to face up to a good deal of the chaotic and frightening self-reflection characteristic of spiritual quest, so as to reinvigorate our culture.

Deep in our pre-history, religion grew out of myth, which in turn may have grown out of attempts by our earliest ancestors to understand dreams. Dreams are a means for both our personal psychic unconscious and the spiritual world to communicate to our conscious egos, often through symbols, images, and metaphor. How do we reply? Perhaps both our private spiritual quests and collective ritualistic religions are our weak and imperfect conscious efforts to respond to that which we do not understand.

Formalized religion grew over time out of more ancient spiritual practices. The most ancient form of spiritual practice we're aware of is popularly called "shamanism." In early tribal cultures and many today as well, the shaman is the individual who specialized in "lifting the veil" to communicate with the spiritual realm, sending messages back and forth that provide healing and information. I see the transition from archaic yet foundational shamanism to a more formal collective cultural religion in the story of Moses and the Ten Commandments. Moses operated essentially as the shaman for his people. As the people for whom he was responsible grew in number, he began to become overwhelmed, I imagine. In such a role he was constantly asked to negotiate between various personal and everyday conflicts among neighbors and family members. Exhausted at the never-ending effort and seeking to ease his burden, he went to the mountain to seek direction for himself. There he was given the insight that the myriad conflicts his people routinely experienced fell into ten generalized categories. As a handy resource guide, he returned to the people and essentially said, "If you simply follow these ten basic principles, your lives will be much better, conflicts will be reduced, and you won't have to rely on me constantly to sort out all your troubles." Such transitions from solitary personal insight to formal organized group rules mark a basic connecting point between the spiritual and religious.

At its best, religion provides shared methods and insights, a common language to be used when publicly sharing a private spiritual experience. The distinction then between religion and spirituality is this; follow the given rules (which are generally completely appropriate) OR go into yourself, looking inward to find the larger lessons and insights. Either direction one takes – a more group-oriented religious practice or a private spiritual quest – can go wrong. And they are not exclusive; religion is intended to be a gateway to the personal spiritual life, and private spirituality involves individual ritualistic practices. But religion can become overly reliant on an increasing number of detailed rules intended to keep a society running smoothly, and thus lose sight of the prime value of the individual. A personal spiritual journey can easily veer off into undisciplined foolishness and adamant egotism, losing perspective of the whole.

Should one seek ephemeral transformation or solid continuity? Both are essential. A religious life is one of continuity, of maintaining the good that has been established. A spiritual quest is a solitary effort at transformation. Yet even the Dalai Lama has recognized this; the great majority of people have no interest in a solitary path. Most people desire to be led, to be given specific direction. Religion provides the secure and comforting foundation necessary for them. The solitary spiritual quest is for the very few – it's not at all comforting, but extremely challenging. One must confront the dangerous dragons lying within one's heart. The well-known saying is that the treasure one seeks is to be found in the place one least wants to go.

And yet this is ultimately our call. Fatima phrases the distinction between the two beautifully for me: "Religions are like windows through which we can observe the stars in the sky. You may move from one window to another, to observe from a different point of view, but you will still be viewing the same sky." This describes the religious approach; but when you are ready, feel free to walk outside and observe the sky directly – that is the spiritual path. Dig deeply enough, and every culture and civilization is found to have a religious foundation. That is essential for a healthy society. But a good religion, I contend, will teach its followers how to transcend it. That is ultimately our destination.

Consider the Transformer

We live by energy. In fact, we are essentially energy. Nikola Tesla said, "If you want to understand the Universe, think in terms of energy, frequency, and vibration." So, the Beach Boys had it right, with their "Good Vibrations"! Certainly, contemporary civilization is reliant on vibrations, the energy provided by electrical systems.

Regarding power and energy, what does a transformer do? Electrical transformers act as intermediaries to step down the enormous power generated by nuclear, coal-powered, solar, or other type of electric production, and the end user. Without a transformer, the wiring in our homes would melt and cause fires from the overwhelming amount of power sizzling down the line.

What is the spiritual connection to this? Jung is credited with saying that religion is a form of protection against a spiritual experience. An intimate confrontation with the divine can easily overwhelm an individual with its power. We can think then of Christ, or the church, as a transformer, stepping down the overwhelming power of heaven to something more manageable for the individual psyche.

We all have individual spiritual experiences (whether or not we recognize them as such) that we wish to share with others, and to gain understanding through that sharing. When we come together to share those individual experiences of the divine, we need some common language, though we inevitably find it to be insufficient. But we try anyway. Coming together in a more structured group in order to understand our individual spiritual longing is how I define religion. In order to clarify as much as possible that shared language, compromises must be made for the sake of social stability. This will satisfy some but never everyone. The intermediary tends to want, and often even need, control, in order to function properly. But the truth is, paraphrasing Heinrich Zimmer, the German linguist and scholar of Indian myth and religion, the most important things (god? the eternal?) can't be discussed, because they transcend thought. The next most important things (religion? spirituality?) are generally misunderstood, because they are thoughts referring to those most important things. The best we can really do is talk about the third most important things. So, we strive as best we can, and look for good interpreters ... good transformers.

The Protestant Reformation of the 1500s was one of many efforts throughout history to essentially dispense with the middle-man, the transformer, provided at the time by the intermediary role of the Catholic priesthood. It seems another such shift is taking place globally now. Historically, very few souls reached a level of insight such as we read in ancient texts, that of sages and saviors and heroes. However, today there are so many "transformers" available to us, not only those we conventionally think of such as Jesus, Buddha, Lao Tzu, Hildegard of Bingen, and Mohammed. We can now add to the list Jung, Mozart, Einstein, Hafiz, da Vinci, and on and on. This may frustrate my more conventional friends, but if souls reincarnate, returning with greater insight acquired over time, this should be no surprise at all. Remember, for several hundred years the early Christian church held reincarnation to be true. As the wisdom of ancient scriptures has been accumulated and integrated into the wider culture, it can be found in many more places than the old scriptures alone. Our greater cross-cultural access and communication means that we have access to truths found in more than just our own local or historic traditions.

Off-the grid living – living self-sufficiently without the benefit of hooking into electrical and sewer systems – is one metaphorical equivalent of dispensing with traditional formal religion for a more direct, manageably scaled spiritual experience. So far, the off-grid living movement has yet to show how it can scale up; it remains a goal for the vanishing few. Is this a goal that the masses can ever achieve?

Some of us can create a manner of living off the grid, independent of connection to wider civilization, usually in an attempt to become as self-sufficient and environmentally benign as possible. So too an increasing number of people are seeking to dispense with traditional, formalized religion, preferring, and able, to find spiritual growth without the need for that intermediary.

Decentralizing both energy production and spiritual authority may or may not win out in the long run, but certainly both are powerful social currents of the moment. Increasingly, individuals seem prepared to dispense with traditional and formal approaches to religion in favor of a more private spirituality, but not all are prepared to cut such a lifeline. Religion is a shared teaching tool to instruct us in our private efforts to grow spiritually. We can think of religion, then, as the "electrical infrastructure" of spiritual life.

Incarnation

There is a well-known quote, attributed to the aboriginal people of Australia: "We are all visitors to this time, this place. We are just passing through. Our purpose here is to observe, to learn, to grow, to love … and then we return home."

So, experiencing life on earth can be imagined as the boarding school of spiritual growth, and we are all students. For some it is elementary school, others graduate school – for some unfortunates it is reform school – and we all return until the lessons are learned and integrated. This idea of reincarnation is by no means rare or unusual. Remember that Christianity too kept the notion of reincarnation for the first couple of hundred years of its founding before, I imagine, the early church fathers realized it didn't support the level of political and cultural control they desired.

Much of the personal spiritual growth that is intended for us takes place without our awareness, but we are best served when this spiritual journey is made conscious with intentionality. The physical places in which we locate ourselves therefore have a significant impact on our opportunities for spiritual growth. If this physical world is the "schoolhouse" to which we are all sent, we have a large responsibility to provide the most advantageous, well-organized, and resourced classrooms possible. This means creating places of grace, beauty, memory, connection, and interaction.

We can understand ourselves as the container for soul. I imagine there came a point in our far distant past – 50,000 years ago is a likely period according to various bits of archeological evidence – when humanity evolved to a point where consciousness broke through and soul embodied into us more fully than ever before. This point in our experience is memorialized in the story of Adam and Eve in the Garden of Eden. Being thrown out of the Garden of Eden is a metaphor for no longer being able to act purely out of animal instinct, but having grown into a moment of conscious awakening and all the attendant fears and responsibilities. Yet the post-Jungian therapist and writer James Hillman makes clear we need to go beyond ourselves, and other creatures, as the only container. Fetish objects have always been understood as able to contain "spirit." An object can contain powerful psychic energy when artists or craftsmen imbue their soul into an object. We say that someone has "really put their soul into it." This is a basic reason art moves us so deeply. This was understood as far back as Pythagoras and no doubt further. His understanding describes to us the various ways such psychic energy manifests in the world: "Consciousness sleeps in a stone, dreams in a plant, awakens in an animal, becomes self-aware in humanity."

We are the containers of soul, and we in turn create more objects for soul to inhabit. The very civilizations we build for ourselves are the greatest such containers. Cities are the cup into which we pour all our hopes and aspirations; we gather all our greatest institutions together in celebration. Just as many places in the natural world contain some power that we revere, so too can such power be created by us. Cities are the containers of containers.

In a conversation with journalist and political commentator Bill Moyers regarding the life of myth and spirit, Joseph Campbell said, "You don't need all this. You can live perfectly well without a spiritual life. It's your life, go right ahead." And he is right. But such an attitude, I'm sure he would agree, sort of misses the point of being alive. We are all on some sort of journey, but it is best conducted with intentional consciousness. We might not think in terms of anything "spiritual" but rather psychological, or simply take on an attitude of kindness and joyful curiosity. We might express this in acts like spiritual meditation, but just as easily in acts like writing music, cultivating a garden, or conducting scientific research. In its broadest sense, the role of urbanism in connection with religious or spiritual practice is to act as the stage where bridges between them can be envisioned, refined, and constructed. The setting in which we conduct our lives and act out our visions, however we define them, is the city.

CHAPTER II

An Evolutionary Spirituality

"I have much more to say to you, but you are not ready to hear"
— John 16:12

For the last 1,000 years, the city of Venice has been sinking on average 2.75 inches every century; the last hundred years have seen over 9 inches. This is mostly because it is built on pilings sunk into a soggy marsh; sea level rise now compounds the problem. Once its location was an advantage; the city began as a hard-to-reach refuge from invading hordes when the Roman Empire collapsed. Through the centuries, when a building sank a bit too much and flooded too often, it would either be raised up above its flood line or be razed and a new higher building constructed over its foundations. But around the year 1800, Venetians stopped this practice. Perhaps they sensed that the city was so magnificently beautiful that it had reached an apex and it was too perfect to change. In any case, modifications ceased, and for the last 200 years, the city has become a fossilized museum, no longer responding to the shifting foundations below.

This is not unlike our contemporary treatment of western civilization's foundational cultural and religious institutions.

Such an image, of buildings being constructed above the foundations of previous structures, is reminiscent of a dream once described by Jung, the preeminent psychological thinker. In the dream, Jung experienced being in the upper story of "his house," which was decorated with contemporary furnishings. In exploring the lower stories, he saw that below him was a main floor with medieval or Renaissance art and furniture. Behind a door, he found a passageway to a lower cellar that seemed to be from the Roman era. From within that space, he descended an ancient staircase leading to a rough cave cut into the bedrock, which held bones and broken pottery, "like the remains of a primitive culture."

I too once had a dream like this. I found myself in a house consisting of many floors with one room each. My task was to ascend to the top by climbing the stairs, but I found my progress slowed by the stairs themselves. They would move backward as I tried to ascend, like trying to climb up a downward-moving escalator. When I finally reached a higher floor, I was told by someone that the stairs would cooperate if, at each floor, I would leave a gift for the ghosts of all the children who haunted the house.

How are these stories connected? Jung's dream, as he came to understand it, represents how the human psyche rests on the old foundations of our most ancient ancestors. We have not only evolved physically, but psychologically as well, with the ancient ways of thinking, feeling, and understanding still embedded within us. Much of mythology essentially consists of these unconscious memories which may precede civilization by tens of thousands of years and more. We each have personal and family stories, which are part of an older cultural history, in turn resting on archaic mythic symbolism, all of which has as its foundation the brain chemistry and neural behavioral patterns developed from millions of years of primordial evolutionary biology. The paleoanthropologist Genevieve von Petzinger points out that the earliest modern humans, physiologically just like us, reach back about 200,000 years. The first signs of "culture" – non-practical, symbolic behavior – are found about 120,000 years ago. Then about 50,000 years ago, a kind of creative explosion took place of creative and symbolic practices indicating that the afterlife was at least as important to our ancestors as this life.

We can see from this that the emergence of a conscious human ego, arising out of unconscious instinct, takes thousands of years, and undoubtedly remains incomplete. The myths and religions of our ancestors tell the story of this process as best they understood. Such a deeply rooted psychological foundation must be understood, respected, and accounted for properly, or else it will rule our lives without us realizing what is happening.

Likewise, our cities are built up, literally, from the ruins of the past. For instance, many of the medieval and Renaissance buildings of Rome were built using the same stones from the ancient empire a thousand years earlier. When we ignore our foundations and stop respecting and building up from the past, we sink back into the mire.

AN EVOLUTIONARY SPIRITUALITY

When we create the future, whether regarding one's personal life aspirations or laying out the street pattern of a new neighborhood, the old ways and habits of being are not to be discarded as outmoded waste, but understood, respected, made use of, and built upon. As Jung phrased it, "the task is to give birth to the old in a new way." This reveals the psychological truth that knowing ourselves requires an understanding of our past in totality – the personal experiences and family stories, cultural heritage, our biological and psychological evolution, and most deeply, the individual conscious and unconscious self, all of which continue to shape us.

The Integral/ Evolutionary Spirituality Movement

What might a new way, built upon the old, look like? At this point in history, the saying goes, there is nothing new under the sun. Even so, our understanding and vision has greatly expanded over the centuries. Scientific discoveries have for the past 500 years gifted us with astonishing new perspectives. Technology has given us a world, for the first time in human experience, in which every culture and civilization is connected to all others and can – *must* – be considered with respect and understanding.

In holding this ability to see for the first time with a truly global vision, we can begin to understand the many ways in which all spiritual quest traditions are essentially the same, differing only in their locally accented stories. As Joseph Campbell and others have clearly shown us, all cultural myths basically tell the same stories, with variations coming through localized geography and history. The tribal stories of peoples from the Arctic to the Sahara to the Amazon, and their rituals and initiations, always speak of personal inward quests to conquer fear, overcome chaos, and develop an organized culture, thus gaining a wider vision. The details generally reflect only whether their habitat is dominated by sand or snow, bison or tiger.

After tens and even hundreds of thousands of years of human experience, however, our very recently gained understanding of the world has changed dramatically with the dominance of rational, quantitative thinking. While our distant ancestors viewed the world as a unity to be respected and left alone, our more recent rational scientific method has for the past 500 years been one of dissection. That is, we have gained our understanding of the physical world through a constant process of picking apart the pieces of a whole into smaller and smaller constituent parts. Louis Mumford describes this scientific process of analysis: "The new system of dealing with mathematically analyzable fragments instead of with wholes gave the first intelligible collective means of approaching such wholes … the method of abstraction led to the discovery of units that could be investigated completely, because they were dismembered and fragmentary." That method seems to have been taken to its natural end, however; it has run its course and become harmful rather than helpful. The transition which seems to be taking place now in scientific thinking is precisely its historical opposite: a search for connections, patterns, and relationships – how all those parts operate together to form greater and more complex "wholes."

This attitude is taking place in the realm of spiritual thinking as well. A group of contemporary thinkers, including Ken Wilber, Craig Hamilton, Brian Swimme, and Don Beck, emerged some years ago around what has become known as Evolutionary or Integral Spirituality. As Wilber defines it, "integral" simply refers to an approach seeking to include as many important truths from as many disciplines as possible, from the East as well as the West, from premodern and modern and postmodern, from the hard science of physics to the softer approaches of psychology and spirituality. The intent is to find the similarities and shared religious and mythological concepts found throughout the world through all of history and integrate them into a deeper and more universal understanding; to make such an evolutionary perspective an intentional, conscious effort of spiritual development.

The Trend Toward Greater Complexity and Connection

There seems to be no discernable, specific end goal that evolution aims toward. The goal of evolution seems to be much more practical – of finding the most appropriate, efficient, and sustainable set of forms and patterns given an ever-changing environment. With this caveat; the trend that the evolutionary process does seem to emphasize over time is that of ever-increasing complexity and inter-connection. In his highly provocative book, *Nonzero*, journalist and author Robert Wright outlines this evolutionary preference and its impact not only regarding biological systems, but those of astrophysics, culture, and political organization as well. To my mind then, we can think of evolution as an organizing system that does not simply move us from bacteria to ape to human, but from simplicity and isolation to complexity and connection. The end result for a human life in this movement toward connected complexity is the fundamental desire and need for meaning.

This search for meaning is, of course, a psychological process. Our growth, psychologically or spiritually, involves continually exploring and integrating new insight and knowledge. This is painful because it requires us to let go of once cherished and reliable assumptions that have become outmoded. Merely becoming a master of maintaining a set of boundaries is inadequate; we must also continually expand our boundaries. We must step outside of the known to accomplish this. Using the conventional western image of this process, Christ is the representation of one who willingly accepts death and renewal.

With this evolutionary perspective, we can consider that the original sin was to have become conscious. This is the story of the Garden of Eden, in which we were originally free of conscious acts and functioned purely on animal instinct. We were cast out of the easy perfection of unconscious instinct when we awoke into consciousness and also began acting out of intention. Yet here we are, bearing an unbearable responsibility. Worse, the follow-up sin of today is to remain only half awake. In our normal semi-conscious state of everyday living, we remain subject to our old animal instincts but with little to no understanding of, let alone control over ourselves.

All in or not at all; once awakened as a species, there is no going back for any of us. Vanishingly few of us are "all in," able to rise to the challenge. I suspect this is the admonishment in the Book of Revelations against remaining "lukewarm," neither awake nor asleep.

In trying to understand the process of evolution and its psycho-spiritual implications, I was struck by the idea of selective breeding. We have been breeding various plants and animals for millennia; the development of civilization itself can be seen as a sort of intentional breeding. Can we think of breeding as "intentional evolution?" This idea is not new but remains a bit controversial. Certainly, a process of self-improvement that we might choose to undertake is a sort of evolution of the self. We are seeking to reach a higher level of selfhood in some fashion … to "breed" a better self. Perhaps in the ancient days beyond prehistory, when humans first became conscious and self-aware as represented in the story of Adam and Eve, we moved ourselves beyond the natural unconscious process of evolution into a process of conscious "intentional breeding," constantly seeking and striving. Of course, part of this has to do with the settings in which we place ourselves. The original setting, according to the Old Testament, was known as Paradise. My understanding of the translation of the term "paradise" means "a walled garden." The natural environment for humanity is thus a place of harmonious balance of the natural and the urban. We need to "breed" more balanced and harmonious cities and towns in which we can consciously, intentionally evolve toward wholeness.

Catafalque, the Apocalypse, and the Ages of Humanity

There is an enormous amount of apocalyptic thinking in the world these days. People from all walks of life seem to have some sense of an impending dramatic shift in the world, if not outright doom. This is not limited to the world of evangelical Christianity; it is found in right-wing politics, left-leaning environmentalism, conventional political economics, New Age spirituality, and the movies cranked out by pop culture. It's as if the collective unconscious of humanity is anticipating that the time is ripe for fundamental change, though the form this might take is an open question. This thinking is not new, but is a repeating theme in history.

Ken Wilbur, the philosopher, mystic, and a leader in integral thinking, has described five stages of human development over the past 35,000 years, from the archaic and magical to our current rational pluralistic perspective. All the previous stages have been marked, he notes, by a deep belief that their values and vision were the only true ones, all others being wrong, threatening, or even dangerous. We now find ourselves at the beginning of yet another stage of human development. This newly emerging stage, according to Wilbur, is distinct in that it accepts truth and value in all previous stages, perspectives, and traditions. There is room for all, and all can contribute; every stage and all perspectives are true, at least to a partial degree, when understood metaphorically. This will define the psycho/spiritual sensibilities of the next age we're moving toward.

Or rather, we find ourselves not quite at the beginning of some new age, but the end of the old. In his massive work, *Catafalque*, Peter Kingsley describes this ending in painful detail. Kingsley, a philosopher and scholar of ancient Greek thinking, focuses this work on the horrifying end of the 2,500-year history of western civilization we now experience, rather than the hope of what may follow. He traces the western heritage gifted to us from the Greek philosophers, rather than beginning with the Christian church, and finds at its roots an unexpected foundation. We understand that the Greeks brought us rationality, logic, and discursive philosophy; this is the gift to the world that the west has to offer. Yet that heritage has at its base quite a mystical, rather than rational, beginning. Two most important Pre-Socratic philosophers, including Empedocles but particularly Parmenides (the two were roughly contemporaries, living about 475 BC) were essentially what we now describe as shamans. As such, they communicated with the spiritual realm, bringing back healing and wisdom to share with the world. This tradition was continued for centuries by the Oracle of Delphi. The rules of logic and rational thinking were transmitted to Parmenides in the form of a poem, by a goddess who appeared to him while on a mystically ecstatic journey to the underworld. The western tradition of logic and rational thinking, which now rejects any form of religion or mystical thinking, has that very spirit as its foundation – a long and rich heritage Kingsley sees as lost now. As a result of this loss of our own heritage, many spiritually inclined westerners look elsewhere, and romanticize, honor, and desire to learn from the traditions of Buddhism and tribal shamanism, for instance. Yet we are almost completely ignorant of our own traditions which have shaped us for generations, without realizing that the ideas and values we seek in other traditions are also to be found in our own heritage.

Jung brings a more detailed understanding of this than Wilbur and takes into account a history far deeper than mentioned by Kingsley. His work as a psychologist went well beyond research into the psychic life of individuals – he ventured to discover the larger story, over the course of tens and hundreds of thousands of years and more, of the spiritual and psychological development of humanity and its impact on civilization, and the emergence of conscious self-awareness out of unconscious animal instinct. His thinking in this regard is iconoclastic to say the least, and remains outside conventional ideas regarding most spirituality, psychology, and history. Even so, many of his insights have become embedded in contemporary thinking, unacknowledged but influential.

A pattern of this evolutionary psychic development of humanity was found by Jung, quite unexpectedly, in the zodiac.

Very roughly speaking, the twelve houses of the zodiac describe a series of constellations which arc through the night sky. The earth not only rotates around the sun and spins on its axis, but that axis also wobbles, creating a shifting scene in the sky. This wobble takes approximately 25,000-27,000 years to complete. This time period is divided into twelve because of the twelve constellations that progress across the sky. This division into twelve goes back at least 2,500 years ago in Babylon and Mesopotamia. Each of these twelve "ages" or periods last about 2,000 to 2,150 years. Currently, we reside in the final stages of the Age of Pisces; coming up next is the Age of Aquarius. Prior to Pisces was Aries, and before that, Taurus.

Looking back several thousand years to the Age of Taurus, Jung notes that at that time – very approximately 4,000 to 2,000 BC – the conventional religious sacrifice in the Middle East was a bull, which as it happens is the symbol for Taurus. Moses, however, as leader of the people of Israel, lived during the Age of Aries, and made it clear that the people were to no longer worship the bull but to sacrifice a ram, or lamb. The constellation Aries is represented by a ram. Centuries later, Jesus shared with his disciples that he was acting in the role of the last sacrificial lamb, and from that time on he would be known as a "fisher of men." Pisces is symbolized by fish. Pisces and the Christian era have coincided for roughly 2,000 years, and we are now heading into Aquarius. What will that entail, with the water bearer as its symbol? Jung understood that water mythologically symbolizes the unconscious. Perhaps the coming era will have as its focus a confrontation, or conversation, or struggle, between the conscious and unconscious aspects of humanity. The outpouring of water seen in Aquarius is represented in the unavoidable threat of sea level rise, both existentially and metaphorically, a new phase in the psychic development of humanity. How should we respond?

All this describes the ongoing process of gradual awakening from our unconscious state of pure animal instinct into ever-increasing conscious awareness. This transition from unconsciousness to consciousness is painfully slow, taking thousands of years for humanity to have merely reached the often pitiful state we now find ourselves. Myth and religion tell the story of this very slow and awkward awakening. The Old Testament, as a series of such stories, is in a sense evolutionary. Many of the very imperfect characters these stories portray, from Abraham to Moses to Job, are a series of precursors to Christ …

approximate versions of an increasingly conscious human. Christ can then be understood as a man to be emulated for his elevated consciousness. The meaning of Apocalypse, described at the end of the New Testament, is thus not so much an end of time as a revelation of a new possibility – emphasizing not simply a shattering end but a coming awakening into a deeper and wider awareness. But the emergence of the new first requires the death of the old.

There are perhaps two overarching reasons for the slow downward spiral of western civilization, leading seemingly to an inevitable apocalypse, both stemming from our lost relationship to our spiritual, religious, and cultural roots. First, we no longer believe in the old stories, viewing them as we do through the lens of rational scientific materialism. We no longer think poetically but rationally. Those old stories, we tell ourselves now, are mere fairytales used to either entertain children or control the masses. A second and more subtle reason perhaps is that we *do* believe them. That is, we have incorporated the lessons of the ancient stories and myths so thoroughly, and no longer need the tales as such. We have incorporated the lessons into our laws, customs, social norms, and moral assumptions to such a degree that the stories no longer seem to hold "transcendent truth" – the lessons are "obvious" to us now after all these centuries. Imagine a schoolchild who advances over time from a basic reader to more challenging literature. A child first learns their ABCs and then sentence construction. From there, grammar rules are learned and incorporated into the skill of composing paragraphs into smoothly flowing prose. So too the moral and psychological lessons of civilization advance over time. Imagine that the ancients viewed the world in a more "pixelated" fashion, but over time, as civilization accumulates and incorporates more lessons, we are able to understand with greater clarity and subtlety.

Now is our time as a civilization to graduate to new lessons of poetic storytelling. No civilization can operate well without religion to provide an operational foundation, but a true religion will teach its followers how to outgrow it.

Kintsugi and the Integration of Values

Viewed through this Jungian perspective, the historic ages of humanity seem to require a regular pattern of growth, brokenness, and regeneration. This mimics the psychological process of individual growth and character development. The Japanese art of kintsugi is a lovely metaphor of this process. It is an artistic act of repair of broken pottery using gold lacquer, in which the brokenness itself adds to the beauty and story of an object, turning a mere piece of ordinary pottery into a work of art. The use of gold is intended to highlight rather than hide the cracks; these act as a metaphor of personal healing –the repair of something broken reveals a hidden beauty.

Unlike a piece of pottery though, it seems we must be shattered emotionally for growth to occur, and it's not optional. No one is immune from the wounds of life: the death of loved ones, traumatic injury and illness, professional failure, disappointments, and disillusionments of untold variety. Once shattered, it is our task to gather together and examine the shards – attitudes and beliefs long-held, character traits, and so forth – of our broken lives to discover how to intentionally re-assemble them into a renewed whole. We ask ourselves, what values do I hold, what do I believe in, what is my purpose in life? Such questions must be asked of oneself, and answered. It is an extremely rare person who does not go through this process; in fact, it is safe to say no one of any emotional or spiritual maturity can avoid this psychic process. The stories of both Christ and the Buddha emphasize this process of spiritual brokenness and re-assembly into the higher self. The process of this psychic rebuilding of the broken self is focused on the discovery and integration of new and larger values and perspectives.

We can think of this shattering and reassembly not only as a personal process of growth but one which entire cultures and civilizations experience as well.

The enormous length of time it takes for a civilization to go through this makes it exceedingly difficult to perceive, however. Consider the way a small child invests so much importance in some object – a blanket or stuffed toy, for instance. That blanket or toy means something of deep value, although the child may not be able to articulate that meaning. That object cannot be taken away or even washed without causing enormous anxiety in the child; every good parent will discover this. Eventually, the object will be discarded or forgotten naturally by the child when whatever value it holds is either transferred to another toy or integrated psychically. This is the process of emotional and psychic growth toward maturity.

This happens to cultures as well. We invest extremely deep meaning in our religious and cultural traditions and institutions. Perhaps we can think of the various upheavals our civilization is experiencing today as the psychic convulsions of having deeply meaningful traditions stripped away too soon by an overemphasis on rationality before the meaning is transferred to new cultural traditions. This is not a new experience in the history of humanity, but it happens so rarely that it is hard to see the progression of growth that it represents.

It has long been recognized that whenever western civilization, with its reliance on rational science at the expense of all else, interacts with a non-western tribal or so-called "primitive" culture, that culture will die, leaving its people psychologically broken. The rational, technical, and essentially meaningless view of the world held by the contemporary west kills the meaningful visions that sustain other cultures. What has not been well understood is that western civilization is now doing this to itself, destroying its own foundational visions; we are killing ourselves by discarding our spiritual heritage. This is what the philosopher Friedrich Nietzsche recognized in his misunderstood phrase, "God is dead." This process is the true meaning of the term Apocalypse. It refers not so much to some violent, fiery destruction of the world – although that seems a quite possible outcome of history – as the destruction of a way of thinking or set of beliefs, values, and assumptions. Apocalypse refers to the destruction of a worldview to make way for a newer and larger vision. Are we on the brink of this at our stage in history?

The larger question examined here of course, remains; how do all these musings on the evolutionary nature of our cultural and psycho/spiritual lives relate to the urbanism we experience in our cities and towns? Let's begin to explore that in the next chapter.

CHAPTER III

The Merging of Urbanism and Spirituality

"A fact is weak unless seen in light of some comprehensive truth"
– Samuel Taylor Coleridge

In a sense, there is nothing new about bringing a spiritual attitude to urbanism. The ancient world assumed that the gods were intimately concerned with city-building, and that a protective deity was essential to the vitality of a city. Macrobius, a Roman living in the early 400s, stated that "it is well known that every city is under the protection of some deity." Athens was overseen by Athena; the tutelary deity of Rome was kept secret on pain of death. Ancient Chinese, Hindu, Thai, and other civilizations had this practice as well. Even in those societies which do not "call in the gods" to oversee a city, the simple act of placing churches, temples, and other religious structures in prominent urban locations is universal. Cities grow and develop for many practical reasons, but can we also say that they are shaped by the larger aspirations of soul?

Incarnation on Earth: A Boarding School Experience

Our essential being is spirit, temporarily inhabiting matter. Think of us all as incarnated spirits, temporarily here on earth as humans; basically, a group of struggling students sent to a boarding school. A well-known quote attributed to the Aboriginal tribes of Australia, phrases this well: "We are all visitors to this time, this place, just passing through. Our purpose here is to observe, learn, grow, and love. Then we return home." We are sent here to learn lessons, and the pedagogical tool used is ... experience. This is incredibly difficult; as the playwright Oscar Wilde put it, "Experience is the hardest teacher. It gives the exam first and the lesson later." Or, from the spiritual teacher Eckhart Tolle, "We are here to experience ... limitation." I would add that we are also to awaken from unconsciousness and discover the opportunities and obligations of conscious self-awareness.

So, experiencing life on earth is our schooling. To repeat an earlier analogy I used, for some it is elementary school, others graduate school, for some unfortunates it is reform school. We're all jumbled together in the same class, and we all return until the lessons are learned and integrated. Much of the personal spiritual growth that is intended for us takes place unconsciously, but we are best served when this spiritual journey is made conscious with intentionality.

Such a view of incarnation assumes the possibility of reincarnation, as we discussed in Chapter I. Is this not a sort of "spiritual evolution," a refinement of soul over generations of time? This should not come as such a great surprise to those of us raised in the Christian west; the Christian world itself held to the idea of reincarnation for its first 500 years. A city grows, changes, and matures in the same way. Over time, a place, either natural or built, can become infused with meaning. City-building is essentially about the creation of meaning ... I am in *this* place, connected to the ideas it represents and the stories that took place here. Meaning may be arbitrary and highly personal, yet it is essential to a fulfilled life. A city or town or village is more than its physicality, and more too than the people who inhabit it. It is an entity unto itself which our ancestors birthed and we nurture and inhabit. It is a living chakra in a sense, a node of living energy.

A fundamental task of humanity is to discover the eternal by experiencing the temporal. The eternal we interpret and discover through myth and metaphor. In our experience of temporal urbanism, that which is eternal or transcendent is understood and shared via symbols, rituals, and art. As spirits now physically incarnated into this world, we are like scouts or explorers sent out to discover some new undiscovered territory; it is the scout's duty to gain as much understanding as possible and report back what has been learned. The conscious ego that I recognize as "me" is the scout, only a small part of a much larger entity of my Self, which transcends time and space.

Perhaps we can say then that the merging of spiritual quest and urban experience anticipates what Jung viewed as the next phase in human psychic development, the reconciliation of opposites. An extraordinarily complex task to be sure, requiring the ability to confront that which we would rather avoid. But, to paraphrase Jung, there is no coming to maturity without relationship to one's environment. This sort of deep relationship and interdependence must now include more than only the natural world – rock and river and tree – but the built world of street and building as well.

Jane Jacobs, Meet Joseph Campbell

Most of us have played the game of identifying famous people we'd like to invite to a dinner party. Ages ago, there was a wonderful TV show, "Meeting of the Minds," which played this out for us. Steve Allen, the founder and original host of "The Tonight Show," put on a weekly "dinner party," in which he invited various historical figures to a salon-type dinner party. Shakespeare, Plato, and Darwin sitting down together over good food and conversation. Two of my own choices would include Jane Jacobs, a foundational urbanist known for, among other things, saving Greenwich Village from destruction, and Joseph Campbell, professor of comparative religion and mythology. They each formulated basic principles in their respective fields; what would they have to say to each other?

Jane Jacobs held that there were four basic conditions of good urbanism. She argued that vibrant activity can only flourish in cities when the physical environment is diverse. This diversity, she said, requires four conditions.

1. Districts must serve more than two functions so that they attract people with different purposes at different times of the day and night.
2. Blocks must be small with dense intersections giving pedestrians opportunities to interact.
3. Buildings must be diverse in terms of age and form to support a mix of low-rent and high-rent tenants. By contrast, an area with exclusively new buildings can only attract businesses and tenant's wealthy enough to support the cost of new building.
4. Districts must have a sufficient density of people and buildings.

Joseph Campbell also developed four fundamentals in his field of study. He explained that myth has four basic functions: mystical, cosmological, sociological, and pedagogical.

1. The **mystical** function is to awaken us to the mystery and wonder of creation, to open our minds and senses to an awareness of the mystical "ground of being," the source of all phenomena.
2. The **cosmological** function is to describe the "shape" of the Universe and our world, so that it becomes vivid and alive to us, infused with meaning and significance. Every piece of creation has meaning and a role to play.
3. The **sociological** function is to pass down "the Law," the moral and ethical codes for people in a culture to follow, in order to define and support the prevailing social structure.
4. The **pedagogical** function is to lead us through particular rites of passage that define the significant stages of life, from dependency to maturity to old age to death. These rites bring us into harmony with creation and allow us to make the journey from one stage of life to another, with a sense of security and purpose.

So, Jacobs and Campbell each have identified four essential characteristics in their respective areas of inquiry. Do they parallel or support each other in any way? Not directly. But, making big intuitive leaps is common in my thinking, leading to my reputation for mixing metaphors and torturing them until they conform. There is something here, I sense, so bear with me as I wander around the possibilities.

What are the mythical, cosmological, sociological, and pedagogical possibilities of Jacobs requirements of urban design? What are the urban elements that embody a good myth? Perhaps an easier way of considering this is to think in terms of archetypes. Archetypes, as first explained by Jung and popularized in Campbell's writings on mythology, are recurring patterns, images, and symbols found in religions and mythologies all over the world. It seems to me that the common theme between Jacobs and Campbell is that both good urbanism and good myths do two things – teach us and connect us. Perhaps we can think of Jacobs' four qualities as fundamental archetypes of urban design.

As compelling as what Jacobs has identified, however, four fundamental archetypes seem somehow insufficient. A more extensive language of urban design archetypes is needed. Architectural theoretician and mathematician Christopher Alexander provides this for us, beyond the fundamentals, in his book *A Pattern Language*. This is the point at which the insights of Jacobs and Campbell seem to merge most fully. *A Pattern Language* is the practical companion to another Alexander work, *The Timeless Way of Building*, which provides a theoretical foundation for the patterns, or archetypes, that Alexander identifies. Alexander's pattern language includes 253 distinct elements of good urbanism and architecture. The patterns he has identified are divided into categories of Regions, Towns, Neighborhoods, Buildings, Rooms, and on down to the details of Construction. The nature of these patterns is both practical (the proper dimensions for spacing ductwork) and wildly playful (design streets to accommodate dancing).

Rather than going through all 253 elements, I'll simply encourage you to find and enjoy the work on your own and dive deeply into these ideas. But don't stop there ... Alexander's magnum opus is a 4-volume work entitled *The Nature of Order: An Essay on the Art of Building and the Nature of the Universe*. No small vision there! Hm, I'd better go set another place at the table for that dinner party.

The Bypass

The term "bypass" seems apt for so many ways in which we seek to avoid problems, discomfort, and complications, whether they are real or perceived. Culturally, Americans have a very strong assumption that we can always find a technical solution to non-technical problems. This is our way of avoiding the need for self-discipline; "There must be *some* way for me to have my cake and eat it too," and our astonishingly successful technology is the tool we use to find that answer. The idea of "innovation" too is overemphasized in this way. Yet most of the world's economy relies not on the creation of the new but maintaining what we already possess. The goal of "sustainability," laudable on its surface, is similarly problematic. What is it we are trying to sustain? From what I can sense, it often implies a desire to "sustain" a particularly self-indulgent, upper-middle-class lifestyle centered around car ownership and the single-family suburban home.

We are all aware of a bypass as a solution to highway traffic congestion. Through-traffic is diverted around a downtown to avoid stoplights, narrow streets, and pedestrians, so cars can move without inconvenience. This fragments our communities, pulling business away from downtown and into suburban settings. A relentless focus on getting somewhere conveniently ends up destroying someplace else.

Bypass is also commonly used in psychological and spiritual communities. Here, the idea of "spiritual bypass" points to a desire to avoid the truly demanding work of psychological growth and healing by engaging in all sorts of superficial rituals and activities which appear positive, but end up merely acting as comforting distractions.

The flight to the suburbs, beginning in the 1950s, is perhaps the largest cultural bypass we have ever instituted. In an effort to avoid the maintenance of older, messy, complicated, and culturally mixed cities, many Americans have chosen to flee to new suburban settings rather than improve the urban communities we already have.

All these sorts of bypasses can work for a time, but the associated costs do not disappear. As long as we can ignore the externalities, fob off and avoid the costs of our decisions, no change occurs. The growth into greater consciousness can often be more painful than we can bear, but there are only two responses. One is to seek a return into the unconscious, via alcohol, overwork, pleasure, and all manner of escapist spiritual practices. The other option is to become even more conscious, through hard work involving humiliating and painful self-reflection, in order to face the very things we fear the most.

As a civilization, however, we can no longer avoid the externalities, no longer take the bypass. The costs have become too high for us to maintain, no matter the call for sustainability. Physically, urbanistically, culturally, politically; fundamental change is required of us, and is found in the development and rediscovery of greater connection and interdependence with each other, and with place.

After decades – centuries, really – of an overemphasis on scientific rationalism and engineered solutions, a rebalancing must take place. We can view the split between rational science/technology and civilization on the one hand, and spiritual insight of nature on the other, as reflected in the terms "patriarchy," the Great Father representing ordered civilization, and "matriarchy," the Great Mother of Nature. We need both, in the proper balance.

How can we understand this transition toward balance? The distinction between curing and healing can give insight here. One way to distinguish the two is understanding their goals. To cure can mean to get back to an original state of health and wellness prior to a wound or illness. To heal, however, requires more – to bring about a new strength and vigor greater than what was experienced before the wound or illness. Viewed in this way, healing is an aspect of evolutionary growth.

A Convergence of Changes

Our world today is experiencing a convergence of simultaneous change. A trend toward connection and relatedness is occurring in multiple arenas. Urbanistically, this can be seen in the work of the Congress for the New Urbanism and its adherents; a spiritual example is found in the efforts of the Integral Spirituality movement. Both the New Urbanists and the Integral Spirituality movement seek to find the best examples of thinking in their respective fields, from all sources, past and present, in order to find those patterns which operate most fully and successfully across all time and cultures.

A movement closely allied to Integral Spirituality is that of Spiral Dynamics. It is essentially a model of psychological and sociological development, with a series of developmental stages mapped by color. These stages move up from archaic to tribal, then warrior to traditional, then modernist to postmodern, and on up to levels of integral and post-integral levels of consciousness. Different writers may ascribe different names to each, but each level represents varying stages of psychological modes of being.

As we explored earlier, the world of scientific inquiry, a prime mover of our cultural imaginations, is shifting away from 500 years of breaking the world apart and down into ever-smaller constituent parts. Now, science is seeking the ways in which those parts are connected to form a whole. Particle physics, for example, is focused on the point at which matter transitions into energy; its theoretical work has become speculative in the manner of spirituality. In the same manner, the work of New Urbanists shows the necessity and greater functionality of the emphasis on fine-grained mixed uses and walkability rather than the auto-oriented separation of uses of the past 75 years.

Our urbanism, like our spiritual and religious lives, is less in need of a cure for its ills than of a healing to move beyond what came before. We have to rise to the occasion, so to speak, no longer avoiding issues of personal or cultural complexity, but addressing and including into a spiritual vision the much wider perspective of reality that science has provided us. Our urbanism must display a greater subtlety and humanity and reflect psycho/spiritual insights of both greater heights and greater depth. Cities and towns have been fragmented, physically torn apart by highways and restrictive zoning, just as the scientific process has fragmented our vision of the world.

The methods of scientific inquiry can be justified – it has produced enormous beneficial success and depth of knowledge – but no such justification can be found for the way we have destroyed our cities and towns. To the extent that they are now being knitted back together, the process is being driven by the insights and methods developed within the New Urbanist movement since the 1990s. The details of this movement will be discussed in Chapter VII. Further advances may await too, in a more artistic approach to the design of place at all scales, emphasizing a more gracious and inspirational public realm. The approach of New Urbanism has developed a set of design tools and policies to create communities of connection and delight. The missing element, I contend, is the intentional creation of places of *meaning*.

Various threads of scientific and spiritual understandings are beginning to reinforce one another, particularly in the fields of evolutionary biology and particle physics. The work of Jordan Peterson, in his "Maps of Meaning" lectures, as one example, shows an intriguing understanding of how belief systems support evolutionary success, both biologically and culturally, and crucially, how those belief systems rest on a foundation of biological evolution and experience. More specific to the design of cities is the work of architect Don Ruggles, who has delved deeply into the manner in which places of beauty relate to health. Relying on work done by the Academy for Neuroscience in Architecture, he reveals for us the way in which millions of years of evolution have hard-wired us to look for patterns that we recognize as revealing either danger or pleasure. Certain patterns in the environment cause us anxiety since they reveal to us, after millions of years of experience, potential danger. Other patterns give us pleasure since they relate to an environment of safety or abundance. These latter patterns we describe as beautiful, and our search for them is at the instinctual level, far older than conscious awareness. Such patterns include what we see in the weather, in plants and animals, geography, and so forth, and are easily translated into the built patterns we create in architecture, art, and urbanism. Beauty is not in the eye of the beholder but is built upon a set of patterns ingrained in our brains. Places lacking in such patterns cause anxiety; those with those patterns bring us a sense of security and happiness. Relative to architecture, the arrangement of elements into a pattern of 3 x 3 is fundamental and has operated for thousands of years. This is likely related to the development of facial recognition during infancy. The arrangement of elements of a house façade, its doors and windows, mimic the facial features – eyes, nose, mouth – of a parent to an infant. So when we see a house in such a symmetrical pattern, we are comforted by the familiarity and security of home and family, though the visual connection remains unconscious.

In other words, neuroscience shows how important beauty is for health.

James Hillman reminds us that objects made by human hands contain soul. Physical artifacts contain soul just as natural objects do. This is an ancient idea but is rarely given respect in the west, except regarding art. Art, artistic artifacts, and music move us so deeply precisely because they contain spirit and soul.

We'll see in a following chapter how the world of real estate development and land planning has made this same transition – from the isolation of suburban sprawl back to the connected whole of traditional mixed-use urbanism. But is there another way of understanding the way in which nature and city lean on each other? A story might help.

The Story of Apsu and Tiamat

Consider the creation story of ancient Mesopotamia. As some of the earliest peoples to create cities, the Mesopotamians had a dilemma on their hands; how to make sense of this completely new way of living, called civilization, which they were in a sense just making up as they went along. The two fundamental creator gods in Mesopotamian religion were named Tiamat and Apsu, the Mother and Father of All. Tiamat as mother represented chaotic untamed and unknown Nature, while Apsu stood for ordered Civilization, the known, understood, and manageable. They procreated and their children were gods, but like human children, they were noisy and disruptive. Apsu became frustrated and sought to control them, which angered the young gods to the point of rebellion, ending in the murder of their father. Even after this horror though, the children continued to live on the corpse of their father. They relied on the order he had provided but did not respect or understand what had been supporting them, killing him and that structure in their selfish ignorance and small-mindedness. Tiamat was of course horrified that her children killed her husband, and in her wrath sent chaos upon them in the form of an army of monsters. The young gods fought back, and selected one from among themselves to lead the battle. His name was Marduk, who was victorious over chaos and essentially took on the role of his murdered father Apsu. He founded a city as a monument to himself and his victory, and from the blood of the chaotic monsters, he formed the first humans. The ordered city was Babylon, populated by monstrous, chaotic humans.

What do we make of such a story? We humans have nature as our foundation, but must have a living basis of structured civilization in which to operate – a culture. Both nature and culture offer blessings and curses, and we receive both according to the respect we show. Nature provides both bounty and chaos; culture provides stable protection but can become deeply oppressive. Culture is troublesome in a way that nature is not, however; it must be constantly renewed, rethought, and updated. As much respect and deference as we must give to our ancestors, we must progress beyond them, or otherwise we live on their "old dead corpse" of outmoded cultural and religious ideas. The old ways are not to be rejected so much as to be updated; that which is of value must be retained but incorporated in a newer, larger perspective. Those ancestors did the best they could, given what they knew and understood; now we must respect but improve upon that work, with deep humility and an understanding of our own shortcomings.

This is the reason I sense so many people despise Christianity now; its wisdom has become ossified, encased in outdated cultural forms and values. This is precisely what Nietzsche meant by "God is dead." But he said more; God is dead, and it is we who have killed him, and we cannot wash off the blood. Nietzsche teaches us today what the Babylonians understood 4,000 years ago; we have arrogantly killed off our foundational values without even understanding them nor realizing the consequences. As a result, we must hope that something larger with a greater inclusive vision picks up where Christianity leaves off; Christ himself anticipated this, saying there was more to learn, and that others after him would do yet greater things.

So too with our cities. As the fundamental physical representation of Apsu – of ordered culture and civilization – our cities have for too long rested upon the old dead corpse of outmoded ideas and values. In contemporary America, these center on suburbia as an escape route from messy urbanism, an unhealthy addiction to the automobile, an extremely isolating desire for convenience, and the acceptance of inelegant technical engineering as the height of achievement. Here at the beginning of the 21st century, a companion to the automobile is emerging as a formative scheme in our image of the city. That is the wired, information-focused "Smart City" of big data, entertainment, and 24/7 convenience.

These seem to be the motivating forces behind our narrow assumptions of what a place can be, and together represent a continued reliance on outmoded thinking. I am convinced this mindset is the final manifestation of 500 years of increasing devotion to technology and engineering as solutions to each and every human trouble. As our culture casts about for its new foundation while trying to slough off its old, outmoded ways, our cities must take on new and more complex meaning. They must be designed to represent and be experienced as the physical embodiment of our evolving cultural values and find new ways of fulfilling our basic and newly emerging psychic, spiritual, and religious needs.

There are thus two new roles required of our urban cities and towns. First, to act as the physical setting supporting the private, individual psycho/spiritual growth of individual citizens. Second, to act as the physical setting in support of a new and as-yet unformed religious cosmology (or several) which may act as the foundation of more broad and inclusive shared cultural values. The urban built environment must evolve into the appropriate vessel for an expanding spiritual vision. One of the highest spiritual aspirations might just be this: the ability to create order out of chaos with respect and humility. The fundamental vision of western civilization is that each individual human has that potential within them. This is what the city represents – the bringing of order out of chaos.

Let me go back to the example of shamanism as a way of elaborating this further. The call to become a shaman typically involves a psychological crisis, in which the candidate must pass through a painful and traumatic loss of self and to re-imagine themselves as a much larger being, deeply connected to the universe, with feet planted firmly in both the physical and spiritual worlds. In a similar process of transition, all of humanity is undergoing a psychological crisis, and it is resulting in greater devastation than ever; in environmental degradation, economic inequality, and social and political instability. Humanity is at a point where it has to awaken into consciousness even further, to break beyond conventional cultural barriers and find the unity we all have together on earth as an expression of the Universe. As this is taking place, we find ourselves with a growing population which is increasingly urban. This global transformation in thinking and understanding will take place significantly in urban settings. We have the opportunity – the requirement, I am certain – to view cities and towns as settings of psychic growth and transformation.

Now, to scale down to the personal again. According to Jung, the first half of life is all about the process of developing a strong, healthy ego, so that we can operate effectively in society. We take on cultural norms, psychological conditions, and so forth. I liken this to putting on layers of clothing. They give us shape and can look pretty good, or pretty ridiculous, and even get us into a fair amount of trouble. All these layers represent cultural values, family history, personal emotional and physiological makeup, tradition, belief systems, etc. Without this, we have no "shape," nor could we function in society. The second half of life, however, must focus on the need to shed all of this, so that we can develop psychologically, transcend spiritually, and connect to our truer selves. Meditation and similar spiritual disciplines we use for such efforts, are best understood not as tools for escape, but as ways to wake ourselves up, make us more open to and aware of the love available to us, the experience of life in us and around us, and the lessons to be learned. This is essentially what we are beginning to experience – must experience – as a whole culture; the breakdown of the old so that the new can emerge.

We are not spirit trapped inside the material world, souls locked inside bodies as if by some unfortunate trick. Rather, our incarnation is intentional, and thus we are spirit *liberated* by the material in order to act, create, and grow. Spirit produces nothing without energetic action in the physical. The combination of spirit and action gives us the ability to imagine things which do not exist, and then manifest them. Our continued awakening into greater conscious awareness affords the opportunity to create an ever-deeper sense of meaning. We might say that meaning is arbitrary, but whether or not this is true, it is apparently essential to psychic health. That meaning is in large part created by the shape we give to place. Jung stated that "formlessness seems to be practically the equivalent of unconsciousness." The spiritual process of awakening into consciousness then means we approach form with ever-greater insight and meaning.

The current American transition away from suburbs and back to cities reflects a new but unrecognized understanding of the patriarchy, by emphasizing the need to rebalance itself toward the Great Mother – less an emphasis on engineered infrastructure, greater focus on its reliance on nature. Civilization – cities, the patriarchal Father – rests on and is reliant upon nature, the Great Mother, the matriarchy.

As a civilization, we seem to have followed a path of religious and spiritual progression as far as it can take us; then diverged from it to follow another path, that of scientific rationalism, which also seems to have reached a turning point. What I have tried to present in these first three chapters is the view I hold of the upheaval that western civilization is undergoing in a multitude of arenas: urbanistically, culturally, and spiritually. Intriguingly, the failings of both our cultural mythos and built environment reflect each other, emphasizing a sort of atomization and isolation. Simultaneously, they both show signs of renewing themselves in mirrored fashion into more intuitive, inclusive, and connected forms.

What are the relevant specifics of the city? What are the stresses of urbanism today, particularly American cities and towns? The following chapters will explore that dilemma.

CHAPTER IV
Changes and Paradigm Shifts

"It is not the strongest of the species that survives, nor the most intelligent, but the one most adaptive to change" – Charles Darwin

The quote above, ascribed to Darwin, is questioned by scholars as to its accuracy. Regardless, I sense he would not dispute the intent. One of the great strengths of our species is an incredible adaptability. We have thrived in every climate, from arctic tundra to burning deserts and steaming jungles. What will be tested in the coming decades is not our ability to survive, but the ability of our systems and structures – physical and cultural and perhaps most significantly, spiritual – to continue to adapt and thrive. What are some of the challenges our urban civilization faces?

Demographics

Over the next 15 years, the global population is expected to grow by 1 billion people. This means having to build the equivalent of a new city of 1.5 million people *every week* for the next 15 years. In the United States alone over the next 40 years, new housing will need to be constructed, equivalent to all the residential units that currently exist in Germany, France, and England *combined*. Are we capable of making the policy changes needed to pull this off? The NIMBY fear of change and density will have to be overcome.

Markets

It is increasingly obvious that the type of land development which local communities allow in their zoning ordinances do not at all match what residents or the market ask for, whether it be in residential, retail, or office development.

There is for instance, a shift from shopping malls which require a car to access, to walkable "town centers" – from acquisitive shopping to experience. Restaurants and entertainment are replacing retail shopping. In just one afternoon spent in the local Trader Joe's grocery store in the Clarendon neighborhood of Arlington VA, a half-dozen people, ranging in age from 20-somethings to retirees, mentioned to me that they specifically enjoy the neighborhood because it allows them to live car-free. My own experience is that after living without a car for almost three years as of this writing, I am saving close to $800 monthly, as I no longer have to worry about payments, parking, gas, insurance, or repairs. Adaptability and versatility are designed into mixed-use neighborhoods, providing the option to live car-free.

It has long been recognized that the United States is vastly "over-retailed." Americans have been turning to consumer shopping for its entertainment appeal for generations, and the development community responded with innovations such as the regional indoor shopping mall. This habit has brought about an enormous glut of wasted real estate. Germany, for instance, has roughly 2.4 square feet of retail space per person, the United Kingdom has 3.8. The United States? 23.6 square feet of retail space per person. What is to be done with all this wasteful surplus?

Co-housing, co-working, and new shared retirement arrangements are appearing in every city. These reflect the "shared economy," a new term that has entered the public lexicon in recent years. Arising out of necessity due to the financial crisis of 2008, the shared economy is a reflection of a young generation unable to find the conventional stability of their elders regarding work, living arrangements, and ownership of homes and cars. Part-time and consulting work, working out of cafés, and living in group settings has become more common. It may very well be that these sorts of arrangements are not permanent and may fade with an improving economy. Yet, the market has responded to these new patterns of living with typical creativity; entire new industries worth billions of dollars have sprung up in less than a decade to cater to new demands" Zipcar, Airbnb, WeWork, and WeLive have all attracted hundreds of millions of dollars in private investment.

What does such a world of a "shared economy" look like regarding urban patterns? At a basic level, a more fine-grained, walkable mixed-use pattern is aligned with this, much more so than conventional suburbia.

CHANGES AND PARADIGM SHIFTS

Climate Change

The United States averages 129 federally declared disasters every year. The big media stories like Hurricane Katrina are just a portion of what the nation experiences year after year. According to InsuranceJournal.com, disasters affected 8% of the US population in 2017; for the year, the federal government authorized $7 billion in disaster funds, in response to wildfires, hurricanes, and earthquakes, among other natural events. Hurricane Harvey alone caused over $8 billion in damages.

Over 40% of the world's largest cities lie within three feet of sea level. Bear in mind that climate scientists anticipate a sea level rise of at least that, and potentially exceeding 6 feet, within the next 100 years. Now, consider where that next one billion people will live, if those largest cities are no longer available. In the United States, the cities and surrounding regions of New Orleans, Miami, Tidewater Virginia, New York, and so many others are already under direct threat. They may not be available to accommodate any new population growth, and in fact may have to decant their populations elsewhere, to nearby surrounding "receiving towns." How will these receiving communities adjust to potentially dramatic population shifts? Will they welcome the influx, and be prepared for it?

Regarding sea level rise, do we retreat or "stand our ground?" Any attempt at triage will have shortcomings. Some places will be deemed not worth the vast expense it will take to save them. What will be left behind in those places we choose to, or are forced to, abandon to natural disaster? Trillions of dollars' worth of infrastructure, of course, but also cultural loss, not to mention landfills and all manner of toxic chemicals which will become exposed. The upheaval and disruption we face will be dramatic to say the least, and will include psychic and emotional pain and possibly a good deal of physical violence as a result.

Beyond sea level rise, other significant environmental challenges stare at us. The many recent wildfires in California reveal to us the number of inappropriate places we have built our homes, and how much land will not be available to us in the future. Changes in temperature and humidity will increasingly affect our choices and settlement patterns.

The phrase "peak oil" has entered the public lexicon, reminding us that our reliance on fossil fuels – the overuse of energy of any source, really – has come at a staggering cost, caused enormous damage to both our environment and culture, and will come to a very difficult end as oil runs out.

The author James Kunstler makes clear in his "Infinite Suburbs" article that the whole of our civilization and its physical manifestation is founded on a false and self-centered notion of the unending availability of fossil fuels. Without oil, the entire structure of our economy and the places we build collapses. With oil, we wreak total havoc on the environment. This is the proverbial rock and a hard place we refuse to respond to but is increasingly demanding our attention. Our personal desire for convenience, and the corporate drive for greater efficiency, are the root causes of our inability to break the addiction.

The Increasing Pace of Change

We've been keeping time in one way or another for thousands of years, using the stars to track the change of seasons and the moon to watch the passing of the months. This was a foundational role for early cities in fact; temples were erected to keep track of planting and harvesting time, and cities grew up around them to support the sacred work. Time, as we understand and experience it today with clocks and timekeeping, is an outgrowth of medieval monastic life. Originally conceived as an aid to get cloistered monks to attend regular prayers at specified hours of the day and night, clocks originally had only one hand to count the hours. Minute hands were added later as an aid to better business management. Now second hands are standard as we focus on the sequence of events in ever smaller increments.

Our daily routines are managed by obedience to the clock. Remembering the original purpose of clocks and timekeeping can remind us to slow down just as easily as to hurry up, and to consider the past as well as the future. Physicists studying the fundamental physical aspects of nature are coming to a very different understanding of time, to the point that its very existence is actually in question. The resolution of that question will come, I suppose, in time.

Allowing for an unplanned future – personally and with regard to the design of cities – creates versatility and the ability to adapt to change. In opposition to this is the desire to create a vision of unending and predictable perfection found in American suburbia's building types and street patterns. A split-level rancher and a cul-de-sac neighborhood aren't supposed to ever change or serve any other purpose other than the original.

Change cannot be stopped; indeed, without change there is only death, but it can be managed to a degree. A regional vision of a complete urban Transect, described in Chapter VII, can provide options for those who seek a slower, or faster, pace of life. Change has become overwhelming to many of us. There is an increasing desire to slow down, stop, even reverse the forward movement of social and cultural change. I think this causes much of our political divide today. Understanding and making use of the urban Transect, that is, valuing urban settings in a variety of intensities and forms, from small village to global metropolis, can help to soften the impacts of unmanageable social change to some degree. Large social, cultural, and market forces aren't going to be automatically redirected by better urbanism, but the two are intertwined. Smaller communities naturally tend to lose out to larger, more cosmopolitan ones, and always have, and that isn't going to change.

Many of those calling for a slowing or even reversal of change often (though not always, of course) do so out of fear, a sense of insecurity, and a feeling of being left behind by the rest of society. To the extent this is legitimate, the unequal and negative impacts do need to be managed. Too much negative change seems to be driven today by market forces that want to profit off our unending desire for ever-greater convenience and variety with ever-decreasing consequences to ourselves.

Lurking among the various impacts of the Covid-19 outbreak of 2020 is the realization of just how fragile the global economy is. Its foundation is a supply chain system stretching thousands of miles, increasingly reliant on "just-in-time" delivery. While many anticipated that the end of the year-round availability of fresh produce shipped thousands of miles would come from the drama of "peak oil," what may have truly made us rethink our current system of global logistics actually came in the form of a viral pandemic.

As long as we can avoid or ignore externalities – that is, the social and environmental costs of an action – the old ways and patterns will continue. This includes not only the way we conduct our economy, but our private psychic lives and personal relationships as well. The cost of broken relationships, whether regarding the global economy, the physical environment, or with the individuals of our community, is externalized or projected onto others who we demand bear the cost.

We as a national and even a global society face unprecedented troubles, in the form of climate change, environmental destruction, economic disparities, political instability, deteriorating infrastructure, and a woefully inadequate built environment. On top of all these, we face a growing human disaster of cultural, psychic, and spiritual crises of meaning and direction. None of these pressing existential threats have any "technical" solution. Because they are at their deepest level not technological nor even political concerns but more deeply rooted in the values and beliefs – and the underlying cosmological vision – which guides our lives and determines our decisions, they can only be more fully approached by the application of a new, larger, more all-encompassing mythic vision.

How an individual responds to such overwhelming and rapid-fire change comes not so much from fighting against such large forces of psychic and historic change, for these changes are in some sense well beyond individual control. Rather, each of us must undergo a process of discerning how to live within the whirlwind of history. That involves gaining, as much as we are able, a sense of history in its broadest ramifications – that is, to act as an eye of calm amidst the hurricane. It has been said that if we cannot meditate in a noisy overheated basement boiler-room, we really doesn't know how to meditate. History is now demanding of us such a meditative approach. The role of the city is to act as the classroom in which we can learn the transformational lessons needed for these larger requirements of humanity.

How do we design such a classroom? The next several chapters will explore the basics of community design, starting with a review of the fundamental mistakes we have made over the past several decades to be avoided in the future.

PART 2

THE DESIGN OF PLACE

CHAPTER V
A Brief History of Suburban Sprawl

"Everywhere is within walking distance, if you have enough time"
– Steven Wright

In a sense, there is nothing recent about suburban living. Over 2,000 years ago, ancient Rome was surrounded by large estates, used by the upper end of society as a retreat from the summer heat of the city. This was more of a seasonal vacation arrangement however, not a permanent pattern of living. What is different today is that suburban patterns have become the default setting for the majority of Americans. At their worst, they reflect our culture of disposability, a throwaway society of immediate gratification without responsibility; disposable plastic household goods, disposable places. How did suburbia come about, and what are the consequences?

The Sources of Suburban Sprawl

For the first time in human experience, suburban arrangements have become a norm. This is a distinctly American form, which has spread to many other nations as well in recent years. Why? Simply because this is what everyone wants? Often it is assumed that suburbia is simply responding to market demands, but the reality is that in a majority of municipalities across America, nothing else is allowed to be built except a conventional suburban sprawl pattern. A number of trends and ideas converged to create this completely new way of living.

My father and his generation lived through two of the most difficult experiences in our nation's history – the Great Depression beginning in 1929, followed by World War II. Coming out the other side of those experiences, perhaps they were emotionally exhausted and needed a little peace and quiet, so to speak. The 1950s are often derided as dull and conformist. Well, of course they were! After any trauma, some recovery time is needed. And so that generation set out to create a suburban utopia of peace and security for themselves.

The roots of the sprawling pattern of suburbia reach back several decades prior to the post-war period, however. Suburban sprawl is characterized by the way in which various activities are isolated into their own specialized areas; single-family homes in a subdivision over here, shopping centers there, office parks elsewhere entirely. This oddity has its roots in a reasonable response to a problem that was simply carried too far. Most mistakes in life, it has been said, are some variation of overcompensating; all things are acceptable in moderation. The fetish of American land planning, of separating out all uses and activities into isolated pods, had a very useful purpose originally. In the 1800s, as society began to industrialize, enormous factories, with their accompanying pollution and noise, were often located in the middle of residential neighborhoods. This compromised the health of nearby residents dramatically. The solution was obvious and appropriate; remove the noxious factories to their own corner of town. Behold, problem solved! Public health improved. This insight was adopted as a cure-all, which unfortunately created an assumption that all uses should be separated from others, to reduce perceived and potential trouble. It remains viable to this day only because of the dominance of the automobile.

Combat engineers and Seabees returning from the war were very definitely a group of "can-do" guys. My father, a World War II test pilot, flying bombers, fighters, and transport planes in the Pacific, would tell tales of having to build landing fields in the jungles of various islands while under fire from enemy troops. The experience of these very capable men taught them to get the job done, with no time or need to take much into account other than practicality and efficiency. Their designs for American streets and infrastructure after the war reflect this shift in values from previous generations, which had the temperament, values, and luxury of time to include aesthetic considerations in their work.

When victory was achieved and the war ended, the need to transition from a wartime to a peacetime economy was critical. The only thing that really ended the Depression was the wartime economy. But with the fighting over, something else had to fill the void in our manufacturing capacity. In order to stave off another economic crisis and political upheaval, the nation had to transition somehow. Factories that had been cranking out battleships, tanks, and bombers instead began manufacturing refrigerators, cars, and all the various products needed to fill up the new tract housing.

Bank lending practices also played into the creation of sprawl. Loans were available for new development and construction in certain areas but not in others, as a matter of policy. Redlining, for instance, was an intentional policy of determining where minority races would be allowed. Loans were made available or not, on either side of these lines. This helped play into the marketing of certain areas as more desirable and exclusive than others. Federal policies regarding financing regulations also added to this. Government programs made financing available for new suburban construction but not for the maintenance or rehabilitation of existing buildings.

Modernist architectural concepts also played a significant role in the creation of sprawl. Corbusier, a French/Swiss architect known as one of the founders of the Modernist aesthetic, famously hated the random and unpredictable nature of cities and sought to bring an almost bloodless and severely machine-like understanding to city design. His plan for Paris involved the destruction of the entire center of the city to make way for a series of skyscraper towers. While this never took place, his concepts were most fully realized in low-income housing projects in inner-city locations of New York, St. Louis, and many others.

The suburban icon, of course, is the automobile. Suburbia as we know it would not exist without it. For a few decades from the 1880s to 1940s, suburbs were compact and centered around a train or trolley station. With the rise of the car, however, trolley lines and bus routes were removed – often intentionally at the hands of car manufacturers and oil companies – with the intent of promoting greater dependence on their products. President Eisenhower's federal interstate highway system helped lock this into place. Soon, suburban design principles were given over almost entirely to the needs of auto traffic, rather than people. A comparison of the medieval core of the city of Florence, Italy and a 20th century American highway interchange makes this point rather painfully. Florence was the heart of the Renaissance, which gifted the western world with astonishing advances in arts, music, and science. A typical highway interchange of today takes up roughly the same land area ... merely in order to make left-hand turns easier so that cars don't have to slow down too much.

All of these trends, policies, and societal desires arrived together at the right time to create what has become a massive problem of unintended consequences. But what exactly is sprawl; to make use of a food analogy, what are the ingredients that go into it?

The Ingredients of Sprawl

For any recipe, good ingredients are key to successful cooking and baking. Conventional suburbia generally makes use of the same ingredients as the traditional urban forms of hamlets, villages, towns, and cities, but not all. It emphasizes its own combination of elements, some quite different from historic patterns. Most significantly, while suburbia may provide the ingredients, it does nothing to blend them together into a palatable meal. So, what are those ingredients of suburbia?

Separation of Uses

Suburban sprawl is characterized by how various activities are isolated into their own specialized areas; single-family homes in a subdivision over here, shopping centers there, office parks elsewhere entirely, with the various pods connected by collector streets and arterials.

Large Residential Lots

Land has always been desirable, and ownership of property is a fundamental asset.

Along with a marketing approach emphasizing an image of English manorial estates, a desire for privacy is a central quality of large suburban properties.

Over-Sized Streets

Streets are designed by engineers according to standards that equate safety with very wide and straight rights-of-way. As with use separation and large lots, a reasonable idea regarding street dimensions got taken too far. The result, however, is that wide straight streets enable speeding – increasing danger, not safety.

Over-Adequate Parking

For so many situations, planning for the worst-case scenario makes good sense. Policies and designs for car parking may not be the right set of issues for this kind of thinking, however. The traditionally busiest day of the Christmas shopping season, the day after Thanksgiving known as Black Friday, sets the tone for parking standards. Every car must be able to find a parking space. The holiday season lasts less than a month; for the other 11 months of the year, acres of parking sit empty.

Lack of Integrated Civic Institutions

Walking to school was once normal practice. In 1970, about 42% of school-age children walked or rode bikes to school. Today, many communities have banned this, making the act of walking a criminal offense. What has caused reasonable communities to take such insane action? For many communities, walking is no longer a safe activity. Small local schools are out of favor, with large multi-acre campuses now the norm. Combined with the separation of uses, land development standards, and speeding traffic on wide roads, schools are now isolated pods, accessible only by car.

School districts feel the need to manage public finances prudently, which is appropriate; yet the goal of efficiency has become primary to the detriment of everything else. Unified campuses are, at least in some short-term ways, more efficient. The same mindset has affected post offices, libraries, and public safety facilities. The cumulative effect, however, is an increasing loss of civility and community life.

Lack of Coordinated Open Space

This image displays what I call the "train wreck" school of site planning. The apartment buildings look like derailed boxcars from a railway disaster. The point to focus on, however, is the random and useless green spaces that result. Too often, communities ask for a numeric standard, a particular percentage of a project's land to be dedicated for open space – quite often, 30%. Beyond that, communities may not ask for anything in detail. And because the provision of open space is left to private developers, no overall vision can really be implemented. The fact that there is no vision is made clear by the mere use of such a vague and generally undefined term like *open space*, rather than the more specific *plaza, square, playground,* or *park*, which have intentional uses associated with them. Thus, developers end up meeting the letter of the law by defining every leftover bit of unbuilt grass as open space, whether it is useful or not. Haphazard preservation is just as harmful as haphazard development because it unintentionally forces development to be haphazard as well.

The Effects of Sprawl

The intent of the suburban pattern of living, originally, was relaxed convenience. This convenient relaxation is no longer found beyond the front door, however. What people often mean when they say they enjoy a suburban lifestyle is that they enjoy their private home. Ask them more specifically if they appreciate the process of shopping, commuting to work, or just dealing with traffic, the answer will likely be a vehement *NO*. Yet this is the price to be paid. The relaxed and convenient lifestyle imagined by the early promoters of suburbia worked really well, for a particular segment of society, for a couple of generations. The Greatest Generation, as it has been dubbed, grew up during the Great Depression, and came of age while fighting World War II. After those experiences, as I've noted above, they were emotionally exhausted, and rightly felt they deserved a little peace and quiet. They created suburbia to meet that need. But the laws of unintended consequences have taken over. The externalized costs of an unsustainable pattern, ignored for so long, are coming due.

Suburban living creates an almost total dependence on the automobile. A machine intended to be a servant of convenience has become the master. Very few tasks of everyday living can be conducted without owning a car. These costs are high; the combined cost of monthly payments, taxes, gas, parking, maintenance and repairs, etc. add up on average to the equivalent of a $50,000 mortgage. In a system designed around the needs of the automobile, the destruction of nature is a bemoaned but apparently acceptable price.

The suburbs end up destroying the very amenity – living close to nature – they were intended to provide. Further, they never provide the benefits of a sophisticated urbanism, which could at least theoretically begin to balance out the loss of natural ecosystems. The vast infrastructure designed to provide for cars is a major source of pollution, leaking oil, exhaust, pollution from refineries, and storm-water runoff from paved streets and parking lots.

The very concept of the suburban pattern revolves around intentional separation and isolation. This is how the longed-for peace and quiet are to be achieved. The suburban model caters to the goal of avoiding as many of life's troubles as possible, while ignoring the fact that it causes at least as many as it tries to solve. This separation is complete; not only physical separation by land use, but housing types separate us by income, race, and age. The consequences of this affect cultural and political values and attitudes as well as daily routines.

The amount of time traveling from place to place is enormous; various estimates conclude that Americans spend the equivalent of two weeks of vacation time on commuting alone. Add to that the amount of time spent running errands, and it's no wonder we dread the traffic that we each contribute to.

Beyond travel, maintaining a large property is also time-consuming and expensive. Mowing grass alone is a chore that few look forward to. Lawn care has become a multi-billion-dollar industry, catering to homeowners who often are required by homeowner associations to adhere to strict standards. It is also a major contributor to water pollution, with chemicals and fertilizers washing into sewer systems and into rivers and streams. The financial costs go beyond the homeowner, however. The fiscal impact on a local government has become more than taxes can bear. The maintenance of streets, water and sewer lines, and other infrastructure bequeathed to us by earlier generations are now reaching the end of their normal lifespans; their replacement is prohibitively expensive. Given the average large lot size (the average subdivided lot during the 1990s was over 1/3 acre), there are often not enough properties on a street to pay for the cost associated with servicing and maintaining them.

As a species, humans are very social, reliant on community for support, even for survival. In fact, the early founders of the New England colonies in the 1600s specifically banned anyone from building a house beyond a certain distance from the village green. It was dangerous to be so isolated and considered antisocial and lacking in contribution to the public good. The wounds that sprawl inflicts are not only financial, political, and environmental but affect our souls as well. As spiritual beings, we are called to connection, not isolation. The current devolution into angry political tribalism is a direct result of this sort of intentional isolation.

I see three aspects of contemporary American life which are leading to our potential destruction: the desire of financial entities for ever-increasing quarterly profits, the corporate desire for ever-increasing efficiency, and the individual desire for ever-increasing personal convenience without any increased cost.

Individually, we desire convenience as much as possible. The development and home-building industries cater to this, but for their own purposes must make efficiency a primary goal. This combination of convenience and efficiency as our highest goals has been leading to our ruin for decades. It has succeeded this long because we have, until now, been able to ignore the environmental, financial, and spiritual costs. No longer.

CHAPTER VI
The Deeper Materialism of Michael Stone

"The biggest environmental disaster facing the world is the American middle-class lifestyle"
"Until we are impoverished, things will not change." — Andres Duany

What architect and visionary urban planner Andres Duany says in the quotes above is not intended, I take it, as a spiritual impoverishment or sense of humility, but something more akin to actual financial impoverishment. I once heard him say in conversation that when we are rich, we can afford to make mistakes; and we are no longer the wealthy nation we once were. Yet as a culture, we continue to make those same breezy, off-hand mistakes of the wealthy.

In a spiritual sense, impoverishment often holds the connotation of a spiritual or psychological crisis, leading to renewal or growth. Can that hope of renewal translate beyond the spiritual?

Accumulating Material Goods – and Letting Them Go

During the blizzard of late January 2016, I was trapped in an Airbnb for a couple of days. With the wind howling and the streets blocked in Old Town Alexandria, VA, there was little to do but cook, watch the snow come down, and talk. As it turned out, my hostess was a psychotherapist and life coach, so conversation flowed easily and naturally in a certain direction. She shared with me the details of her ongoing experiment – to live in extreme simplicity, with the goal of owning no more than 100 objects. Quite an intense aspiration, which could easily veer into what I consider mere survival, rather than living. A noble effort at personal discipline, but perhaps not in the midst of trying to entice paying customers to a new Airbnb business!

Consider the opposite extreme. The average American household possesses about *300,000* discreet objects, reports the LA Times. Hair dryers, frying pans, socks, toys, pillows, power drills, spoons – the average household contains more TV screens than people. How healthy can such an approach to life be?

Here is a twist for any spiritually-minded individual; in order to delve more fully into a spiritual life, we must fall more deeply in love with the material world.

By this, I mean not a *materialistic* approach of acquisitiveness, but a deeper appreciation of and connection to the physical world in which we find ourselves. This goes beyond a love of nature – forests, wildlife, the power of the sea which comes easily – but a profound sense of reverence for human creations as well. Not just music and the arts, but technology and urbanism as well. While many cultures believe the natural world, as well as human beings, are imbued with spiritual presence, psychologist James Hillman sensed we must accept that the work of humans also embodies true spiritual life. My view has always been that we are not incarnated in the physical world in order to escape it, transcend it, and avoid physicality, but to dive deeply into it, learn from it, and participate in it. We are offered the opportunity to appreciate, love, and participate in this physical universe. The incredibly difficult trick is to do so without the desire to possess or control.

Spiritual Materialism or Materialistic Possession

In a 2013 TED Talk, Buddhist teacher Michael Stone describes an approach to life he has termed "deeper materialism." I ran across this randomly and it affected me very strongly. His talk was profoundly moving to me, and I can't hope to communicate as eloquently as he, but I can summarize a few takeaways that struck me regarding the value of considering a Deeper Materialism.

Spirituality usually refers to what is behind the physical, in an invisible "other place." So, we have to make it visible somehow in order to relate to it; this is the role of the arts and design (and I would add, urbanism). Someone has to make a decision regarding what that looks like. Spiritual practice, and religion, is invented by humans in every culture – but what is it, what is its purpose? It also changes when it encounters a new culture. Culture is changing significantly now, all over the globe, and therefore, a new "operating platform" is needed.

Materialism in our culture is superficial; it is an acquisitive attachment to things. How is our materialism related to our spiritual practice? Spiritual enlightenment often means total detachment from the world. But what if we scrap our whole idea of spirituality, and replace it with a deeper love of the material?

Stone's idea is that we are not materialistic *enough* – we don't love the physical world deeply, as a gift – either the natural or human-made world, neither lakes and forests, nor sidewalks, buildings, or communities.

Spirituality and enlightenment too often take us up and away from our experience of life; then we split off into something too abstract. Meditation, for example, is generally thought of as a method of clearing the mind to attain enlightenment and thus, avoiding the need to be reincarnated. This is "vertical" practice, an attempt to escape this world. Stone seeks to replace this historically conventional "vertical" transcendence of escape, with "*horizontal*" transcendence – not by going up, out, separating, but *connecting* through relationship. Relationship then, is the key to a deeper materialism.

Detachment and Connection – Two Types of Meditative Practice

There are two ways this deeper materialism is already coming to fruition. We can see this in our ordinary, everyday experiences.

Yoga has become ubiquitous in hospitals, churches, prisons, etc. It gives us a type of spiritual experience without religious dogma – yoga means "intimacy" in Sanskrit – it gives us greater intimacy with our experience in the moment. Since we have such very short attention spans now, yoga provides us a means of focusing deeper attention to our material life.

Along with yoga, farm markets are now everywhere. Why? People aren't merely going to get fresh produce to cook, they are participating in horizontal transcendence, connecting with something much bigger than their own lives. A farm market is a series of relationships – farmers, consumers, community – the urban and rural supporting each other.

A third example might be found in what economists have dubbed the "shared economy." This is found in people choosing Zipcar membership rather than car ownership, and co-working arrangements rather than isolated private offices. Experience rather than possession. The decline of conventional retail is occurring at the same time we see an enormous rise in fine dining; consumers are choosing experiences over "stuff."

A Deeper Urbanism – A Spirituality of Embodied Connection

If Mr. Stone asks us to consider a deeper materialism, how does that relate to urban form and life? What constitutes a deeper urbanism? Relationship is the key to a deeper materialism. Relationship is about connection to and respect for all things – trees, animals, stones, technology, the arts – and urbanism. And good urbanism, in my view, is about providing two things: choices and connections. Urbanism then, is a physical manifestation of Relationship.

The love of and experience of nature allows us to appreciate the creative energy of the Universe and benefit from its power. But love of and participation in urban life at any scale or intensity, whether village or city, provides us the opportunity not only to appreciate but to *participate* in the ongoing act of creation. Urban life is a collection of human aspirations, of spiritual longings made physical, the cup into which we have poured all dreams, ever since we began to build cities more than 6,000 years ago. The Buddhist cosmology includes the story of the god Vishnu, who sleeps and dreams the world into reality. Even more ancient, the shamanic tradition understands this world to be first a dream of ours, which is then made real by our actions.

If the enterprise of creating cities and other urban forms is to continue, then sustainability becomes a core concern. A primary need for achieving sustainability, according to the architect Steve Mouzon, is *Love*. Sustainable urbanism, according to Mouzon, is not better technology, more efficient window systems, driverless electric cars, or high-performing HVAC equipment. Rather, it is found in creating places that we love, and therefore take care of and maintain. Without this, we end up being willing to treat places as disposable, abandoning them for the outer exurbs, wasting their embedded energy and beauty. This, I think, gets to what Stone is talking about. This sort of deeper urbanism can bring us into a more direct understanding of our connection to each other, the natural world, and our dependence on and connection to the earth.

How does a city or town foster this? Certainly, this includes quality design and materials, from the details of street furnishings and public art to the skeletal structure of street pattern and open space. Beyond this, though, urban settings provide something else. I write this after participating in the Women's March, here in Washington, DC ... exactly one year after that blizzard. From one year to the next, my thoughts have turned from how to best arrange a personal material life, to conversations on how best to organize our shared public material life. Looking out the window of a café, watching hundreds of other participants streaming by, I am aware that I have seen – and been a part of – the creation of collective memory.

The German psychologist Erich Neumann wrote of his concerns regarding the rise of Mass Man, as opposed to Group Man. The Mass Man arises out of the shadow of mobs, into unthinking political and emotional hysteria. Group Man, however, comes together with an intentionality of mutual support for individual growth. Such group participation is afforded by urbanism – village or metropolis – in the form of the smaller-scale democracy of neighborhoods and associations. A deeper urbanism, that physical manifestation of our collective spiritual longings, is the place where we can own this without possessing or being possessed. But we have to slow down, pay attention, and participate. Urbanism is the result of and setting for that intentional coming together.

CHAPTER VII

How to Bake a City

"Eternity is in love with the productions of time" – *William Blake*

I love to bake bread! Actually, I'm a terrible baker and only a moderately competent cook, but my favorite room has always been the kitchen. The act of creating something both nourishing and delicious is a pleasure in itself, and doubly so when my loaves bring a smile to someone's face. The preparation of food and the feeding of others is a fundamental act of service.

A number of years ago while experimenting with an oatmeal loaf, I was struck by the idea that the baking of bread is analogous to the design of a neighborhood, village, or town. The process of baking a loaf of bread is superficially straightforward enough, and the design of a good community is not rocket science. Both, however, require getting the details right, and some subtle understanding of basic principles.

What follows below is an outline of essential design elements and principles of New Urbanism, and the manner in which they are arranged and melded together. Going along with the baking analogy, I title these the ingredients, recipe, and menu of community. A look at the rules by which we create place, the little details we use to spice up community, and the way we view how much is enough – the dreaded "density" – is also discussed.

The Ingredients of Community

The first thing in baking, of course, is to pull out all the necessary ingredients. Bread typically includes flour, sugar, salt, sometimes milk and eggs, and yeast or perhaps baking powder and soda. What are the ingredients needed to physically create a neighborhood or city? I count a "baker's dozen" of these ingredients, as follows.

Walkable Size

Throughout history, the places we build have been sized by the simple need for walkability. The ancient Greeks, it has been said, determined the size of a town or city based on the number of citizens who could easily hear a speaker at a political gathering. The appropriate size for a neighborhood in France, goes another story, has been based on the number of residents needed to support a bakery. In mid-20th century America, a neighborhood was defined by the area served by an elementary school. Today, the measure is walkability, bringing a wide range of uses and activities within an easy walk from center to edge of a neighborhood. This is a range of 5-10 minutes, or a quarter to a third of a mile.

Mixed Uses

Mixing things together means not just horizontally along a street or block, but vertically as well. Those uses can include residential, commercial, office, and even some civic uses. Shops and restaurants should line the street, with residential activity above. In this way, enough variety of uses are brought close together to make walkability viable.

Variety of Housing Types

This might include large and small single-family detached homes, townhouses, duplexes, condominiums, and rental apartments in various configurations. One of the catchphrases of the day is "cradle to cradle" design. Popularized by William McDonough and others, this applies to the functionality and environmental sustainability of products, and their ability to take into account future generations. As it might apply to community design, the availability of a variety of housing options provides residents the ability to remain in their neighborhood even while life transitions require moving to a smaller or larger house.

Network of Intimate Streets

The conventional traffic arrangement of streets in the post-war era has been a dendritic, or hierarchical pattern. That is, many smaller streets feed into a few larger streets. A cul-de-sac feeds into a local neighborhood street, which then decants into a collector, which in turn feeds an arterial, and ultimately a limited-access highway is a recipe for traffic jams.

In contrast, a traditional community pattern of streets and blocks provides options and is more easily understood. The standard arrangement is a grid pattern, but what is important is not that the streets are straight and arranged in a clean grid but that they connect, with blocks not exceeding about 500 feet in length. In this way, walkability is promoted, and choice is provided. Traffic is dispersed rather than concentrated, so if one street is blocked for some reason, different routes are still available.

HOW TO BAKE A CITY

Central Square or Green

Every community needs a central open place, a heart, for gathering, playing, protesting, and celebrating. A good size ranges from one-third acre to one acre, not more. Normally the space is green, but hardscaped plazas are common. This is the space by which the community is often identified, creating memory through public holiday celebrations, farm markets, etc.

Parking Arrangements

A very typical daily American experience is the hike across vast expanses of asphalt from a parked car to the destination storefront. Because of the design priority given to the car, parking is normally placed between the street and buildings to make it visible. We end up viewing a sea of parking as normal; the dull pain this visual blight causes is hardly felt anymore. Yet parking should be thought of as infrastructure or a utility. These are necessary but unattractive, and so should be mostly hidden from view. The vast majority of parking should be placed *behind* the buildings it is intended to serve. Placing some parking out front is actually very useful, however. This is done by placing the parking not between the street and the building, but between the street and the sidewalk. This on-street parking creates a buffer between moving traffic and the sidewalk, increasing the comfort level for pedestrians.

Sidewalks

In this list of ingredients, one aspect recurs most clearly: the pedestrian experience. Sidewalks need to be wide enough to accommodate a number of people, plus various furnishings such as signage, mailboxes, bus stops, plantings, and outdoor dining. In residential areas, sidewalks should be at least 5 feet wide so that two people can pass or walk together easily. In commercial areas, width needs to increase to 12 feet, and up to 25 feet if outdoor dining is included.

HOW TO BAKE A CITY

Rear Alleys and Lanes

Alleys and rear lanes provide secondary access to a lot. This is valuable in order to allow for large delivery trucks and emergency equipment. They also allow various unattractive utilities to be hidden, such as trash, electrical and gas structures, and parking, allowing for a more attractive streetscape.

Shallow Setbacks

Virtually all conventional zoning requires that buildings be set back away from streets or sidewalks a minimum distance. A novel approach turns this on its head, setting a *maximum* setback distance. The intent is to create the sense of an outdoor room; to do so, proportions must be created to give a sense of enclosure. A maximum ratio of 6:1 is desired, regarding distance from façade to façade across a street to building height.

Outbuildings

Secondary structures on a lot, aside from the main house, are known as outbuildings. These can serve any number of purposes. Typically located at the rear lot line along an alley, the standard use is a parking garage. They can also be imagined as a bedroom that has migrated away from the main house. An outbuilding can provide additional living space, a rental unit to support the mortgage on the property, a home office, an in-law suite, or a children's rumpus room.

Porches

We've all had to fumble with a pocketful of keys, looking for just the right one, while standing at the door of our house, getting soaked during a rainstorm. Beyond sheltering us while fumbling for keys, however, a front porch serves other vital purposes. It gives a sense of welcome, but also serves as a middle ground, a transition from the public street to the private home. Residents can choose to use the porch as a psychological safety buffer from the world or engage with passersby from the relative comfort and security of the porch. This is particularly important when the call for shallower setbacks is considered.

Flexible Buildings

By this I mean the ability of a building to be put to a variety of uses over time, as the market dictates. Versatility is key. One of the limitations of conventional suburban residential and commercial architecture is the inability of a structure to play more than one role. A split-level rancher will never be anything but a single-family residence, while a traditional townhouse can easily be transitioned to office, retail, or restaurant use, and back again.

Variety of Open Spaces

Specific types of public spaces are crucial to the health of any community. Several different types are useful, ranging from formal plazas in the center to informal greens and naturalistic parks at the edge of a community; playgrounds, ballfields, tot lots, and so forth provide specialized infrastructure for particular activities. Typically, a variety of small scattered open spaces are more valuable to the life of a community rather than a few large, centralized parks.

The Recipe for Community

The next step, of course, is to mix the ingredients together. This has been surprisingly lost in American urban planning for the past 75 years or so, though an ancient concept. As we have seen in Chapter V, the sprawl model of community design doesn't get around to this mixing. In fact, it intentionally avoids this. But would we serve our guests only the ingredients of bread? A cup of flour, a tablespoon of sugar, a raw egg?! Yet regarding the design of community, this is what we have accepted in post-WWII America, resulting in the mess of suburban sprawl. Single-family homes in one area, apartments elsewhere, more expensive homes isolated in another corner of town, shopping along the highway, office parks hidden away in yet another isolated pod. Not so tasty. What do we get when we mix these ingredients together? Depending on how they are mixed, there are three outcomes: Neighborhoods, Districts, and Corridors.

These two images each show a collection of the necessary ingredients, but they add up to very different experiences. Inclusion of the right elements is not enough; they must be mixed together.

Neighborhoods

Neighborhoods are the fundamental building block of community. Primarily residential in nature, they also will include some mix of commercial and civic elements, geared to serving the nearby residents. Their identity is both a physical and emotional map. Generally, they are small enough to be easily walked from one end to another and have some identifying civic or commercial institutions as an anchor. A neighborhood can be considered similar in scale to a village; when two or more villages connect, they become neighborhoods and form part of a larger town or city. Conversely, villages are neighborhoods that are unattached to others, standing free amidst undeveloped agricultural, forested, or other open land.

Districts

While neighborhoods are predominately residential, they contain some other uses and activities mixed in. Some uses, however, just don't "play well with others" and need to be isolated in their own single-use areas. Such areas are known as districts and might be defined by noxious activities dominated by industrial, warehousing, or transportation uses. Some districts may remain mixed but are dominated by civic, commercial, or institutional uses such as a university, an arts and entertainment district, or downtown.

Corridors

Neighborhoods and districts have centers in which we gather together, but they also have boundaries and edges. These linear boundaries can be thought of as corridors or hallways. They might be natural such as a river or stream, ridgeline, or steep topography, and also contain elements of the built environment, such as train tracks or a highway. Along an urban corridor, there might be placed various land uses directly related to the transportation type; warehousing, big box shopping, car dealerships. Corridors can be seen as both positive and negative; they divide one neighborhood from another, but they can also connect.

The Menu of Community

So, we have, metaphorically, mixed all those ingredients of community and served our guest a wonderful slice of freshly baked bread. But just as we would not merely serve guests a cup of flour and a raw egg, neither would we serve them only bread, but also perhaps a salad, a main course, dessert – in other words, a full meal. The way in which this is provided in community design is through what is known as the

Transect.

Merriam-Webster's online dictionary defines "transect" as "a sample area (as of vegetation) usually in the form of a long continuous strip." In common parlance, the noun is not capitalized. However, the field of New Urbanism and the Center for Transect Studies does capitalize the noun, and uses it in a very specific and meaningful way.

The Transect is a concept developed in the field of environmental studies as a method of understanding ecosystems, and how they connect, transition, and relate to one another. A Transect can be thought of as a slice of the landscape, transitioning along multiple ecosystems. Each ecosystem has its own distinctive flora, fauna, geology, and hydrology. So, for an ecologist, a Transect might include the ocean floor, the beach, marshland, scrub pine, and on to hardwood forest.

To an urbanist, the Transect has a slightly different set of ecosystems, those of the human environment. The urban Transect was developed by proponents of the New Urbanist movement, led by Andres Duany. It includes six general categories in a gradient of development intensity. These are as follows:

T-1 – Preserved wilderness and natural areas which are deemed too valuable, delicate, or otherwise inappropriate to develop, including wilderness, natural areas and parks, steep slopes, wetlands, etc.

T-2 – Rural and working landscapes such as agriculture, which may be developed in the unforeseen future.

T-3 – Sub-urban, and low-density in character, dominated by single-family homes with little to no mixed commercial uses.

T-4 – General neighborhood, remaining primarily residential but of a higher density, including townhouses and occasional apartment dwellings and corner stores mixed in with single-family homes.

T-5 – Neighborhood center, a focal point for a neighborhood featuring increased commercial and some civic elements clustered to serve the immediate area.

T-6 – Downtown core, the most intensely developed area, featuring concentrated office, retail, and civic elements of a city. Residential is limited to apartment and condominium buildings.

These Transect zones can be thought of as a range of informal to formal, completely natural to intensely urban, simple to sophisticated. Any element, or ingredient of community can be designed in a more formal manner or less so, and when designed in context of its Transect zone, all elements are appropriate and acceptable. A wooden split rail fence, for instance, is appropriate in a rural setting, but out of place in midtown Manhattan. In this way, all aspects of development are appropriate in the right context.

Likewise, a range of settlement patterns is also needed, including a hamlet, village, town, and metropolitan city. No one form of community is best; providing a range of options is always preferable, so we need to respect the desire for and provide a variety of options across a region.

The transition points from one ecosystem to another are the places where so often life flourishes in new and unexpected ways. The meeting of the forest and field, the ocean and beach – these are porous borders in which species mix, hydrologic patterns shift, and geology transitions. At a grand scale, the borders represented by the meeting of continental plates converging and separating creates the most wonderful (though dangerous) landscapes. Such a transition point, as when a residential neighborhood meets the downtown, may bring a sense of excitement and anticipation.

The Cookbook of Community: Zoning Ordinances and Holy Scripture

When we find some wisdom or valuable knowledge which we think of as foundational, it gets put into a book so that later generations can make use of it. These sorts of "instructions for life" are generally thought of as inviolate, not to be changed, but adhered to as eternal truth. I see them differently though; while the wisdom of the elders must be given respect, their words are often more appropriate as guideposts that need occasional reviewing and updating. Cookbooks too are to be taken as only a starting point for serious foodies. My favorite soups were found in recipe books, but as I became comfortable with the process of making them, I gained enough confidence to deviate from the directions by adding new ingredients. My favorite bean soup now has three new ingredients that were not originally called for, making it more popular than ever among those who have tried it.

Zoning ordinances are taken by many communities as akin to scripture, and seemingly are updated only slightly more often. Indeed, if a conflict arises between what a community desires in the built environment and what the zoning ordinance demands, zoning will win out. Zoning by nature tends to hold the conservative goal of maintaining a predictable status quo of property values. In fact, zoning generally doesn't put into place those things which are desirable, but instead prevents a perceived problem – better the devil you know than the devil you don't know. Zoning ordinances are the legal implementation of a community's comprehensive or master plan which is aspirational in nature; yet zoning requirements are inevitably in conflict with the aspirational goals of the community. As long as Americans view residential real estate primarily as a source of private wealth creation, as an investment rather than a home and savings, this will continue.

Works of scripture too tend to be written over a long period of time, but are eventually finalized and set in stone. They are stories, however, so in order to have power, they must be written in a language familiar to our ears. Think of the difference between a list of ingredients in a recipe and those found in prepackaged foods at the grocery store – if the ingredients can't be pronounced, it's probably not good food. Likewise, if the language in a holy book doesn't resonate with our contemporary understanding, it won't inspire. If zoning language is too out of synch with that of a community plan, it won't result in well-designed places.

A common response to this failure is the inclusion of language requiring that 1% of a project's budget be set aside for public art. But this provides hardly even a band-aid in treating the wound of failing urbanism. The response is not merely a higher dollar set aside for art to hide the ugliness of what we build. The great cities of Paris and Rome achieved their gracious power not through a 1% set-aside for beautification but through a completely different set of values and priorities. The places we build reflect the values we hold.

Cookbooks change more quickly than scripture, as they should. Medieval recipes are not de rigueur today, while the Old Testament remains highly influential. Of course, culinary tastes don't have the same impact on our lives as do the mythic stories we use to organize the world. As our understanding of the world changes and becomes more complex, the old stories begin to sound inadequate. Jesus alluded to this when he spoke to the disciples in the Gospel of John, saying, "I have more to teach you, but you are not ready to hear." He was an evolutionary, it seems. We should be too.

Counting Calories – Or, a Few Words About Density

Why are we afraid of things we don't even know how to define? We have a cultural notion that density of place is always a negative, that less density is always better, that more density can only bring on disaster, generally including increased traffic and an unspoken influx of "those people." This American propensity stems all the way back to Thomas Jefferson, who had a strong dislike of cities, preferring instead to emphasize a nation of "yeoman farmers." He set the pattern by creating a system of land division for the Louisiana Purchase, essentially intending to settle the entire space with farms each set on 160 acres. Cities were for Jefferson a necessary evil at best.

What exactly is meant by the word "density"? In a sense it is nothing more than a numerical calculation, the number of housing units per acre or people per square mile. The number might be large or small, but it is only a number. There is no magical figure to be achieved; it is a mere quantity. There are innumerable design variations to achieve the same numeric density, through small or large lot detached homes, townhouses, duplexes, stacked condominiums, garden apartments, etc. Professionals use a variety of techniques to come up with a number, making the concept of density even foggier. Net versus gross density, residential units per acre, people per square mile, Floor Area Ratio – these are all meaningless to the public, offering no particular vision of what a place might look like or how we might experience it, which is, after all, what we really care about.

The problem of density illustrates how the professional world of land planning has lost its way, preferring to determine value with an arbitrary number rather than a qualitative experience. The general public, however, usually has a very poor understanding of what it is they seem to fear. A high-density number is almost always a proxy for some other deeper fear, of some unknown. The public imagination equates density with crime, poverty, traffic, a loss of property value, and people who are "not like us."

Is it possible to fear too little density? This is beginning to happen for practical, not merely aesthetic reasons. California has recently experienced an emerging alliance between young real estate developers and the environmental movement whose goal is to increase density in order to relieve the lack of affordable middle-class housing. Instead of NIMBY (Not In My Back Yard), the new cry is YIMBY – Yes In My Back Yard.

Our experience of a place is not quantitative but is completely qualitative: architectural quality and details, landscaping, amenities, ambiance, etc. Most fundamental, beyond detailing and decorative embellishments, is the basic urban structure, the "bones" of streets, block arrangements, building setbacks, and the like. When planners focus on the experience of place from the ground level up, rather than the achievement of a numeric standard, worries over density seem to evaporate. Places of equal density can look and feel wildly different. A place of lesser density than what the public may desire can be quite unpleasant, while a place of higher density may be wonderful. The places we admire and enjoy the most are always more dense, by whatever measurement is used, than we realize. To play off the food analogy again, the goal of a good recipe is not to set a preordained amount of salt, but to create a delicious meal. Likewise, the goal of urban planning and design is not the attainment of a perfect numerical balance, but the creation of an enjoyable and lovable place. Our experience of a place is more important than numbers. Do we feel comfortable? Is it a pleasant place of enjoyment and memory?

An excellent method for understanding this is known as a Visual Preference Survey (VPS). While not a fully scientific method, a VPS can give the public a way of comparing development patterns of varying densities and formats, along with sense of the sorts of places they enjoy most. A VPS consists of a series of up to a several hundred photographs depicting different land uses, street scenes, building and open space types, and so forth, which participants then score based on the appeal of the image. A ranking of desired outcomes can then be developed.

A study conducted in 2014 by the National Association of Homebuilders (NAHB) looked at the characteristics of development in the United States. Titled "Typical American Subdivisions" and written by Paul Emrath, the vice-president of NAHB, it states that the median gross density of residential subdivisions in metro areas is 2.9 dwelling units per acre. Density as a numerical standard, however, gives very little sense of the character of a neighborhood. Two places of the same density can provide dramatically different experiences. A density of four units to an acre, for instance, can be made up of four single-family houses spread out equally on quarter-acre lots, or four narrow townhouses clustered in one corner of the site. The assumption that lower density results in a more pleasing experience isn't always true.

Density then turns out to be a false concern. What might seem like too high a number of units is softened, to return to the cooking analogy once again, by the "herbs and spices" that are added to the recipe of community. This includes the various design details implemented: landscaping, street furniture, architectural detailing, color, etc. We add these spices "to taste" as a typical recipe allows.

Beyond this, lower-density communities have trouble financially supporting the infrastructure and amenities that people tend to desire from a neighborhood. When a community has a solid foundation, we tend to describe it as having "good bones." In our own skeletal systems, bones without enough density tend to become brittle and break, a condition known as osteoporosis. Both our bodies and communities need a basic level of density, it seems.

We have looked at what is involved in cooking up a fine meal – ingredients, recipe, and menu. Imagine too that we have indulged ourselves in the immersive environment of a fine restaurant, knowing our calorie count is manageable. Now comes the maître d' with the tab. Can we afford what we just ordered? The next chapter will take a look at that concern.

The Charter of the New Urbanism

Before we do that, I must acknowledge and give credit to the source of the material shared here. For thirty years I have been an active member of the Congress for the New Urbanism and continue to be deeply influenced by the design and policy values it promotes. I identify myself professionally by my association with it. Adopted by the Congress for the New Urbanism in 1996, and published as a book a few years later, its Charter outlines the principles which are the source for the material of this chapter. It is reproduced below; its language should be disseminated as widely as possible among all those even tangentially involved in the shaping of our physical communities, including designers, policy advocates, and elected officials.

The Charter of the New Urbanism

The Congress for the New Urbanism views disinvestment in central cities, the spread of placeless sprawl, increasing separation by race and income, environmental deterioration, loss of agricultural lands and wilderness, and the erosion of society's built heritage as one interrelated community-building challenge.

We stand for the restoration of existing urban centers and towns within coherent metropolitan regions, the reconfiguration of sprawling suburbs into communities of real neighborhoods and diverse districts, the conservation of natural environments, and the preservation of our built legacy.

We advocate the restructuring of public policy and development practices to support the following principles: neighborhoods should be diverse in use and population; communities should be designed for the pedestrian and transit as well as the car; cities and towns should be shaped by physically defined and universally accessible public spaces and community institutions; urban places should be framed by architecture and landscape design that celebrate local history, climate, ecology, and building practice.

We recognize that physical solutions by themselves will not solve social and economic problems, but neither can economic vitality, community stability, and environmental health be sustained without a coherent and supportive physical framework.

We represent a broad-based citizenry, composed of public and private sector leaders, community activists, and multidisciplinary professionals. We are committed to reestablishing the relationship between the art of building and the making of community, through citizen-based participatory planning and design.

We dedicate ourselves to reclaiming our homes, blocks, streets, parks, neighborhoods, districts, towns, cities, regions, and environment.

We assert the following principles to guide public policy, development practice, urban planning, and design:

The Region: Metropolis, City, and Town

–Metropolitan regions are finite places with geographic boundaries derived from topography, watersheds, coastlines, farmlands, regional parks, and river basins. The metropolis is made of multiple centers that are cities, towns, and villages, each with its own identifiable center and edges.

–The metropolitan region is a fundamental economic unit of the contemporary world. Governmental cooperation, public policy, physical planning, and economic strategies must reflect this new reality.

–The metropolis has a necessary and fragile relationship to its agrarian hinterland and natural landscapes. The relationship is environmental, economic, and cultural. Farmland and nature are as important to the metropolis as the garden is to the house.

–Development patterns should not blur or eradicate the edges of the metropolis. Infill development within existing urban areas conserves environmental resources, economic investment, and social fabric, while reclaiming marginal and abandoned areas. Metropolitan regions should develop strategies to encourage such infill development over peripheral expansion.

–Where appropriate, new development contiguous to urban boundaries should be organized as neighborhoods and districts, and be integrated with the existing urban pattern. Noncontiguous development should be organized as towns and villages with their own urban edges, and planned for a jobs/housing balance, not as bedroom suburbs.

–The development and redevelopment of towns and cities should respect historical patterns, precedents, and boundaries.

–Cities and towns should bring into proximity a broad spectrum of public and private uses to support a regional economy that benefits people of all incomes. Affordable housing should be distributed throughout the region to match job opportunities and to avoid concentrations of poverty.

–The physical organization of the region should be supported by a framework of transportation alternatives. Transit, pedestrian, and bicycle systems should maximize access and mobility throughout the region while reducing dependence upon the automobile.

–Revenues and resources can be shared more cooperatively among the municipalities and centers within regions to avoid destructive competition for tax base and to promote rational coordination of transportation, recreation, public services, housing, and community institutions.

The Neighborhood, The District, and The Corridor

–The neighborhood, the district, and the corridor are the essential elements of development and redevelopment in the metropolis. They form identifiable areas that encourage citizens to take responsibility for their maintenance and evolution.

–Neighborhoods should be compact, pedestrian friendly, and mixed-use. Districts generally emphasize a special single use, and should follow the principles of neighborhood design when possible. Corridors are regional connectors of neighborhoods and districts; they range from boulevards and rail lines to rivers and parkways.

–Many activities of daily living should occur within walking distance, allowing independence to those who do not drive, especially the elderly and the young. Interconnected networks of streets should be designed to encourage walking, reduce the number and length of automobile trips, and conserve energy.

—Within neighborhoods, a broad range of housing types and price levels can bring people of diverse ages, races, and incomes into daily interaction, strengthening the personal and civic bonds essential to an authentic community.

—Transit corridors, when properly planned and coordinated, can help organize metropolitan structure and revitalize urban centers. In contrast, highway corridors should not displace investment from existing centers.

—Appropriate building densities and land uses should be within walking distance of transit stops, permitting public transit to become a viable alternative to the automobile.

—Concentrations of civic, institutional, and commercial activity should be embedded in neighborhoods and districts, not isolated in remote, single-use complexes. Schools should be sized and located to enable children to walk or bicycle to them.

—The economic health and harmonious evolution of neighborhoods, districts, and corridors can be improved through graphic urban design codes that serve as predictable guides for change.

—A range of parks, from tot-lots and village greens to ballfields and community gardens, should be distributed within neighborhoods. Conservation areas and open lands should be used to define and connect different neighborhoods and districts.

The Block, The Street, and The Building

—A primary task of all urban architecture and landscape design is the physical definition of streets and public spaces as places of shared use.

—Individual architectural projects should be seamlessly linked to their surroundings. This issue transcends style.

—The revitalization of urban places depends on safety and security. The design of streets and buildings should reinforce safe environments, but not at the expense of accessibility and openness.

—In the contemporary metropolis, development must adequately accommodate automobiles. It should do so in ways that respect the pedestrian and the form of public space.

—Streets and squares should be safe, comfortable, and interesting to the pedestrian. Properly configured, they encourage walking and enable neighbors to know each other and protect their communities.

–Architecture and landscape design should grow from local climate, topography, history, and building practice.

–Civic buildings and public gathering places require important sites to reinforce community identity and the culture of democracy. They deserve distinctive form, because their role is different from that of other buildings and places that constitute the fabric of the city.

–All buildings should provide their inhabitants with a clear sense of location, weather, and time. Natural methods of heating and cooling can be more resource-efficient than mechanical systems.

–Preservation and renewal of historic buildings, districts, and landscapes affirm the continuity and evolution of urban society.

CHAPTER VIII

Money, Finance, Taxation:
The Practical Necessities of a Spiritual Urbanism

"Money is coined energy" – C.G. Jung

This is perhaps the point at which the spiritual and material truly meet; if spiritual ideals and aspirations are to be translated into physical reality, resources need to be marshaled and organized. How do we determine priorities? Money and finance are tools to achieve greater goals, not ends in themselves. When it comes to creating a spiritually focused urbanism, money and finance are essential, practical, and rather unforgiving tools in the service of aims traditionally seen as very impractical. There are ways the two can work together more smoothly; in this chapter we'll consider some possibilities.

Money as Stored Spiritual Potential

It is easy (and necessary, I think) these days to call the very nature of capitalism into question. The national and global structure of finance that it has created over the centuries has made possible astonishing accomplishments but has clearly gone off track, wreaking havoc in its single-minded pursuit. Critics rail against it as a deeply flawed ideology, and call for its replacement with various, usually vague, options of a more socialist or communitarian approach.

Capitalism in America goes back to the earliest English settlements of the 17th century (Jamestown, the Mayflower voyage), which were underwritten by venture capitalists as money-making schemes. Then the Debt Recovery Act of 1732 set the tone for the American vision of real estate. It allowed British financiers to seize more than just personal property to recoup debts owed by American colonists, but also land and anything on the land. This set a precedent for land to be used in place of money; real estate became capital.

I'm not convinced, however, that capitalism is an ideology. As the internet entrepreneur and author of *Four Hundred Years of American Capitalism* Bhu Srinivasan describes it, capitalism is less an ideology than an operating system, similar to what drives my laptop. For a computer, an operating system is the nexus between hardware and software. Similarly, capitalism functions as the point at which the hardware (commodities such as ore, lumber, and land) are joined together with ideas, aspirations, and intentions. As an operating system, however, it is in need of a full-scale upgrade after too many minor regulatory fixes and patches. These upgrades must include not only legal constraints but a reassessment of fundamental principles. Generally, I sense the trouble with capitalism as we experience it today, and certainly regarding real estate, is a matter of scale and concentration.

The problem with capitalism is there aren't enough capitalists. It has become a system of a few big players rather than being open to many small participants. Money is itself a benign tool, neither good nor bad; it all depends how we choose to use it. Like freedom, how we put it to use is the essential concern. What is the intention, and how are the costs and benefits discerned? These are best answered at the smallest scale possible, the individual, and the creative vision they carry. Money is a tool to be used in the process of making something. Our efforts to heal the wounded pattern of urban settlement must focus on enabling the individual to participate with the most impact. This is the work of the local small-scale real estate developer.

A Matter of Scale

If it makes sense to think of money as stored spiritual potential – or potential of any kind, really – how long should it be held, for what purpose, and by whom? And significantly, how much of it? I've heard one pundit say that there is simply too much money in the world, held in too few places, all sloshing around looking for the next place to land. Disaster seems to recur whenever too much money chooses to invest in one place all at once – the silver market in the 1980s, dot-coms in the 90s, and real estate in the 00s.

Getting the scale right is crucial. In his book *Scale*, the particle physicist Geoffrey West considers the growth and longevity of mammals, and finds that the larger animals tend to live longer and have a slower metabolism. With every doubling of average weight, a species becomes 25% more efficient in its use of energy and lives 25% longer. This is the result of the geometric pattern of the various networks that bring energy into, and remove waste from, a creature's body. He then applies the same research to the life of cities and has found a seemingly universal "Rule of 15%."

His findings indicate that the doubling of the population of a city will result in a 15% increase in various positive attributes of civic life: higher wages, education, health and longevity, infrastructure cost savings, etc. In other words, the larger you are, the less energetic input is needed per capita. The offset is, unfortunately, a commensurate 15% increase in negative qualities as well such as crime and disease. This is a universal global pattern across all nations. There is an efficiency of scale to cities. While West does not state a maximum potential size of cities, they can obviously become unwieldy; but clearly, we can see that addressing the issues of appropriate scale means being in harmony with natural systems.

How does this relate to the reality of ordinary real estate development projects and their impact on a community? The problems and complications of contemporary life are increasingly large and complex. I've always felt that because of this, we generally need large solutions. Regarding the creation of community though, bigger is not always better; a better way to phrase this might be that we need smaller solutions that can be replicated and scaled appropriately. Designing and building intimate places requires many small efforts, each providing a distinctive look, feel, and story. As a rule, large projects designed and developed by few entities result in uninspiring, predictable placemaking. Getting the scale right is crucial; while large projects are often necessary and valuable, and may have an efficiency of scale, as a default setting, they can overwhelm a community with bland design responses and loss of history and connection.

When we think of urban redevelopment projects, we tend to imagine big problems that require big solutions, resulting in mega-efforts involving millions of dollars and a dramatic change in the look and feel of a community. Local government tends to promote this sort of large-scale effort, in the policies and zoning regulations they adopt.

Scale is a significant predictor of the feel of a project. Smaller scale projects are nimbler and more responsive to local situations, have a more immediate impact, and allow for individuals to participate in the creative process, offering variety and opportunity which in turn creates a commitment to place.

Large projects can be necessary, wonderful, elegant, and a positive influence. But they are naturally expensive, and thus geared to high-end markets only, to the exclusion of the middle class and poor, and often focus on treating the urban setting as an entertainment playground rather than a living, working neighborhood.

What every community brings to the process of land development is its limited supply of land. A very common error made by local governments is to assume that community redevelopment requires large and complex projects, feasible only by large corporate development and construction firms with the resources to gather the millions of dollars needed. Of course, the results are intended to increase the local tax base.

But how well is the community served by this assumption that bigger is always better? Quite poorly, according to urban planning consultant Joe Minicozzi. His innovative approach to the pattern of development and the fiscal impact it has on a community emphasizes the *per-acre value* of land. Does the physical form of development determine taxable revenue? Consider his analysis of the City of Asheville, NC. He compared two fundamentally different patterns of development to determine their impact on the city; that of the large-scale suburban pattern represented by the local Walmart, and a traditional 6-story downtown mixed-use building. His findings are dramatic. The essentials of each are as follows:

	Walmart	Mixed Building
Acreage	34	0.20
Tax Value	$20 MM	$11 MM
Value/acre	$0.588 MM	$57.9 MM
Property Tax/acre	$6,500	$634,000
Retail Taxes/acre	$47,500	$83,600
Residents/acre	0	90
Jobs/acre:	5.9	73.7

Repeating this analysis in cities all over the nation, he found that on a per-acre basis, the finely-grained mixed-use pattern of traditional cities always outperforms the suburban sprawl model. There is no question as to which pattern is more fiscally responsible to the community. We see that the essential issue is pattern and scale, not merely the amount of development, that is crucial in defining the health of a community.

Municipal Tax and Finance

There was a time when local government actually led the development process, rather than simply setting rules and waiting for the private sector to implement its vision. Washington, DC was essentially constructed in this manner. President George Washington hired Pierre L'Enfant to design the city; the blocks formed by the streets he laid out were then parceled out and offered for sale to the public by the appointed commissioners who raised the money needed to actually build the infrastructure.

Not all governmental activities are intended to have a quantifiably positive financial return. In fact, the role of government is to provide those aspects of civilization that private business cannot. This is why government cannot be run like a business. The point of most publicly provided services has nothing to do with providing an efficient return. The cost of parks and recreational facilities can be quantified but not valued, for instance.

We have already touched on the way municipal policies and ordinances affect the form and thus the financial stability of a community. The work of civil engineer Chuck Marohn and his *Strong Towns* initiative encourages localities to understand the long-term costs of maintaining the infrastructure required of the development they permit. He has found that the typical single-family zoning that makes up the majority of land within American towns does not allow for enough homes to pay for the ongoing maintenance of streets and sewer pipes. In other words, conventional American development is designed for financial failure. We have been able to externalize – ignore, really – the costs of our pattern of living for several generations, but no more. Our ancestors gifted us, roughly during the period from the 1910s to 1930s, excellent streets, bridges, water lines, and sewer systems. They did not, however, consider the replacement costs. All of a sudden, and all at once across the nation, all this infrastructure has reached or exceeded its operational lifecycle and is at the point of total collapse. Our cultural assumptions for the single-family home means that the replacement cost far exceeds our ability to pay for it; there aren't enough houses per linear foot of street on a typical block to pay for its maintenance.

The experience Marohn describes in his work with Lafayette, Louisiana is typical of almost every municipality in America. The cost of replacing all the city's decaying infrastructure was roughly $32 billion. The total value of the entire tax base in the city, not just the real estate, was a mere $16 billion; not even close to what was needed. To put the issue in personal terms, the average household in Lafayette will have to see their annual property tax bill go from $1,500 to $9,200, just to maintain their current infrastructure. In other words, 20% of household income is needed to maintain, repair, and replace the roads, sewers, and water lines. This is not unique to Lafayette, but the standard fate of essentially every community in the US.

Real estate development has been the backbone of municipal fiscal policy for generations, but without honest accounting of maintenance and replacement costs for infrastructure, it has been revealed to be a giant Ponzi scheme.

How can a community begin to scale back its operations in a way that can encourage local participation at a smaller, more local, and financially sustainable scale? The "Pink Tape" and "Tactical Urbanism" movements move us in the right direction. The regulatory and review processes of land development are notoriously slow and convoluted, shutting out many creative solutions. The idea of replacing "red tape" with less onerous "pink tape" is welcome. This is essentially a movement to streamline the review process, ease the regulatory burden, and clean up zoning ordinances.

Tactical urbanism is a set of bottom-up techniques for temporary experimentation on the built environment, to test the viability of physical changes before substantial amounts of money are spent. The testing of ideas is short-term and low-risk. This is the source of the fairly common "pop-up" retail movement. One example is to temporarily convert a series of on-street parking spaces into green space with seating, or a dining area for adjacent restaurants, before committing to actual construction.

These are all changes in vision and approach for municipal governments. What is the role of development in all this?

The Small-Scale Developer as Impresario

Real estate developers were once considered heroes in their communities rather than greedy environmental terrorists. In fact, statues were erected in their honor and towns were named after them. Well, granted, most of that was self-promotion, but still, they provided all the basic essential elements of civilization that we cannot do without; our homes, shops, and places of work and entertainment. Yet we despise their work. Why? Perhaps, as discussed above, much of the problem has to do with scale.

When at their best, a real estate developer reminds me of a Broadway impresario. An impresario has almost nothing to start with; no money, no theater, no play or playwright, no director or actors. They have two invaluable things though: contacts, and a vision. They are like matchmakers, seeking out others who do have the skills, abilities, and money to bring the vision into reality. Likewise, there are four essential elements a land developer may not immediately control but needs to assemble: land, capital, entitlement (zoning, various building permits and approvals), and tenants. In order to achieve this, they need to be generalists, not specialists, and have a wide but not necessarily deep set of skills. They don't need to have all the answers but need to understand what questions to ask.

The way in which a developer asks questions and determines answers is a process known as the *pro forma*. Also affectionately known as "making stuff up on paper," it is essentially a spreadsheet of assumptions regarding how a building will make money, testing out how much a project will cost to complete, and whether and how much it might earn. On one side, the costs include purchasing land and financing the project, the price of materials, costs relating to design, consultant and approval fees, marketing, ongoing maintenance, and so forth. Whether or not it will make money depends on whether the market will bear the rent or sale price needed to cover all costs plus some profit. For small rental buildings, the standard is known as "The Rule of 100" – every $100 of total project costs needs to generate $1 in rent (given certain interest rates, etc.). Thus, a total project cost of $100,000 must generate $1,000 in monthly rent. Is that worth the effort or not? Will the market bear that rent? If so, the project might work; if not, the project doesn't make sense (cents?).

An old adage in the architectural profession is that "form follows function." That is, the shape of a building is derived from the uses intended for it. In the world of investigative journalism, a parallel adage is to "follow the money." Putting the two together, we come up with what those in land development have come to realize as a deeper truth – "form follows finance." Money is a commodity, just like lumber or nails, but the difference is that money is a *created* commodity. And just like other commodities, money can be bought and sold, and comes with a price. That price is the major factor in determining the shape and quality of our buildings and the places they form.

The term "mortgage" goes back to at least the year 1283, coming from the Latin "mortuus vadium" meaning a death pledge. Serious business. Unlike residential mortgages, commercial mortgages for development range from 5 to 20 years, and generally have an amortization period longer than the term of the loan, perhaps up to 30 years. In a typical scenario, a lender might make a loan amortized over 30 years but due in only 7 years. This would result in manageable monthly payments over 7 years with the great majority of interest and principal due in one final balloon payment. For example, a developer with a $1 million commercial loan at 7% would make monthly payments of $6,653 for 7 years, followed by a final balloon payment of $918,127.

The way real estate is financed creates enormous pressure on developers to cut corners, reduce risk, and emphasize predictability and conformity in the products they offer. The issue of scale once again becomes significant. Smaller, less complex projects have less inherent risk. What we need to emphasize is fewer large and complex development projects run by corporate builders, and instead many smaller projects by smaller, local "mom-and-pop" development teams and individuals, working in incremental steps.

To reiterate, the problem with capitalism is that there are not enough capitalists. Where are these small local developer capitalists to be found? John Anderson, of the Incremental Development Alliance, is out to create them. IncDev, as it is known, seeks to build capacity at the local level for an army of small-scale property developers through a series of multi-day "boot camp" training seminars. Attendees are trained in every aspect of real estate development. Developers are generalists, not specialists, and need a wide but not deep skill set. How to assess a property, create a pro forma, build relationships with local officials and other actors, ask for money, manage the project, and reduce overhead are just a few of the topics covered.

Having taken the training myself, I can attest to the value of these seminars. The greatest takeaway, however, is not so much the technical knowledge needed, but an understanding of the right attitudes and values needed to succeed in small-scale development. Reducing complexity with simple repeatable building types and smaller overhead costs reduces risk and enables the ability to "over-deliver." The essentials include building trusting long-term relationships with neighbors, lenders, and officials. In all this, small-scale incremental development is more like gardening than farming.

For the small local incremental developer, work is focused not merely on the project site but the surrounding context. The neighborhood as a whole is what is of concern – getting to know the neighborhood, its people, and its history, not just the individual building site. Projects are selected as part of a neighborhood in which a long-term visionary impact can be made which, over time, can add up to a significant impact on the whole area.

There's an analogy between an incremental approach to land development and urban redevelopment, and the process of personal healing. The conventional approach to healing emotional or psycho-spiritual wounds is some large dramatic life-changing event, quite often to be found in a high-priced weekend retreat or seminar. The reality, however, is slower and more subtle. Small everyday changes in habit and routine are generally more workable and long-lasting. So too with the work of real estate development. Incremental development, done by small-scale local developers, is the equivalent process used by both nature and the soul, whereby larger universal patterns of health emerge out of small beginnings.

Efficiency, Sustainability, or Something Else?

The term "sustainability" is an assumed fundamental in any environmental or urban conversation today. It has even become central to corporate business language as well. However, to the extent that sustainability is assumed to mean some series of more efficient systems and technologies, it will fail.

What does the word really mean? There are more than enough definitions to choose from. Whatever definition we choose, we have to answer a basic question: what is it that is going to be "sustained?" If sustainability is merely an attempt to find a way to keep old familiar patterns in place, the purpose is defeated. This is my basic complaint regarding a more "efficient" automobile, for instance; a more "efficient" fleet of vehicles won't produce a more "sustainable" transportation infrastructure. This merely results in a more efficient pattern of unsustainable habits.

Sustainability is not merely an issue of more efficient technology, but more deeply of lifestyle and values which derive ultimately from our cosmological vision. Living a simpler lifestyle means less energy is needed – production versus consumption. The search for greater efficiency can easily veer into nothing more than an attempt to continue unhealthy patterns. In fact, the word "sustainability" implies just that – an attempt to keep in place habits that aren't in themselves sustainable. If we can find some work-around though, our habits won't have to change. So, the question must be asked, when we seek to promote sustainability, what are we trying to sustain? Perhaps looking for sustainable sources of energy in order to maintain an unhealthy consumer lifestyle isn't where the best solution will be found.

As the writer James Howard Kunstler points out, our conceptions of efficient systems tend to be highly unsustainable. A soybean field of 1,000 acres may be efficient as an agricultural business model, but highly unsustainable without enormous amounts of energetic input in the form of fertilizer and equipment. A thousand acres of marsh and woodland is highly sustainable but not at all efficient; it is full of redundant systems and species, each relying on the other for support.

Sustainability based on increased efficiency may simply not be possible. Better technology is only half the equation, the "supply side," so to speak. The "demand" side, that of our consumer desires, habits, and lifestyle, is of greater impact. Habits and lifestyle, of course, are shaped by our psychological view of ourselves and our world - our spiritual cosmology.

Efficiency and sustainability seem to be fundamentally at odds. And yet, in the world of finance, efficiency is pretty fundamental. Corporations rely on it for profits, and citizens expect wise and efficient use of municipal taxes. In all sorts of ways, a community must be efficient in its allocation of limited finances. While sustainability has become everyone's goal, greater efficiency won't always give it. There must be a balancing act between the two, or at least, a method of prioritizing between the two. A community must be efficient in its goal of sustainability, but as architect Steve Mouzon has observed, a primary element of sustainability is lovability. This echoes architect and founder of the Arcosanti project Paolo Soleri's quote: "Lovableness is the key to a living city." Unless we deeply love something – person or place – we won't work to sustain its existence. All the love in the world won't produce a sustainable place if there isn't enough money to create it, but otherwise, what's the point? Love motivates much more than a desire for a balanced spreadsheet.

In the process of decision-making, a hierarchy of values is often especially useful. As a community seeks to transition from conventional auto-oriented suburban sprawl to traditional pedestrian mixed-use urbanism, the following hierarchical perspective should be considered as a guide for decision-making.

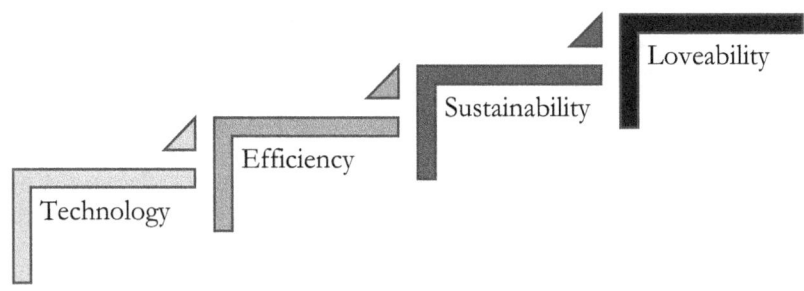

- ☐ **Technology** is a useful tool but only in the service of the higher good of efficiency;

    - ☐ **Efficiency** is essential but subsumed to the service of the higher good of sustainability

        - ☐ **Sustainability** is essential but only in the service of the higher good of lovability;

            - ☐ **Lovability** is the expression of the human soul and is creatively supported by an urbanism of meaning and memory

PART 3

THE EXPERIENCE OF PLACE

CHAPTER IX
Embodiment and Place

"The real question is, can a 5-minute walk be a journey of discovery?"
— David Dixon

The old cliche is that we all want to find the "meaning of life." The unfortunately phrased question posed by Arthur Dent in *The Hitchhikers Guide to the Galaxy*, "What is the meaning of life, the universe, and everything?" sends him unwillingly on all sorts of wild and unexpected adventures. Joseph Campbell thinks differently, writing, "People say that what we're all seeking is a meaning for life. I don't think that's what we're really seeking. I think that what we're seeking is an experience of being alive, so that our life experiences on the purely physical plane will have resonances with our own innermost being and reality, so that we actually feel the rapture of being alive."

This desire for experience can be thought of almost as an obligation; our spirits and souls demand it. As Thomas Moore phrases it, the soul has an irrepressible desire for enchantment. A common understanding in many spiritually-minded communities is that we are essentially spiritual beings who are trapped inside of matter. They say it is our task to liberate ourselves from this material world. I say the opposite; we are not spiritual beings trapped in matter, but spirits liberated into a certain freedom by our physicality. Spirit cannot act unless incarnated.

Humans are largely irrational creatures. The good city will appeal not only through rational values of practicality and sustainability, but by telling stories and allowing for positive sensory experiences. We use the senses as a sort of "spiritual technology."

In the end, Arthur gets some of each: a little meaning, and a lot of experience in his galactic travels. We don't need to go flying off quite so far for such adventures; we can find it much closer to home. What then does the city offer us regarding the experience of being alive?

The Flaneur

When I was 24 and could find no intentional plan or direction for my life, I decided to live in Brussels. Ostensibly, this was an agreement with my father to prepare for a career in the Foreign Service – hang around the European Commission headquarters, hone my French language skills, make a few connections. Instead, I volunteered with a Flemish nonprofit construction company, building an orphanage and drug rehab center.

I made the right choice.

Trying to get myself acclimated to a city divided into two unwilling halves (French-speaking Walloons, the Flemish with their Dutch language), I decided the best way to discover my way around was to intentionally get lost. I lived near the Jacques Brel Station in Anderlecht, so I took the metro to the far northeastern end of the line, in Stokkel, and walked back, to see what there was to see. Of course, it was a bit too much of an all-day and night hike, but it was a wonderful experience, with so much to discover. There was nothing in particular I wanted to see, I just wanted to be in the middle of something new and unknown. The jumble of languages: Flemish, French, German, Italian, Greek; the jumble of architecture: medieval, industrial, Art Nouveau, modernism; the tangle of hopes and fear. This was 1984, when the Euro-punks were convinced Reagan was bringing George Orwell back to life.

This was basically how I spent all my free time for a year, when not swinging a hammer – wandering new streets, trying to catch snippets of conversation, window shopping, discovering the pleasure, normally limited to Belgians and Brits, of sitting at an outdoor café drinking beer in a heavy drizzle. Late night was best, when delivery vans banged more loudly in the otherwise silent streets, and I had random meetings with Nick Cave's roadies in a back alley after a show. I wasn't looking for anything in particular, but I knew the wandering itself was important. I am, and always had been without knowing it, a *flaneur*.

A *what*?

Dictionary.com defines the term as an idler, dawdler, loafer. A very thin, shallow, and offensive definition; Merriam-Webster isn't any better. A playful term is a good alternative: Coddiwomple (v.) – To travel in a purposeful manner towards a vague destination. But I prefer my own definition: a passionate yet detached wandering observer of city life.

The first use of the term is generally given to the French writer Charles Baudelaire in about 1854. The habit, however, may have its literary origin with Louis Mercier, a writer and newspaper reporter more than 50 years earlier. He wrote about everything he saw, the everyday life of ordinary people on the streets, and ended up publishing 12 volumes of sketches.

Not a dilettante nor a dandy, who are cynical, detached, and intentionally create scenes, a flaneur is a calm observer, bearing witness to the lives of fellow urban dwellers. A flaneur is generally singular, isolated. The true Parisian flaneur will definitely make eye contact with passers-by, but never smiles or gives greeting. It is a private meditative spirituality. Being naturally gregarious, I can't help but strike up brief conversations with strangers, perhaps crossing the metaphoric line between private spirituality and the sociability of religion. Who knows what may come up in such brief conversation – personal stories, cooking advice, travel tips, humorous pet stories – random stories from people one might otherwise never meet. The city is usually considered to be a lonely place, but only if you're unwilling to take a few chances. Oxford University literature professor Christopher Butler is said to have understood the flaneur as seeking a form of transcendence, to "find the eternal in the transitory." City life is almost universally said to have a negative impact on the human psyche, but what are the positives? The flaneur is out to find them. Without necessarily intending a meditative or prayerful effort, flaneurs are open to it merely by reducing themselves to the act of observing, of being present in the moment.

The intentionality of having no intentions allows the opportunity for the unexpected to break through. It is meditation in motion: observing and being fully present to the moment, letting it go, releasing the experience, and being open to the next. The flaneur is giving a new twist to the perhaps overused term of the moment, "mindfulness," generally described as being present to and observant of one's own internal state of being – breath, heartbeat, emotional state. But can flaneury not be an equivalent effort at being present to one's external surroundings? The sounds and activity of the surrounding street, sidewalk, people ... by simply observing, taking it all in and letting it all go, we can find our center no matter the setting.

How to Walk Down the Street

Until recently, I have not put much thought into walking. Walkability and neighborhood walk scores, yes; but the physical act of walking really had not crossed my mind. For an urbanist, walkability and the experience of place is fundamental, a real joy. For a spiritually curious individual, awareness of self and surroundings is just as essential. Now, I'm increasingly paying attention to how I walk. I've found that the simple act of walking down the street can be an opportunity for more than merely getting from one place to another, even more than pleasant entertainment. There are several different ways to do it I suppose, depending on your goals – and how busy the sidewalk is.

I try to be aware of both the act and experience of walking, using diverse sources of inspiration. On crowded, busy sidewalks, my practice of Tai chi comes to mind. A few years ago, a mentor suggested I take up Tai chi or Qigong as part of my spiritual practice. Back in high school, I took a few years of Shorin Ryu karate, so the idea made sense to me. I tried a Tai chi session and it immediately resonated. I've been taking classes ever since.

If Tai chi is at all on your radar, you likely get an image of a slow-motion exercise that groups of retirees practice in public parks. Far more than that, Tai chi is a foundational nexus between Taoist philosophy and martial arts. A basic concept of Taoism is *wu-wei*, which means non-action or non-doing – that is, acting in a natural, uncontrived way. The goal of spiritual practice is, according to Lao Tzu in his work, the *Tao te Ching*, the attainment of this purely natural way of behaving.

Another way of thinking about wu-wei is "action that does not involve struggle or excessive effort." The concept of "effortless action" is foundational to Tai chi. As a martial art, it assumes your opponent is larger, stronger, and faster. Therefore, do not act as the aggressor, but allow your opponent's energy to work against him. Be fluid like water, it teaches – few movements are ever made directly, but rather obliquely. Walking against the flow of a crowded sidewalk is much the same. One cannot simply barge ahead – passersby, trash cans, pets on leashes, and abandoned scooters have to be avoided. A rather good attitude for life in general; Tai chi can be thought of as meditation in motion. As I walk a busy sidewalk on Connecticut Avenue in DC, or King Street in Alexandria, I find myself weaving in the side-to-side dodge of Tai chi, avoiding the aggression of the oncoming flow, and focusing on the moment, the simple act of taking one step after another.

In calmer settings such as a neighborhood park or residential street, a different source of insight inspires me. Walking comes as naturally to us as anything, but the Zen Buddhist teacher, Thích Nhất Hạnh, in his small book, *How to Walk*, reveals the simple act of walking as an opportunity for gratitude and joy. He taught "mindful walking" for seventy years. Meditation, he shows us, is not always sedentary. He imparts a number of practical tips, some basics that I'll share here. First, set for yourself a simple intention to enjoy and be aware of the basic process of walking. Focus solely on each step and breath. Make a contract between yourself and a particular place to practice mindful walking. Choose a particular stretch of road, or around a certain block, or while running a specific errand on foot. Finally, match your breathing with your pace. Perhaps begin with two steps as you inhale, three steps with each exhale. Adjust according to topography and your own comfort.

What makes a sidewalk conducive to these sorts of meditative walking, crowded or not? Perhaps the closest that sidewalk design comes to promoting, or at least accommodating, meditative walking, is found in the art of walkable placemaking. Our experience of sidewalks is, of course, at a basic, personal level. The act of meditation is what we bring to the place.

Sidewalk design can be a lot more complicated than we think! Although meditation is not a design criterion I'm aware of, there are lots of roles sidewalks have to play, and their design takes some subtle consideration. Just as the cartway of a street has distinct lanes for travel, turning, and parking, so too do sidewalks, particularly in commercial areas. Physically, they have four layers:

> **Frontage zone** – adjacent to property lines and building facades, this transition space gives room for outdoor dining and space for displays, signage, and merchandise from adjacent retail shops

Thoroughfare zone – for pedestrian travel, at least wide enough for two people to comfortably walk side-by-side

Furnishing zone – used for tree wells, planters, landscaping, lighting, transit shelters, and furniture such as benches, trash cans, and kiosks

Edge zone – a small clear area used for people getting in and out of parked vehicles

Sidewalks aren't designed with a layer designated for meditation, but they can provide plenty to meditate on, and pay attention to. Done gracefully, all of this adds up to a positive and immersive pedestrian environment, both pleasing and practical. Are mindfulness and walkability at odds here? While meditative walking is typically an inward-looking effort, a well-designed sidewalk, with good adjacent uses and window design, also offers the outward-looking meditative setting for that third sort of meditative walking discussed earlier, that of the flaneur. Sometimes a little space to breathe – or walk – is all we need to start a new path.

Café Life

"Community is about how we treat others who are like us; civility is about how we treat the stranger on the street" – David Brain

A number of years ago, I started a consulting practice in Lancaster, Pennsylvania out of a small unit in an apartment building I owned at the time. I had a great set-up: one room with a great window view for a desk where I would write; a second room held my drafting table and drawing needs. Cozy, convenient, efficient.

I couldn't stand it. Within a couple of weeks, in spite of interesting projects to work on, I realized I was bored, lonely, and easily distracted.

The first lesson I learned about operating a consulting business had nothing to do with financial management or client relations, but my own personal habits and traits. Mornings are *not* the time to expect creativity from me; that's the time for the dull routine of reading mail and other mindless necessities. After about 3:00 in the afternoon, I get more energized for several hours. But unless standing at the drafting table, I find myself unable to crank out the work needed. I tend to wander about. An office setting is usually too quiet and dull somehow, meaning I get distracted by the smallest things. Too much quiet while I work is somehow unnerving. Many writers will recognize this tendency.

Fortunately, just a couple of months after I started my consultancy, I discovered three excellent cafés within walking distance. Salvation! Now, some years later, I have moved to the Washington, DC area and returned to the world of consulting but now without an office. Naturally, I have reverted to form and continue to work out of cafés and coffeeshops.

There are over a dozen spots in Washington, DC and the close-in suburbs of Arlington and Alexandria, Virginia that I have occasionally patronized. A few, though, have become favorites and part of a regular rotation of mine; this way I get to experience distinct neighborhoods in the area, and a lot of different personalities. Each of these spots has a different vibe, and the buzz of human activity and conversation actually helps me focus and concentrate because I have to intentionally shut out all the surrounding stuff to get anything done. And so, I do; I'm more productive there than in any other setting.

Boccato Lounge/CoWork Café in the Clarendon neighborhood of Arlington is the close-by, walkable neighborhood spot closest to home. Additionally, it is part of a growing trend toward shared office space. During weekdays, the majority of the café space is given over to a membership-based co-working arrangement offering patrons internet access, printing, and other infrastructure of the working world. Saturday nights generally include live music; the overall effect attracts a wild diversity of local university students, start-up business entrepreneurs, immigrants, and families.

Near Farragut Square in downtown DC is a Peet's Coffee Shop. It's much more of a professional crowd, not so sociable given its location in the heart of DC law firms and K Street lobbyists. But when taking a break from reading or writing, I might overhear a conversation between a political operative and potential congressional contender, or two attorneys working on developing language for a new constitution in Afghanistan. The headquarters of the National Geographic Society is a half-block away, bringing in the occasional writer or photographer with stories of exotic adventures. The large glass façade allows me to witness the whole world going by. Never a dull moment!

Misha's in Old Town Alexandria is a small, funky coffee roaster, and plays great jazz all day. It has the most "local" and intimate feel, and with a yoga studio upstairs and an architecture school across the street, there is a creative feel to it as well. A bookstore around the corner offers me an occasional welcome diversion from … well, reading and writing.

The spot I have visited longest is a Starbucks. It's such a lovely setting in Old Town Alexandria and in a historic building dating from 1765, which to an urbanist like me is irresistible. Plus, it's adjacent to a waterfront park along the Potomac River, so I can take a break to commune with the water and ducks when necessary. It's a bit touristy but it's always filled with friendly and interesting regulars changing throughout the day: bankers at breakfast, retirees in mid-day, teenagers after school lets out, maybe a few homeless later in the evening. All of these groups intermingle and accept each other's presence easily. I've been going there since moving to Alexandria in 2011, so the baristas and a few other regulars know me by name.

Teaism is an Asian restaurant/tea shop in the Penn Quarter area of downtown DC, attracting an odd mix of alternative/vegetarian patrons, lost tourists, and straitlaced agents from the FBI headquarters around the corner. There is a window seat at which I often sit, overlooking the National Archives. That way, I can keep an eye on the Declaration of Independence, Constitution, and Bill of Rights, which seems particularly important these days. And there is a koi pond in the dining area!

So many elements of public and social life have been increasingly privatized. Community swimming pools have been replaced by backyard pools, movie cinemas by home entertainment centers. In such an increasingly privatized, fragmented, and isolated society, these cafés offering sociable gathering are increasingly important. In fact, entire books have been written on the subject. The term "third places" was popularized in the world of urban planners and sociologists through the book *The Great Good Place* by urban sociologist Ray Oldenberg. Third places are where people congregate other than work or home. Traditionally, common third places included country stores, barber shops, hair salons, soda shops, and taverns. Today in the early 21st century, a coffee shop is the standard third place.

As described by Oldenburg, third places share several common features. First, they are neutral, meaning that all people can come and go as they please. If you don't go to your third place for a few days or weeks, your return is welcomed; if you disappear from home or work for days or weeks at a time, though, your eventual return would be greeted with suspicion and anger. Secondly, social status is diminished so that all members of society are welcomed; the status we have in society is leveled in such places. Also, conversation among complete strangers is common; in fact, many cafés and coffee shops include large common tables shared by individuals, encouraging interaction by strangers and mixing groups of people that otherwise might never interact.

Having lived in Belgium a number of years ago, I experienced the local café essentially functioning as a public "living room" available to all. After dinner, a typical evening in our little Flemish village was spent at the local, where entire families would gather. Grandparents might be found playing chess at tables with the family dog lying at their feet, while parents sit at the bar or play darts; children would be scattered all about doing homework or playing. Third places are filled with, and almost defined by, such collections of regular patrons. New people and strangers are, of course, completely welcome, but the spirit of place is set by the friendly camaraderie that develops among a small but dedicated crowd of regulars. As with so many elements of urban settings, the success of third places depends on what individuals bring with them. Third places tend to hold an intention of social interaction, and so, in my experience, their patrons almost universally arrive with a sense of open friendliness.

We humans are a social species. While in America we have come to deeply value privacy, I sense we have reached our fill of it; privacy has crossed over into isolation. Each of the places I have chosen as my third places are almost always packed with people, some chattering wildly together, others quietly reading. There is the opportunity to interact, or not; to experience the energy and vibrancy of other people, hear their stories, in an intentionally sociable space which, at the same time, offers the option of not interacting at all. There is a cultural shift going on across the nation these days, and this renewed "café society," as an aspect of a renewed desire for more urban settings, is proof. A growing public demand now is seeking experience, rather than purchasing and shopping for the latest new thing – restaurants and cafés over retail shopping. This reflects, I believe, a growing sense of need for deeper connection, purpose, and meaning in a society struggling to find new spiritual and psychological grounding.

Living Car-Free

Sometimes, disaster can strike and what seems like a life-changing mess turns out to be a great prize. So it was when my car was rear-ended at a stoplight one recent summer. Waiting patiently for the light to change, I was slammed into by a drunk driver at 45 mph, and three cars were subsequently declared a total loss; one person was still undergoing rehabilitative treatment two years later. This was the fourth such rear-ending accident I went through in four and a half years of a long commute. Such an annual event I can do without!

I was provided with a loaner vehicle through insurance. Less than a week later though … yep, the loaner got rear-ended at a stop sign! I took this as a signal from the Universe that the time had come to live the life I've always wanted.

I relocated to Washington, DC from Lancaster, Pennsylvania several years ago with the express desire to live car-free. Feet, bike, and the Metro would be my transit tools, supplemented by Zipcar whenever the desire to leave town might strike. The issue was finally forced on me, and I couldn't be happier. All sorts of benefits stare at me now, not least of all from the household budget. Several line items have disappeared from the budget spreadsheet: monthly car payments, insurance, maintenance, gas, parking tickets.

Avoiding drunk drivers rear-ending my car is a pretty good benefit too.

I'm blessed to live in a manner that allows this sort of freedom. From my home in Arlington, Virginia, I can walk to every conceivable daily necessity. Walk Score gives my address a rating of 91 (frankly I don't know why it's not 100!). Within a 10-minute walk, I can reach three grocery stores, two pharmacies, a library, schools, a university, churches, gyms and a YMCA, the County courthouse, more restaurants than can be counted, parks, numerous bus lines, and a Metro station.

Most of the time, however, I mount my bike to reach my favorite haunts: downtown Washington, DC is a 20-minute ride away, Old Town Alexandria a 25-minute ride. My bike gives a greater feeling of freedom than a car somehow. The world around me is more immediate and accessible. I regularly find myself hopping off the bike to take a photo of some architectural feature I hadn't noticed before, to commune with a Great Blue Heron that just landed nearby, to watch the planes fly overhead as they land at National Airport, or to chat with other bikers and random pedestrians as we pause at an intersection.

I divide my travels into five layers based on what distance is comfortable and practical for various travel modes. "Local" destinations, in my mind, are accessible by walking or biking. "Nearby" travels are accessible by bike or Sprynt. "Medium" travels are by bike, or Metro if a station is near the destination. "Regional" trips for me are generally within the Beltway around DC, using the Metro or Zipcar. "Out-of-town" trips get Zipcar or Amtrak, and National Airport is a quick 15-minute Metro ride away.

Hang on, you say, back up; what is Sprynt?

Sprynt is a small and brand-new transit company, a start-up which just began service less than two months prior to this writing. I chatted up the driver of one vehicle who gave a quick business plan-style sales pitch. It is a hyper-local transit option, for trips too short to drive and too far to walk. Its service area is extremely limited, running only along the corridor of Wilson and Clarendon Boulevards, between the Roslyn and Ballston neighborhoods of Arlington, VA. And amazingly, it's free to riders, as it relies solely for revenue on advertising, placed on the vehicle and shown on screens in front of each of the five passenger seats. The company operates only a handful of vehicles which are not much more than specialized golf carts, upgraded enough to be comfortable and street-legal. Riders make use of an app in the same way they might call an Uber. Expansion may eventually include the same sort of limited operations in the Crystal City area of Arlington. Similar transit start-ups have shown up in a very few other cities as well; the intent is to find a convenient niche in which to compete with Uber and Lyft.

More recently, Sprynt has been supplanted by an influx of motorized scooters, available for rent on a per-ride basis. These scooters are dockless, meaning a rider can pick them up anywhere, ride them to a destination, and simply walk away. The corporate owners (Bird, Lime, Jump, etc.) pick up the scooters for recharging wherever they are left. The result, however, is a mess, with riders who have no responsibility for the vehicle leave them lying about like so much litter, blocking sidewalks and bike paths. Convenience uber alles! Grr.

How we connect to and move about the world makes a difference. We observe the world differently, interact with it and the people around us more intimately or less, depending partly on the methods of transportation available to us. A good community is designed to promote choices and connections. I'm blessed to have so many options in front of me.

The Night-Time Flaneur

I've found the quote to be true, from the English poet Rupert Brooke: "Cities, like cats, will reveal themselves at night." But it takes some hunting.

One of the basic strategies of New Urbanist downtown revitalization is the creation of the "18-hour place." The intent of such an approach is to activate a place at all times of the day, early morning through late night, so that the core of a neighborhood center, or a downtown, is actively used by a variety of different people, for different purposes, for the fullness of a day. The goal is to achieve places that are safe, memorable, enjoyable, and financially viable. This assumes an intimate, fine-grained mix of uses, including residential, shopping, entertainment, office and commercial, perhaps even some small-scale artisanal/craft manufacturing.

But what goes on when almost everyone is asleep, during those other six hours? What insights, spiritual and urbanistic, can be revealed to us on the streets at 3:30 in the morning? As Christopher Butler reminds us, the urban wanderer known as a flaneur seeks to discover the eternal by exploring and observing the transitory.

I began my own practice of "flaneury" far from the city, however, having spent most of my youth on a beach on the Chesapeake Bay. It was a somewhat isolated neighborhood of small summer vacation cottages surrounded by salt marshes on three sides. The only social spot was a fishing pier which included a bar with burgers and fries, where I learned to play pool and pinball while listening to Lynyrd Skynyrd on an old jukebox. I also spent lots of time wandering around the beach and marshes by myself, particularly at night when Mom thought I was asleep in bed. Beautiful shells, strange and stinky seaweed, rocks, tangled driftwood, and the occasional wooden shipwreck figure prominently in my memories. My friends and I would build bonfires on the beach and stay out until sunrise appeared over the Bay. Sitting on a sand dune late at night, surrounded by reeds and bayberry, watching the moon behind the waves all night, was a transforming experience. Although I often complained of being bored, as teenagers so typically do, it was, in retrospect, a damned good childhood. I've never seen a reason to stop this sort of late-night wandering and exploration. City or salt marsh, town, forest, or beach, it all provokes in me a sort of curious and detached wonder. I was inspired during a recent summer, as a result of enduring a very long walk home after a late-night social event, to make this an intentional adventure; to choose locations that intrigue me, experience them at a time when no one else would think to, say between the hours of 3:00 and 4:00 a.m., and share whatever appears. Such an undertaking has its inherent dangers of course; my being a white male makes it somewhat less so for me.

Dyke Marsh and Crystal City, July 27th

For several reasons, I chose to begin these adventures in flaneury outside Alexandria, not in the city itself, but in a park just outside the Beltway, along the Potomac River in Virginia. For a full urban experience, the complete Transect should be involved, not just downtown. So, a little bit of preserved nature set the tone. The location is also near the first boundary stone which gave Washington, DC its shape – that seemed apt as a point of beginning. Finally, my Tree is located there. I have formed a pretty close connection with one particular Linden tree; I read, write, and meditate under its branches, and it acts as a calming and centering influence, a doorway for my spiritual explorations, so to speak.

And what better time to begin, of course, than under a full moon? The full moon of July is known as the Hungry Ghost Moon in the Chinese tradition. I consider us all hungry ghosts in our essence, spirits temporarily embodied as humans. When the hunger to grow and experience becomes overwhelming, we become incarnate, and like vampires, seek out what we need to feed, grow, and experience.

Vampires did appear that night in a sense, in the form of bloodsucking mosquitoes. More than I could bear ... so much for meditating quietly with my Tree to ask Spirit for support and insight. Other than their buzzing though, what became apparent quickly was silence. At 2:30 a.m., the usual sounds of traffic along the George Washington Parkway, playing children, even the quacking of ducks, had stilled. The only activity I found came from unexpected encounters with wildlife. I had a staring contest with a beautiful red fox, and a race on my bike with a startled baby rabbit. I lost both times.

The start of this nocturnal flaneury was a good eight miles from home, and I was on my bike. To get away from the buzzing vampires and eventually get home, I decided to continue the night by riding back along Route 1, from Alexandria to Arlington. This took me through Crystal City and past the Pentagon. I quickly remembered that even at this time of night, even very light traffic on suburban streets is far more frightening than on more urban ones. Suburbia as a design model is completely focused on cars, and averse anything unusual or unexpected, such as a bicyclist.

Crystal City is an essentially linear corridor of 1960s-era office buildings running parallel to the Potomac River near National Airport. It has been trying to reposition itself as something more than a soulless office canyon and is slowly perking up with residential and entertainment uses. For the most part, though, it still feels strained; street-level commercial activity in what felt like every third building consists of enormous gym clubs, each displaying dozens of stationary bike machines. I noted the irony and rode on.

In various urban parks, Arlington County has seen fit to begin placing wooden bars across the seats of park benches to discourage the homeless from sleeping rough in public spaces. Perhaps this was one of many causes of the homeless camp I stumbled upon in a side corner of the parking lot at Target. So many of our municipal management and land use decisions end up not really solving a problem so much as merely shifting it elsewhere. Not unlike much of our psychic lives, I suppose; putting a patch over a problem doesn't make it go away, it just pops up again elsewhere in some other form. Perhaps homelessness should be thought of not as a problem in itself, but a symptom of some larger failing.

Aside from mosquitoes and some homeless brethren, the most common sign of life at 3 a.m. comes in the form of maintenance workers. The late-night silence was broken only by my pedaling until a jackhammer shook me out of the calm. Sewer and street repairs have to take place sometime, and a crew of workmen were hard at the task of repairing a broken pipe. We rely so much on this hidden infrastructure and rarely give it a moment's consideration. So too our lives rely on our unconscious, the unseen, foundational infrastructure of our larger Self. Aren't dreams like those workmen, appearing at night to repair and maintain our psychic health?

14th Street, Shaw, and Blagden Alley, August 14th

While the evocative sensual experience of the first adventure was silence, on this occasion it was the cool temperature and soft breeze. It's definitely *not* what is expected of an August night in Washington, DC. On a bike at 3 a.m. in shorts and a t-shirt, it was almost too cool. It helped wake me up though, and somehow gave a sense of timelessness to the night.

The quiet, deserted hour of 3:00 in the morning in DC is still much more active than in Crystal City, with quite a few bikes on the street, mostly restaurant workers heading home. Even a pedicab was still cruising for paying passengers, with more hope than success. The lights inside the iconic Ben's Chili Bowl revealed a few people still hungry enough to risk heartburn.

Away from the shuttered bars and restaurants of 14th and U Streets, on 9th, things calmed down even more. Traffic was thin enough so that I felt like I owned the streets, riding down the center without a care. The homeless and late-night locals want to know what I was up to … if I'm not out to score drugs, what the hell am I doing here now?! One tried to give me the usual patter, his practiced line about needing money since, by the grace of God, he just arrived from Carolina. He figures me out quickly enough to drop that and we chat about life a bit before moving on. Turning up an alley, I must veer to avoid a couple of what I thought were old paint cans, only to discover they were the booted feet of a homeless man sleeping in a doorway.

The alleys of the Shaw neighborhood no longer have the amount of trash or graffiti I remember from my semi-punk days in the 1980s, but still enough to make it clear that it isn't completely gentrified, still has something of a scrappy edge. Completely different worlds can occupy the same space for very different purposes. It's pretty clear to me that the newcomers have almost no sense of the history of the place they have come to dominate. The juxtaposition of hipster renovations and the long-time working class give a sense of adjacent secret intimacies, with neither culture truly knowing the other, yet influencing each other in ways they may not even recognize. Blagden Alley and Naylor Court strike me as excellent examples of this. The near-downtown neighborhoods of DC were at one time crisscrossed with service alleys, home to horse stables, warehouses, workshops, and barely habitable housing for the underclass. Those that remain today went through a prolonged period of decline, eventually dissolving into almost complete abandonment. For about the past ten years though, Blagden Alley been the home of upscale restaurants and residences, craft cocktail lounges, coffee bars, and creative class consulting outfits. Its defining feature is the public artwork adorning various walls and garage doors.

To really get a feel of what the place has been over time requires a late-night visit, when the current life does not dominate, and the energy of history can be more easily felt. Blagden Alley lies at the confluence of three worlds: the downtown professional crowd, uptown creatives, and long-time working-class African Americans. These edges where various cultural ecosystems meet are much like natural points of transition: ocean and beach, field and forest, jungle and savannah, day and night. At such places, different species and different cultures intermingle and make unexpected magic happen. The trick is not to unbalance the fine line of intermingling, which I think has been the challenge of urbanism and civilization from the beginning.

Whatever insights can be found on deserted night-time streets are perhaps available to us during daylight hours, but there are other things to focus on then, limiting our ability to take it all in. Spending time on the streets at the late hours before dawn is a bit of a waking dream; the unconscious of the city rises more easily to awareness. A city is all about the gathering of people, but really making sense of both the place and its inhabitants, for me, often comes by observing a place in their absence.

Bridges

At least three times a week I find myself riding the bike path along the Potomac River, from Arlington south to Old Town Alexandria or into downtown Washington. It's an excellent ride, with wide vistas, closed-in woods, watery marshes, and views of the great American monuments – the Washington Monument, the Lincoln and Jefferson Memorials – across the scenic river. The experience inspires me, calms me, excites me every time.

So my frustration can be understood when one day I was greeted with an enormous gash in the greenery. A wooden fence had been erected around a construction site right on the river. Argh! What the hell was the Park Service/Corps of Engineers/Department of Something or Other, up to?! There was no one on-site to ask. Raggle Fraggle Snaggin #*&!&%#@*!!! For a couple of weeks, I raged at this affront to nature.

Oh, of course. Finally, a small sign was erected, giving an explanation: staging and construction zone for the repair of Memorial Bridge.

Like so much of America's infrastructure, Memorial Bridge was falling apart, badly. Carrying 68,000 vehicles per day, the bridge is undergoing three years of repair work at a price tag of $227 million. This should extend the life of the bridge by a good 85 years. I've heard that most of the world economy has less to do with innovation and creation of the new, and much more to do with repairing and maintaining what we already have. As a former landlord, I know that maintenance of the old can be much more expensive than construction of the new.

This isn't just any bridge across a river though; it is a metaphor for our national history. As early as the Andrew Jackson administration, a grand bridge was envisioned to symbolically unite the northern and southern states. No specific location or design was determined until the bridge as we know it was proposed in 1886. Designed by the famed McKim, Mead & White, its construction was not complete until 1932. The location, set in the years after the Civil War, is unusual. Bridges are normally placed and aligned so as to increase commercial activity. Not so Memorial Bridge; the alignment does not connect two vital economic cores, but instead by either accident or intention, has a mission of telling a story. This can be easily seen in the two terminated vistas at either end; the Lincoln Memorial at one, and Robert E. Lee's plantation home (Arlington House) and the National Cemetery at the other. The bridge acts as a visual reminder of the unity of the nation, the rift that occurred during the 1860s, and the desire to restore, and maintain, wholeness.

Of course, bridges only fulfill their objective if both sides are open and receptive. Around the turn of the last century and into the 1920s, our grandparents and great-grandparents gifted us with invaluable infrastructure in the form of transportation networks, bridges, water and sewer systems. They did not, unfortunately, take into account the ongoing costs of maintenance. All at once and everywhere, we find that all these systems are crumbling. Our sense of national unity is crumbling as well – we find that not everyone wants connecting bridges, metaphorical or otherwise. The longer we wait to repair the damage, be it political, physical, or interpersonal, the harder and more expensive it gets. Regular small maintenance projects and occasional large renovations are needed to avoid the loss of connection.

Most of life's lessons have to do with relationships; how to create and maintain, repair them, keep them healthy, strong, and positive. Perhaps the construction and maintenance of bridges is a good metaphor for the basic work of our lives. We are, each of us, little neighborhoods, so to speak, part of a larger whole, separated by rivers of misunderstanding. As a transportation corridor, a river acts to connect two distant points. By its very nature, though, it also divides, depending on where you want to go. The next time you cross a bridge, remind yourself of the importance of maintaining strong connections with others, especially those unlike yourself. The political and cultural divide we find ourselves in these days is affecting us as a nation in our personal relationships. We need to put enormous effort into the repair and maintenance of our connecting fabric, by which I mean both public infrastructure and personal relationships. Get to work repairing those bridges, everyone.

A Stage for the Senses
On November 23rd, 534 BC, Thespis appeared onstage wearing a mask in the role of Dionysus. This made him, according to Aristotle and others, the first actor ever; that is, the first human to take to the stage as a character other than himself. Previously, all performances were either storytelling or musical and choral productions.

The ancient rituals and celebrations that our ancestors reveled in, from prehistoric tribal dances around a small fire to medieval mystery plays, continue to this day. We see this in the Mummers Parade in Philadelphia and, of course, Mardi Gras. New Orleans seems to practically organize its life around Second Line parades. These sorts of celebrations and dramas have the ability to define a city.

The ancients made use of ritual in an attempt to affect events in the outer world. Today, we need ritual to affect change in our personal inner worlds. I first learned the value of ritual through my experience growing up in the Episcopal Church. In young adulthood, I was able to compare that complex ritualistic experience with that of the Mennonites, for whom elaborate ceremony is intentionally avoided and thus almost completely lacking. Yet even they cannot fully rid themselves of something so basic to human experience. Participating in ritual, whether elaborate or plain and simple, is a fundamental human desire, even a need. For us, ritual is how the seen and unseen serve one another.

When my children were young, I tried explaining what was happening during the Episcopal church services we attended. The first half of the service, we listen to stories, I told them. The second half, we participate in the re-enactment of a story. At ages five and seven, they just were not interested. Perhaps they have some semblance of appreciation now – that ritual, whether religious or secular, set in a church, sports stadium, or concert hall, brings meaning and direction into our lives.

The psychotherapist James Hillman argued that young males in particular have a fundamental need for ritual in order to mature properly. We see this most clearly in the victory celebrations of competitive team sports and in the military. In general society, however, we have downplayed most rituals as being naïve, meaningless, or manipulative. Perhaps this loss is a source of the anger, frustration, and angst we see in adolescent males today in America.

Rituals, in their social and public aspect, need a setting in which to be performed. Except for older and larger cities, civic space has become hard to find in the US. As an example, after winning the World Series, the Anaheim Angels naturally wanted to hold a victory celebration. The story, perhaps more apocryphal than true, is that since no city square or plaza existed for such an event, the victory parade was held on Main Street in Disneyland, followed by a rally in a parking lot. A contrasting approach to the design of civic space is given by Christopher Alexander, who in his book *A Pattern Language* suggests that streets be designed to accommodate dancing. To give Disney their due, however, the appeal of the Main Street USA setting does just that; their land planners operate as stage designers, and clearly understand better than most that the city street is intended for festive public display. This is why the Main Street USA setting in Disneyland remains one of the most popular tourist attractions in America. We enjoy it so much because we cannot enjoy anything like it back home.

Nature is its own stage for its own performance. Much as we must have a deep connection with the vibrancy of green living nature, it somehow isn't sufficient for humans. We have an inescapable desire – need – to create. We must create not only the performance but the stage on which we act. This need demands to be both expressed and experienced through the senses.

As biological creatures, we have evolved a set of senses with which to take in and interpret the world around us. As spiritual beings, these senses allow us to experience and savor that world and give it meaning. This life of the senses is not unchanging though; we develop the skills to make use of it, and the senses are foundational to higher development. The urban thinker Louis Mumford stated in his book *Culture of Cities* that "the daily education of the senses is the elemental groundwork of all higher forms of education." The experience of the city is the immersive environment so well suited to this education; he felt that the medieval town in particular was an "omnipresent work of art." What are some of the ways the various senses take in the city?

Sight - Humans are an extremely visual species. About 90% of the sensory input we receive is visual, and two-thirds of our brain activity is spent interpreting visual stimuli. Does what we see indicate danger or safety? Does it delight us or worry us?

Those things we interpret as safe and delightful we consider to be beautiful. We desire both ordered pattern and unexpected whimsy, and we find this in color, texture, and motion. These are the elements of the built environment, both in the permanent and intentional design of place, and the temporary and playful ways people make use of space.

Sound - The city is usually thought of as full of the irritating noise of trucks and construction, which cannot be denied. Yet the sounds of a city can delight as well, such as the splashing of a fountain, the chattering of children, and the snippets of conversation overheard on a sidewalk. Formal and organized concerts are scheduled in parks and plazas, but more random music is sometimes available too. Recently, there emerged a movement among cities to randomly scatter pianos on sidewalks and corners, available for anyone to make impromptu music.

Smell - Like sound, the smell of a city is historically a negative in the public imagination. The rise of coffee shops and roasters is combating this admirably, though. So too are small artisanal bakeries and restaurants with sidewalk seating. The smell of an artist's paint outside a gallery provides an unexpected and unusual addition to the palette of a city's sensory experience.

Taste - How do we taste a city? Food has become an enormous driver in urban revitalization efforts. This is found not only in sidewalk cafés and outdoor restaurant seating, but particularly with food trucks roaming the streets and gathering near pedestrian centers. In larger cities, the tradition of small vendors on the street selling roasted chestnuts and pretzels continues. The latest twist is the banana bike traveling around the streets of Seattle and Washington, DC, passing out free bananas, courtesy of a corporate sponsor.

Touch - The most obvious element of a city is its collection of buildings. We touch these constantly, at least when we grab the door handle when we enter. Some buildings seem to invite touch in their use of materials or unusual shapes. Street furniture, particularly benches, are absolutely made to be touched. Every aspect of the built environment has been touched by someone. Someone laid the brick, poured the concrete, planted the trees. To the extent we interact with the city with a playful, thoughtful, artistic touch, the spirit of those artisans and workers gives life to us. But we touch not only with our hands; the one aspect of any city which we simply cannot avoid touching is the sidewalk. Normally so humble, a good sidewalk may delight with color or a playful pattern in its brick or stone. It can also be the canvas upon which a memorial can be created, as in the "Extra Mile" series of bronze markers located in the sidewalks of downtown Washington, DC. Even manhole covers give opportunity for art.

Time - The forgotten sense that we all share is that of time. This connects us not only to the past but ought to remind us to pay attention to the future as well. Our ancestors gifted us with so much; what will we leave for our descendants? We must make sure what we provide them is worthy. Time is experienced through the cycles of days and seasons. A city will memorialize time through festivals and rituals repeated through the years. Most people will gain a sense of the spiritual in an urban setting through art festivals, music, spectacle, etc., where all the senses are put into play.

The more day-to-day method of staying connected to the past in a city is, of course, the retention and re-use of old buildings. A more subtle way though might be the honoring of ruins, where older buildings and structures are *not* put to economic service but kept anyway, as reminders and teachers.

Such memorable experiences create place out of mere location. We expand our souls this way, in our interaction with the soul of place. We grow beyond the limits of our time and place by digging more deeply into *this* particular time and this place.

Dreaming and Waking in the Streets of Paris

The Paris that the world has fallen so deeply in love with did not exist until about the early 1870s. Prior to that, the city had remained largely unchanged in its form for hundreds of years, an overcrowded medieval mess of narrow, crooked streets lined with buildings sagging with age. There were certainly grand spaces – the Louvre and Tuileries – but the city as a whole was a cramped maze, impossible to traverse. The lack of water and sewer facilities gave rise to filth and regular outbreaks of disease.

Emperor Napoleon III appointed the bureaucrat and civil servant Eugene Baron Hausmann to oversee a massive renovation of Paris with few, if any, restrictions. From 1853 until 1870, Hausmann oversaw the construction of an extensive water and sewer system, numerous parks and civic buildings, and, most notably, the demolition and renovation of multiple neighborhoods throughout the city. Today we recognize this work most easily in the many boulevards and avenues that boast grand vistas and are lined by elegant architecture and sidewalk cafés. Parisians of the time were grateful for the renewal and delighted by the elegance of the new spaces, though, as is always the case, they were frustrated by the massive dislocation and high-handed dictatorial manner with which Hausmann operated. In the end, he built far more housing than he demolished, and gifted the city with an immediate improvement in public health. By 1870, however, citizens had had enough, and he was forced to resign. The legacy he left is a city universally considered one of the most beautiful in the world. Having lived in Paris for several years as a small child, and visiting again numerous times as an adult, I have been shaped, emotionally and urbanistically, by the juxtaposition of these two worlds – the ancient and earthy medieval warrens lying between the elegant and airy cosmopolitan boulevards.

As to Hausmann's accomplishments, I'm intrigued by the psychological impact of the two experiences – walking the classic boulevard of grand vistas and the ancient closed medieval passages. Regarding the mythic symbolism of the psyche, I consider Hausmann's straight, formal, and cosmopolitan boulevards as representing our rational consciousness and the ragged, disjointed medieval passages as representing the irrational, unconscious dream state. In the interstices between the boulevards, the ancient crooked passageways still exist. We wander semi-lost among the bent little alleys and then unexpectedly cross onto a grand sunlit boulevard; it is much like awakening from a dream state. We turn a corner and then dive back into the dream, in and out of consciousness, alleyway to avenue and back. The street, whether bright avenue or murky alley, is a thread, the warp and woof woven into our life fabric.

CHAPTER X

Urbanism as Storytelling:
The Narrative Arc of a City

"Frankly, there isn't anyone you couldn't learn to love if you knew their story"
– Mr. Rogers

Humans are at heart storytellers.

Why are stories important to us? Beyond simple entertainment, they are the original educational tools – the script consultant Dara Marks calls stories "the human instruction manual." Beyond serving a collective educational purpose, stories are also important to us personally. As mythologist Michael Meade reminds us, "The lost home that we are seeking is ourselves; it is the story we carry within ourselves." How do we go about sharing stories, both collective and personal? Well, it helps to be near others, and urban environments, whether city of empire or simple small village, have always offered the perfect setting to create those relationships necessary to storytelling.

One of the basic emotional needs we have is to be understood by the people most important to us. We want our personal story to be heard and accepted. When we are denied this, all sorts of psychic and spiritual wounds are inflicted. Moreover, stories are a key to expanding our circle of empathy, a basic aspect of psycho/spiritual development. These personal stories, while private and individual, are part of a larger collective narrative, repeated millions of times over the centuries. Seemingly small and insignificant at times, our little private stories are actually epic in nature.

What Makes Us Distinctly Human

As a species Homo Sapiens, we have not always been storytellers, but as humans we have been. This is the transition we experienced upon awakening from purely animal instinct into conscious awareness. As a species we, of course, have always acted out of our animal instinct. We also dream about those instinctual acts, as do some other species. But as we came into consciousness, we began to ask questions about those dreams. What do they mean? Why do we act in the ways we do? What is this world around us? We would tell each other our dreams in an attempt to understand and find meaning in them. Sometimes lessons were learned. The stories from the dreams would become ritualized as a way of re-enacting and remembering. These became mythic. Those rituals became formalized; eventually, they were written down. The writings became formalized into religious and political institutions. These myths tell the psychological story of our awakening into consciousness as an attempt to understand who we are and our place in the universe. Stories are simply a fundamental aspect of being human.

Why Cities Exist

Buildings, as Jordan Peterson reminds us in his "Maps of Meaning" lectures, are externalized clothing. That is, they operate as a barrier to protect us from some of the physical and psychological dangers of the world. By extension, a city too is a form of "externalized clothing," providing a layer of protection. But clothing has become more than merely practical – it offers us a way to display ourselves and our values – just as our buildings and cities have. Some are more gracious than others.

Most writing on the origins of urban living concentrate on commerce, increased efficiency, and protection from outside invaders. For instance, Malcolm Gladwell, a popular writer known for his ability to find unexpected connections and trends, has shown how cities succeed because of their ability to create wealth and reflect fundamental patterns of nature. For the author Geoffrey West, a particle physicist writing about the field of biology, cities exist for their efficiency. In his book *Scale*, he describes his discoveries regarding the way biological organisms, cities, and corporations grow, live, and die. He relates how the various biological systems that make up a body all scale wither up or down, so that, in a sense, a shrew is simply a scale model of an elephant. His essential finding, the "Rule of 15%" I discussed in Chapter VIII, is applicable to both biological systems and urbanism – with every doubling in population size, a city sees a decrease of about 15% in the cost of infrastructure, and a simultaneous equivalent 15%

increase in various socioeconomic benefits.

In a very real but counter-intuitive sense, then, living in a city is a way of living in harmony with natural principles. Doesn't always feel like it though, does it? But harmony with nature involves more than simply being surrounded by greenery; it includes patterns and systems as well. A natural pattern for humans, beyond those of practical, financial, and commercial concerns, is that of storytelling. One aspect of storytelling is imagining things that don't exist in the physical world. This is our distinctive human ability; with it, we can act not only out of instinct but with intention. This imagination can be used to either lie or to discover and communicate transcendent metaphorical truths. The latter is the softer, less "technical" purpose of a city.

The iconic writer on urbanism, Louis Mumford, recognized this, bringing together the practical and symbolic, telling us that "the chief function of a city is to convert power into form, energy into culture, dead matter into the living symbols of art, biological reproduction into social creativity." For an even more succinct perspective than Mumford's, we can turn to Shakespeare to discover why cities exist; in his simple line he reminds us, "All the world's a stage." Cities provide us the best settings to tell our stories. There are all sorts of venues a city normally provides us for storytelling, whether we are on the stage or in the audience – concert halls, libraries, opera houses, lecture halls, college auditoriums, art museums, church sanctuaries, the humble coffee shop. A classic stage for storytelling, though, is one not thought of as such: the sidewalk and street corner. This informal setting is the most common stage on which we find ourselves, chatting with friends while walking or during chance encounters with acquaintances or random strangers. Some sidewalk locations are so well-situated for finding an audience that chance encounters become semi-formalized. Centuries ago, London instituted a specific spot for the telling of stories, known as Speakers' Corner. Since the 1700s, everyone has had the right to set up a soapbox and speak their mind to whatever audience cares to stop and listen. An urban setting, then, whether grand metropolis or small town, provides us with all the excellent settings for hearing and telling our personal stories.

But a city does more than provide us with an audience to hear our story; a city also has a story to tell us. Ancient cities were often laid out as the physical reflection of some cosmological or spiritual order, an attempt to recreate heaven on earth. Dozens of cities in ancient cultures – Mayan, Aztec, Chinese, Egyptian, Indian – show patterns reflective of cosmological or cultural belief systems. Like participating in an elaborate religious ceremony, residents might have had the daily sense of being immersed in, and participating in, a grand mythological story. Perhaps surprisingly, even Washington, DC was designed with such a pattern in mind. Simply being in a significant place, walking down the street, can provide the opportunity to participate as an actor in a story or play. The ancient Andean city of Tiahuanaco in Bolivia, built well over 1,000 years ago, seems to have been designed expressly for this purpose. As the seat of a pre-Incan empire, it has apparently acted almost solely as a tourist attraction for the expression of the empire's cosmic significance. Some archeological researchers speculate that the builders intentionally kept the place unfinished, constantly changing and under construction. We can try to approach this experience of immersive participation in a smaller way today, by learning the history of our local town or neighborhood, viewing ourselves as a continuation of its founding story.

The City as Archetype and Dreamscape

A city and its inhabitants tell each other their stories. Most epic stories throughout history, certainly the great ancient mythologies, have their origins in our unconscious, and come to us primarily through dreams and works of art. Can the experience of a city provoke the unconscious to speak to us in this fashion? I would say yes. If we consider the city as a classroom populated by our fellow "students of life," as a resource for the writing of our own story, and also view the city as having a story of its own to tell us, we find a new source of inspiration and growth. Since epic stories rise from the unconscious, we can liken the city to the collective unconscious and its inhabitants to the personal unconscious. The city provides various stages for individuals to tell the stories of their personal unconscious. In turn, inhabitants of the city provide an audience to which the city can present its story, the collective unconscious common to all humanity. We write and live out our personal stories in the places we live, whether that be city, town, village, or suburb. We imprint onto certain places our memories of meaning – I attended an uplifting concert here, a joyful reunion with a friend happened there, my child attended that school, I lost a lover there. We define ourselves partly by our relationship to place; we love or hate a place because of memory, much of which may be unconscious. Some memories fade simply because of time, others are repressed because they evoke pain. And just as memory can fail or not be as accurate as we hope, so too do places change.

Stories we tell from our personal narratives form chapters, or perhaps more accurately sub-plots, of the larger story of the collective unconscious seen in the epic of the city. We can think of urban form as a metaphorical labyrinth through which we can process our personal story, meditating upon the images we find while walking the streets. What goes on down that alley? That building is beautiful and important; perhaps I should explore it. I need to cross this intersection to reach that restful park. Who are those people gathered over there? Urban form can provoke such little questions in us, and in turn dreams are provoked from these little scenes. Some of what will be shown to us in such urban stories will be beautiful, some not; we should accept and be grateful, for both beauty and ugliness are inescapable teachers.

Beyond our individual stories, a city, whether thousands of years old or only ten, has a story of its own to tell. The story of a place includes specifics of both time and place, some of which is universally transcendent. The story comes to us in various ways such as traditions, annual festivals, parades, and local legends of the people who came before us. We can think of these as the acting out of dreams. Dreams are the vehicle by which the unconscious, both the personal and collective, speaks to us. Dreams seem odd to us, and can be hard to interpret, because the unconscious speaks a much older, non-verbal language that our conscious self then must interpret. And so, we hold festivals of art, food, dance, music, parades, and costumes to help us interpret unknown mysteries.

How does the city speak to us, and how do we speak back to the city? The city and its inhabitants provide content for each other's stories. The city and the collective unconscious it represents both teach us the bigger picture, the larger stories of what they aspire to, through our dreams; we in turn shape the city with the inspiration it gives. In this way the conscious and unconscious affect each other, a two-way conversation. But what comes to us through dreams will have a will and destiny of its own that our mere conscious selves can only blindly fight against or follow faithfully. The latter always proves the right path.

Urbanism and the Narrative Arc of Storytelling

The outline of the great story of human experience is unchanging, though the details vary over time and place. This great story has been dubbed "The Hero's Journey" by the writer of comparative mythology, Joseph Campbell. The journey has six elements, forming a narrative arc for any adventure story. These are the Call to Adventure, the Road of Trials, the Abyss, Transformation, Apotheosis, and the Return.

In trying to work out what the narrative arc of urbanism might look like, I toyed with the concept of the Urban Transect but felt that assumed too obviously that stories are reflected in a particular urban pattern – your story isn't complete unless you finish in the heart of downtown – which I'm not convinced is true. In any such an arbitrary attempt, the storyline for the mythologizing of urbanism includes both physical aspects of design and situational/cultural elements. What I provide here is an incomplete set of ideas and relationships. We all have a different take on the ways urban experience and personal myth relate. A basic one is how the act of walking down the street reflects the progression of an inner spiritual journey. On the next page are the elements of Campbell's classic "monomyth"; to the right are ideas about how that matches up urbanistically. Readers will find others.

Campbell's Monomyth	Potential Urban Equivalent
Call to Adventure (disruption, awakening, refusal)	**Gateways** (airport, train/bus station, exit ramp)
Road of Trials (tests, expansion, helpers, mentors, synchronicities)	**Streets** (intersections, signage, lighting, crosswalks, street trees)
The Abyss (belly of the whale, meeting the angry god/goddess, temptation)	**Abandonment** (blight, political stalemate, failing infrastructure, cul-de-sacs, trash, sewage, homelessness)
Transformation (rebirth, new attitudes/behaviors, revelation and vision)	**Renewal** (meeting strangers, renovations, revitalization, adaptive reuse)
Apotheosis (final death and rebirth, ultimate reward)	**Public Space** (participatory politics, ritual, community, home)
Return (mastery of both worlds, reconciliation of opposites, freedom to live fully, the Self)	**Building on a Foundation of Nature** (urban systems as natural systems, inclusion, compassion, the urban transition from mere location to Place of Meaning)

There are any number of ways a city must be like a good story in order to succeed. Not unlike Campbell's elements of a mythological story, the screenwriter Andrew Stanton, in a wonderful TED Talk, gives a number of guidelines for developing a memorable story.

- A story must promise us it will tell us a truth that deepens our understanding of who we are as human beings.
- Stories allow us to understand the differences and similarities between ourselves and others.
- The greatest commandment of storytelling is "make me care."
- A story must make and keep a promise that it will lead to something that is worth your time.
- Storytelling without dialogue is the purest form. The audience

wants to work for its reward, to participate in the story.
- A story must invoke wonder.

Cities would do well to emulate these guidelines.

"Who are you?" This simple line, delivered in a scene in the movie *Lawrence of Arabia*, is essential to any story, and inspired Stanton in his own writing for such hit movies as *Finding Nemo* and *Toy Story*. A city will pose this question to us as well when we think of it as a story in which we are immersed.

A successful city holds possibilities for each of us to create a personal story, to see ourselves in it, and to tell us a story in which we participate and through which we seek to learn who we are. But we'll never know what the ending will be.

CHAPTER XI

The Interplay of the Natural and Urban Worlds

"Man's course begins in the garden, and ends in the city"
– Alexander MacLaren

A conventional understanding of nature for a contemporary American is expressed as pristine wilderness untouched by humanity. This consists of green woodlands, furry creatures, rivers and lakes, seaside, and mountains, all imbued with positive traits of beauty and goodness. Usually stones and rocks are included in such a perspective as well, but for the most part, nature is thought of as the grand and the beautiful. This represents the outlook of western thinking of only the last several generations, which splits nature and humanity apart. This understanding of nature is fairly recent and by no means universal in human experience. A comprehensive vision of "nature" is needed that includes human creations. The city can no longer be viewed as something apart from nature. We often need to escape the city and dive into field and forest as a refuge from too much civilization – the concept of "forest bathing" has recently appeared. But would it not be better to create an urbanism from which no escape is needed? The term "paradise" means "walled garden" – so paradise assumes living in culture and nature *joined together.*

What is "Nature?"

A dictionary definition of the term "nature" is fairly all-encompassing: "The phenomenon of the physical world collectively, including plants, animals, the landscape, and other features and products of the earth, as opposed to human creations." The popular imagination seems more specific; when we say we want to go relax in nature, we typically envision lots of beautiful and calming scenery, absent the unexpected dangers that much of nature presents. Our thinking about nature seems much too narrow; perhaps this is because it is an idea, a human invention. One way of narrowing down what "nature" includes lies in deciding what is not natural. Well, what does that encompass, other than things that are man-made (please excuse the gender specific use here)? Everything.

The follow-up question must be, why are man-made things not natural? Are humans not part of nature?

All creatures have instincts, including humans, but what we additionally possess is conscious intentionality. Perhaps this intentionality is the source of our suspicion against ourselves. Our intentions can be equally injurious or supportive. A frog does not have to decide what it means to be a frog; a human, however, has the possibility – even the obligation, I would say – to determine what a human life can be. How we decide that question has enormous implications.

Is nature limited to planet Earth? Were the Apollo astronauts in "nature" when walking on the moon? Is the Kuiper Belt at the outer reaches of the solar system part of nature? This is certainly not an environment we were physically designed for, nor is the Marianas Trench at the bottom of the ocean. What we must consider as part of nature is not always pleasant or appropriate. However we define nature, we feel disconnected from it, from something fundamental that we should – by nature – have a strong and vibrant relatedness with. But we don't.

The Split

Nature has not always been loved. Over the centuries, different cultures have had various views. Those people and cultures most intimate with "nature" have a greater respect for the dangerous, destructive powers within the natural environment than those of us in the contemporary western world. For many, if not most, ancient cultures, nature was dominated by a dark and dangerous aspect. The city is the last place we contemporary westerners think of when considering "nature," but it has often been understood as a safe refuge from the dangers of chaotic wilderness. Followers of the Judeo-Christian heritage will recall that the Old Testament reviles the city as a dangerous evil – up to a point. After the Israelites wandered the desert wilderness for 40 years, they built themselves a refuge: a city, Jerusalem.

There are several ways to consider the separation we feel from nature. To the extent we feel such isolation, it is self-induced because we have turned "nature" into an idea filled with cultural assumptions and parameters. Two of our approaches to thinking about nature and our separation from it strike me as most significant.

The first regards what we seemingly hope to find in a connection to nature. Nature is foundational, of course, but is it always good and positive? Not to the gazelle about to be snared by the lion, nor the deer buried under a storm-induced mudslide. What we consider nature is not always kind or beautiful. Its systems operate without any apparent regard for outcomes. Perhaps what we seek is not nature itself, but its beauty. The psychologist James Hillman has stated this most clearly; the split we experience is not between the human and natural worlds, but in what humans are seeking. While we certainly belong to nature – it has been our home forever – it is not nature in itself that we desire today, but the beauty it contains. This is the beauty of non-human forms of aliveness that we sense in a tree, a bee, an elk. The rolling flow we see in clouds overhead or the ever-changing-yet-always-the-same tumble of water in a rushing river reminds us of the life within ourselves. This connection with the beauty inherent in life is what we seek; nature then becomes the vehicle rather than the destination.

A further connection we desire, along with beauty, is the creative act which nature represents. Living nature is creativity unleashed in unimaginable, ever-evolving ways. Traditional cultures have understood that the creativity of life is not limited to the world of plants and animals. Human artifacts can be imbued with life as well, such as totems, icons, talismans, and other ritual objects. This is why certain works of art move us so deeply; they are containers of Soul. Our contemporary worldview of exceeding rationality has killed the "aliveness" of human artifacts, however. Objects can no longer have soul to the rational western mind.

The second break with nature we have forced upon ourselves is a split between living, green, or organic nature, from what I think of as "structural nature." These are two aspects of the same thing, yet we tend to disregard the structural.

Living Nature

When I speak of living nature, I envision those green, organic aspects of creation, animal and vegetable, which exhibit active life, as well as water and wind, whose movements and motion can also give a sense of life. How do we integrate living nature into the urban environment? More than a few writers and designers with greater skill than mine have explored this extensively. The most obvious is the inclusion of street trees. A well-arrayed network of connected parks, large and small, both active and passive, is a universally positive aspect of any successful modern city.

Various technical means of incorporating green nature into urbanism are gaining prominence. Two in particular seem most significant. First, a new method for managing stormwater is becoming more widespread. The process known as "daylighting" involves bringing back into the open a river or stream that has been buried and channeled into sewer pipes. In decades past, many such streams became "sewered" for new development or a street to be built above. Allowing rainwater to flow naturally restores the land and its normal hydrology, creating a habitat for various creatures and bringing a finger of living green back into the city. Green roofs are a second technical method of bringing more green life into urban settings. The intent is, once again, related to stormwater management. When rooftops – those that are reinforced strongly enough to bear the weight – are covered with soil and planted with various groundcover, grasses, or shrubbery, they manage to hold rainwater for a period of time before it is released, thus reducing stress on the sewer system and thus the local riverine system. The added benefit is increased living greenery, including the possibility of rooftop gardens. In both these instances, water is viewed as a resource to be cared for rather than a problem to be quickly dispensed with.

Agrarian Urbanism, a relatively recent movement that considers agriculture in urban settings, includes rooftop gardening and goes a step beyond – several steps, actually – to consider the entirety of the urban pattern as a setting for the garden. The general concept as devised by Andres Duany and others is that the standard convention of including retail and entertainment as aspects of community is no longer sufficient. The growing, processing, cooking, and eating of food is so basic a human activity that to organize a community around this makes perfect sense. Accommodations are made for a variety of growing methods, no matter the intensity of urban development. It is distinct from urban agriculture in which cities are retrofitted for farming (occurring in places like Detroit) and agricultural urbanism, in which a community or neighborhood is associated with an adjacent farm, such as a Community-Supported Agriculture program (in New Urbanist developments such as Serenbe and Hampstead). The concept makes use of the Transect (the manner of viewing urbanism from most to least intense activity), finding appropriate methods of food production at each level of development. Beyond the edge of community might be located large tractor farms for field crops; smaller farms and orchards within the less-developed community edge; rear-yard gardens in general neighborhoods; front-yard gardens and designated community gardens in more dense neighborhoods; rooftop and balcony gardens and window boxes for the most intensely developed town center. This sort of agrarian-based urbanism, specified by location along the Transect, becomes the ultimate in organic, locally-sourced food, as well as structuring a community through the nurturing of both people and nature.

Structural Nature

There are elements of the physical environment which are not "alive" in the conventional sense, yet still exhibit dynamic movement. This is found in the flow of a river, the billowing of clouds, the shifting of entire continents due to plate tectonics. Our love of nature must include more than a desire to be surrounded by greenery and cute furry animals, but to be in harmony with these systems and patterns as well.

I've mentioned an example of such patterns in Geoffrey West's "Rule of 15%" in his book *Scale*. This is similar to the "Quarter Power Rule," or Kleiber's Law which governs living organisms, stating that for every doubling in size, a creature requires only a 75% increase in metabolic rate. This implies that the urban pattern follows laws of nature just as living species do.

I describe such systems, patterns, and tendencies as the structural aspect of nature. The image that helps me make the most sense of this is that of a trellis. The rules, patterns, and structures of nature act as a trellis or skeletal foundation upon which the living green side of nature can manifest, grow, and flourish.

This trellis is less physical than conceptual. It can be understood through geometry, mathematics, statistics, and the principles of particle physics, for instance.

Being personally quite incompetent in these fields, I find this skeletal trellis more accessible through the lens of sacred geometry. This is discussed more fully in Chapters XV and XVI. The basic premise of sacred geometry, however, is that geometry acts as the method by which invisible laws, concepts, methods, and systems are revealed and made visible. It describes the geometric and numerical concepts upon which the physical world literally takes shape. Geometry then is the method by which the principles of physics and mathematics manifest themselves physically. It is found in proportions such as the golden mean (the ratio of 1:1.614) and pi (3.14159). Nature seems to find certain patterns and proportions more useful than others, and we find them not only useful but beautiful too.

Urbanism as an Aspect of Natural Systems

In our thinking about the "nature" of nature, perhaps we are experiencing a misalignment of imagination. The fundamental images we conjure for ourselves regarding the natural world may themselves need to be questioned. A new metaphor is needed to give us better clarity.

The ideal for what we consider natural is perhaps too pure, too unattainable. That ideal is the concept of wilderness. The image we have of wilderness – of land untouched by any human presence – is no longer appropriate. At this point in history, there really is very little pure wilderness left on the planet. Humans have had their impact on almost every single corner of the earth. Plastic residue is found in the deepest ocean depths; global warming is reshaping Antarctica. Indeed, human intervention is now required to maintain even a minimal level of untouched landscape. The seemingly passive goal of leaving wilderness alone now requires an intentional act. For better or worse, because of our impact on the landscape, we have an increasingly profound obligation to manage both the land and our interactions with it.

This can only be achieved by the most difficult task, that of changing our assumptions and habits of thinking. The idea of "wilderness" assumes – with good cause, I must admit – that every human action is negative. That leaves us little room for error, unfortunately, and a reduced capacity to participate in a connection to nature.

A better way of imagining the land is not through the lens of untouched wilderness, but of the garden. A garden provides a place of nurturing relationship for people. It acts as a reconciling space between the seemingly opposing values of wild nature and human creativity. A garden can be thought of as a mandorla or vesica piscis in this way. When we think of a garden, we come into relationship with the land as caretakers; given our horrific mistreatment of the land for so many generations, this is a critical aspect of healing.

The ways in which we interact with this global garden varies, of course, with the level and type of activity. The most comprehensive approach I have encountered regarding regional land management is the concept of the Transect. As noted earlier, the Transect allows for a full range of activities, both built and preserved, based on location from most to least intense. This is crucial because while many preservationists rightly condemn haphazard land development, the opposite is equally dangerous – haphazard preservation is just as problematic because it then forces random haphazard development. The Transect is useful not only conceptually to give a vision of what, where, and how to build and preserve, but it also can establish legal, enforceable standards.

It is easy enough to visualize the manner in which living organic "green" nature is incorporated with trees and parkland into urban settings even without the Transect, though incomplete. How is the "structural" side of nature reflected in urbanism? The basic layout of the street and block pattern, infrastructure, building types, and transportation systems al take on this role, including the manner in which these are in harmony with geometry and West's Law of 15%, among others. A growing movement known as "biomimicry" (the emulation of natural systems to solve human problems) is also making itself felt in urban design. This often assumes that elements of architecture and urban spaces be curved in the way a vine might curl, for instance. It can also reflect a more angular, geometric understanding since nature is both "organic" and "structural."

The elements and physical patterning of human urban places form the structural aspect of nature, creating a trellis upon which the living green side of nature can then manifest, grow, and flourish. In discovering the manner in which a city or town can best reflect both the organic and structural aspects of nature – in asking the land itself what pattern is right for that specific place – urban design then becomes a type of geomancy.

Healing the damage we have inflicted on the land must include urban as well as natural systems. This entails healing ourselves and requires a new mindset. Thinking of both nature and urbanism as sacred space is a core aspect of this.

How is this reflected in urbanism? Two similar terms reflect this sacred understanding of place. The ancient Celtic concept of the *nemeton*, a sacred grove in a forest, reflects sacred nature. The Greek term *temenos*, the title of this book, refers to the sacred plaza in front of or surrounding a temple, and is the urban equivalent of sacred space.

The Temple of Canova in Possagno, Italy, and the fronting "temenos" or plaza

THE INTERPLAY OF THE NATURAL AND URBAN WORLDS

An unexpected way of experiencing nature, whether in forest or city, is taking a deep dive into the unconscious, through meditative practices and what Jung terms "active imagination." When these various components of nature are considered together, the urban setting is then seen as absolutely a part of "nature." But whereas both the living and structural components of nature operate purely through dynamic instinct and laws, the human psyche adds the much more complex layer of intentionality. In his "Dream Analysis Seminar," Jung speaks to this in an unexpected way, arguing that the meditative process itself is a way of experiencing nature. "Savages are not dirty – only we are dirty. Domesticated animals are dirty, but never wild animals. People who have got dirty through too much civilization take a walk in the woods, or a bath in the sea. They may rationalize it in this or that way, but they shake off the fetters and allow nature to touch them. It can be done within or without. Walking in the woods, lying on the grass, taking a bath in the sea, are from the outside; entering the unconscious, entering yourself through dreams, is touching nature from the inside and this is the same thing, things are put right again."

In James Hillman's understanding of beauty, and Jung's idea of meditation as a method of interacting with nature, we can see that nature often functions more as a vehicle for us than as the final destination. Perhaps we might be better off with a more wholistic perspective; rather than thinking of ourselves as passively within Nature, we are actively a part of Creation.

One final approach to the distinction between nature and urbanism is offered by Jordan Peterson, the controversial psychologist from the University of Toronto. Nature, he says, is that which lies outside culture. Nature represents the unknown; culture is comprised of what we know and understand. Civilization – culture – is a limited domain of competence, while nature is an unlimited domain of mystery. This is, of course, a culturally-derived understanding! In this perspective, the unknown and unmanageable chaos of nature is represented by the Mother – the Matriarchy – while the rationally systematized order of civilization is represented by the Patriarchy. Both provide danger and security in equal measure; Mother Nature feeds and nurtures us but can destroy us just as easily; the ordered Patriarchy of civilization can protect us but also become horrifically oppressive and violent. They must be valued and respected equally and balanced appropriately.

Psychologically speaking, learning and growth occur by confronting the dangerously unknown and mysterious: strangers, disease, disappointment, death. These are not just found out in the wild, lying just beyond the light of the campfire. Are such unknowns not also found in an urban setting? That too is nature in the city. The intent of psychic growth is to bring our vast mysterious unconscious contents into the light of conscious understanding. Our task is to increase our range of competence, familiarity with, and acceptance of the unknown. Or to put it metaphorically, to bring nature into the city.

PART 4

A DEEPER URBANISM

CHAPTER XII
Sacred Urbanism

"The City is the solid exhibition of the communal soul"
– James Hillman

The city has always held a special place in the human imagination. This is seen easily enough in the mythical places in which we imbue highly aspirational meaning; Atlantis, Arcadia, Cockaigne, El Dorado, Shangri-La, and so many others. Such imaginary places reflect our longing for a manifestation of our highest hopes. And yet they remain illusory, no longer even providing inspiration for the places we do build. For the past five hundred years or so of western history, we can see a reduction in the intentions of city-building that used to be as places reflecting the values of our society, down to mere engineered infrastructure. Or perhaps a more apt way of thinking of this is as a diminution of our values. From the security of the Medieval and the elegance of the Baroque periods, on to the Industrial and now Post-industrial, both artistic and poetic sensibilities have been diminished and set aside … what could possibly come next?

I sense a deep need for an emerging City of Meaning. Any space can become sacred, depending on what the dweller or visitor brings with them to contribute. The space itself, though, can promote, evoke, or remind the visitor, and perhaps even help create a new sensibility, if designed with that intent. "There is a community of spirit" the Sufi poet Rumi reminds us; "Join it and feel the delight of walking in the noisy streets, and being the noise."

A Human Instinct

The creation of physical community is not just a human effort. Bees build hives, ants build colonies, prairie dogs build prairie dog towns. It is instinctual to these species, and I think to us as well, or has perhaps become so as we have evolved over time. But in addition to instinct, we also act out of intention. The creation of place, for us, is not just a practical need but a fundamental way in which we project into the world our hopes and aspirations, our vision of the universe and ourselves. We dream of that which does not exist, and then make it manifest. All those aspects of civilization we hold so dear – art and museums, education and universities, music and concert halls, courts of justice, cathedrals of spiritual reflection – have always been brought together in memorable urban settings since we began building cities so many millennia ago. A city or town is the cup into which we pour all life's lessons. It is the manifestation of our collective spiritual journeys. Our intentions are not always clear or well-thought-through, but the process is sacred and fundamentally human.

We build not only for ourselves but our descendants. What we build is not a blank slate but reflects to some degree what we inherited from our ancestors. Thus, we cannot truly understand what we are doing unless we consider what our ancestors left for us and what universals we will pass on to the future. The poet Rainer Maria Rilke wrote, "We are continually overflowing toward those who preceded us, toward our origin, and toward those who seemingly come after us … It is our task to imprint this temporary, perishable earth into ourselves so deeply, so painfully and passionately, that its essence can rise again invisibly, inside us. We are the bees of the invisible, we wildly collect the honey of the visible, to store it in the great golden hive of the invisible."

The founding of a place is to define the center of a known and secure territory, set against the unbounded, unexplored periphery, as historian of religion Mircea Eliade reminds us. That center is marked as the point at which heaven and earth come together in service to one another.

The Mandala: Urbanism as Cultural Shadow Work

The artwork known as a mandala, most famously created by Buddhist monks in the Himalayas and the tribal peoples of the deserts of the American southwest, is the psychological equivalent of the union of heaven and earth, according to Jung's research. He considered the mandala as spiritual work of the highest form, a meditative process of reflection on creation and the self. The word "mandala" itself simply means "circle" in Sanskrit, representing wholeness and completeness. To achieve this wholeness, we must reflect not only on the "goodness and light" but the darkness within as well, the shadow side.

The shadow, in psycho-spiritual terms developed by Jung, represents aspects of ourselves that we have rejected and repressed, for any number of reasons, as being undesirable or negative. These aspects are not always negative, dark, or "evil" but are at odds with how we wish to see ourselves, or how we wish to be understood by the world. Shadow material often is developed during childhood through experiences which cause distress or emotional pain. We may suppress these memories in order to avoid the pain; the unintended consequence is that this suppression also blocks the process of psychological growth. We all possess a shadow side – it is a natural aspect of our spiritual psyche – but good emotional and spiritual health requires that we become aware of, accept, and integrate our shadow material into our conscious awareness.

Beyond the individual shadow, there is also a collective shadow inherent in all humanity. This is easy enough to see in the daily news and history books.

Urban life certainly has its shadow aspects, elements which are inherent to civilization but too ugly for everyday viewing, so to speak. Trash, garbage, and sewage are by analogy the physical shadow of contemporary urban life. I suppose any land use rejected by the public, in NIMBY (Not In My Back Yard) fashion, might be considered our city's shadow: industrial uses, trucking and warehousing, low-income housing, drug rehab centers, etc.

The general attitude is, "Out of sight, out of mind." Toss out the garbage or flush the toilet and be done. Yet all this waste doesn't disappear; it goes somewhere and must be dealt with. Landfills and sewage treatment plants take care of this for us because it simply has to be managed. The volume and toxicity of the refuse and waste we produce is astonishing, but only recently have we really felt the need to think about it.

Coming to terms with one's shadow is typically part of a personal spiritual awakening or a psychological shift, often forced on us by stressful circumstances. We need to do the same for our cities. Our infrastructure is crumbling from decades of neglect, and the environment is certainly experiencing unprecedented stressors, but our collective response is beginning to look encouraging. Like an individual seeking to explore and integrate their shadow side, communities are beginning to bring their "dark side" into view and find ways to turn problems into opportunities. The move toward "daylighting" is perhaps the most obvious and encouraging example. As development took place early in the life a city or town, very often natural streams were channeled into underground pipes as part of the municipal stormwater system; streets would often be built on top of the former stream or creek. Daylighting uncovers these buried waterways, turning them back into natural corridors, bringing green open space, as parkland and wildlife habitat, back into the urban setting.

Another example is the efforts of the Solid Waste Authority in Lancaster, PA. Faced with the continuing need to deal with an increasing volume of trash on limited land, the Authority came up with the rarely-used solution of co-generation. Rather than viewing trash as a problem to deal with, it viewed trash as an opportunity. The trash is used as a resource, fuel for an electric generating plant, complete with exhaust scrubbers to eliminate as many air pollutants as possible. The remaining ash is much cleaner and takes up significantly less land.

Stormwater has also been conventionally seen as a nuisance, a problem to be dispatched as efficiently as possible. Out of the parking lot, off the street, into the sewer pipe, and done! Yet the long-term negative effect is at least two-fold. The first is to eliminate aquifer recharge, lowering the groundwater table. The second problem is that of pollution, particularly in older cities. Historic communities often have combined sewer systems; rainwater and sewage are conveyed in the same pipe. This might not be too bad during normal rain events, but heavier storms overload the system, requiring the treatment plant to be bypassed; raw sewage is then dumped directly into streams and rivers. As a method of easing the pressure on such combined systems, stormwater management policies now seek to allow rainwater to soak back into the ground, or be detained so that it can be slowly released and not overwhelm the system.

The move toward a more sustainable approach to the messier aspects of modern life is reflective of spiritual healing. Any difficult issue, be it psychological in nature or the management of community infrastructure, is best served when we acknowledge the existence of the negative, bring it out in the open, and work to turn what was once viewed as a problem into an opportunity. A spiritual journey is not always joy and light; we have to dig deep and uncover a lot of crap to find spiritual gems.

The process of "group shadow work" is not the most popular

form of therapy — conventional therapy favors one-on-one encounters — but any time a group comes together, its leaders are on the lookout for shadow material to arise. Informally, society also engages in shadow work, though in awfully slow and messy ways. Political debate and policy analysis, journalism, novels, protest of various sorts, social commentary, all may be thought of as a sort of uncoordinated process of cultural shadow work. The work of any designer who shapes the physical landscape not only impacts space, but society as well, by determining how and where it can operate. The best design must then include a deep process of self-reflection … what values am I permanently imprinting on the city and its future? My ego or larger and more eternal values?

Design on the land is improved when it reflects the process of drawing a mandala. A mandala is a geometric design, square or round, containing spiritual symbols intended to evoke a state of spiritual meditation or to create sacred space. The construction and drawing of a mandala is always unique; no two are alike, as they display a relationship between particular deities and the individual practitioner.

Chakras and the Transect

Humans are nothing if not expert at inventing systems to make sense of their world. Thus, the joke: The brain wants two things: a problem to solve, and an answer. It doesn't care what they are; this is how the game of golf was invented.

And yet systems are an enormously useful navigational aid, whether we consider psychology, economics, political science, history, or spirituality. Two systems have captured my attention as ways of organizing and understanding ourselves and our communities: the chakras and the New Urbanist concept of the Transect. Other systems of understanding such as Maslow's Hierarchy of Needs, the writings of Ken Wilber, and Spiral Dynamics, might fit in as well. So, what are chakras and Transects, and how could they possibly relate?

In Hindu and Buddhist thought, a chakra is an energy point or node in the "subtle" (non-physical) body. Chakras are the meeting points of the subtle energy channels called "nadi." Nadi are believed to be channels in the subtle body through which the life force (prana, or chi in Chinese systems) moves. Various scriptural texts and teachings present a different number of chakras. It's believed that there are many chakras in the subtle human body, but there are seven chakras considered to be most significant.

The chakra system and yoga arose during the second half of the first millennium. The seven basic chakras exist within the subtle body, overlaying the physical body. These seven chakras are said to correspond to the seven main nerve ganglia which emanate from the brain and spinal column.

The first three chakras, starting at the base of the spine, are chakras of matter. They are more physical in nature. Chakras five, six, and seven, are more spiritual in nature. The fourth, or heart chakra, is the link, the connection between the material and spiritual.

In the concept of the Transect we find another system of understanding the world around us. Transects and their zones were discussed in Chapter VII, but let me refresh your memory for sake of this comparison I'm about to make.

A Transect is a way of understanding nature, viewing a slice of the landscape to examine changes across the environment. Each ecosystem has its own distinct combination of plant and animal life, hydrology, and geology. For an ecologist, a Transect might move from the ocean floor to the beach, then marshlands, low scrub pine forests, and on to upland hardwood forests. Each of these settings has distinct characteristics of flora and fauna, geology, and hydrology, yet flow into one another as a continuum.

The urban planning and land development movement known as New Urbanism has made use of this concept and extended it into the human-built environment. For an urbanist, the Transect is both a theory of urban patterns and a system of classifying land uses, potentially organized into a zoning code. To a New Urbanist, the Transect is understood as a gradient of development intensity and of human living arrangements, from most rural to most urban. Moving across the urban Transect reveals changes in design, patterns, and physical structure. As a method of seeing the best way to mix – or separate – land uses appropriately, all development types become appropriate if located and designed properly. When the various elements of the built environment are properly located, the whole becomes greater than the sum of its parts, what Andres Duany describes as "immersive environments." It should be noted that this understanding takes into account the fact that places change over time.

There are six generalized Transect zones, moving from the most natural and informal, to the most urban and formalized (also discussed in Chapter VII):

T-1 Natural/Preserved
T-2 Rural/Reserved
T-3 Neighborhood Edge
T-4 Neighborhood General
T-5 Neighborhood Center
T-6 Urban Core

In the New Urbanist model, community is characterized by mixed uses and walkability; the needs of pedestrians are emphasized over the automobile. Each of the Transect zones has its own set of characteristics, including building alignment, size and mass, street typologies, parking arrangements, types of open spaces, housing options, and densities, among other details.

For my own purposes (and as a way to make the comparison with Chakras balance out!), I add the mythical Seventh Transect, the perfected City as imagined throughout history, from Plato's Republic and the Shining City on a Hill, to Italo Calvino's Invisible Cities, and my own imagined places of beauty and harmony. Perhaps we can even place the Garden of Eden in this context, as a longed-for home?

How do they relate? Both the chakras and Transect zones represent centers of energy.

The first three Transect zones – Preserved, Reserved, and Neighborhood Edge – are the most "earth-bound," that is in greatest relationship to the natural world, as are the first three Chakras – Root, Sacral, and Solar Plexus. In them, we find our physical security, the source of stability in the material world, the foundational elements required for civilization, and the basic social and personal relationships of daily life. The fourth Chakra and Transect – the Heart and Neighborhood – represent the transition between the physical and spiritual. This is Home, where we experience the deepest connection to Love, Compassion, and Ego on a daily basis. The final three Transect zones, Neighborhood Main Street, Urban Core, and the "City of the Imagination," as I term it, are the points at which we experience greater communal connection and increasing opportunities for self-expression and communication, the gathering of wisdom and knowledge, and the ability to transcend our limited routine.

TEMENOS

The Chakras

Root
Survival, instinct, security, stability in the material world

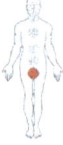

Sacral
Emotion, energy, relationships, sexuality, intimacy, creativity

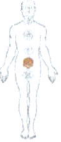

Solar Plexus
Energy and will; Effectiveness, social identity, metabolism, self–esteem

Heart
Love, compassion, trust, forgiveness, balance, openness, empathy, ego, hope

Throat
Communication, self–expression, listening, speaking, writing, healing

Third Eye
Imagination, insight, visions, intuition

Crown
Consciousness of and connection to the universal; Transcendence

The Transect

T-1 Preserved
Wilderness, wetlands, slopes, habitats, nature preserved in perpetuity

T-2 Reserved
Working land, agriculture and agrarian, managed forests, grazing. Intended to remain open but some limited future development potential

T-3 Neighborhood Edge
Privacy; the point at which nature begins to yield to urbanism. Essentially residential with some civic amenities

T-4 Neighborhood General
Home, intimacy. Primarily residential but with some small local commercial as well as civic activity

T-5 Neighborhood Core
Main Street. Shops and offices with residential above. Gathering places such as parks and cafes

T-6 Urban Core
The focal point of regional activity; the most active, formal, and stimulating

City of the Imagination
The New Jerusalem, the City on a Hill, the City of David

Not every place needs all six (or seven) Transect zones to create a fully-developed community. But as humans, we need the full, rich experience of each. All seven chakras are inherent to us, and we experience each on a daily basis. Balance is key, both for personal health and communal harmony.

The Begijnhof as a Spiritually Inspiring Form

Throughout most of history, cities were more often than not surrounded by a protective wall. This was common as recently as the 1600s, after which the weapons of war became powerful enough to make walls useless as protection. During the Medieval era, cities grew not just as centers of growing commerce, but from both the security and competence found in cloistered monasteries. As Mumford states in *Culture of Cities*, "The cloister in both its public and private form is a constant element in the life of cities." One of the most distinctive of these cloistered forms is that of the beguinage, or begijnhof in Flemish usage.

For over 200 years, during the late 1100s through the 1300s, Europe underwent significant upheaval, suffering through war, famine, plague, and crusades. Under the feudal system of the time, strict rules for class and gender were in place, with few options for women. They could live with their families until they married, then live with a husband until widowed, then with a son. The only other choice for an "honest" unmarried woman was to become a nun.

As a result of the turmoil of the era, there were so many unmarried, widowed, or abandoned women in northern Europe that out of necessity, a new role and lifestyle emerged for unmarried women to work honestly and live culturally acceptable lives. They were known as the *beguines*, and lived together communally, dedicating themselves to prayers and good works. They were laywomen, though in dress they resembled nuns; they didn't take vows or belong to the hierarchy of the Catholic Church but lived independent lives, free to own property and businesses. Theirs was a movement with no vows, rules, constitutions, or commitments.

At first, homeless women built rough cabins near each other outside the walls of towns where they were able to help each other raise children, plant gardens, and sell their handiwork in the market. These ghettos of poor women were easy prey to bandits and worse; in response, the women organized and raised funds to build protective walls and gates around their small neighborhoods. This naturally gave them a group identity and status. Some of these walled communities grew so large in the 13th century that they housed thousands of women and were virtual towns within the town, with markets, breweries, churches, hospitals, cemeteries, and administration halls. Younger women lived in convent-style apartments and the older or more well-to-do women lived in individual houses. By the end of the 12th century, nearly every town in Flanders had at least a small beguinage even if it didn't have a regular convent.

The end of the Crusades, an improving economy, and a gap between major outbreaks of the plague restored the balance in numbers of marriageable men and women. Fewer women turned to life in a beguinage because they had more attractive alternatives. Occasional rounds of official harassment from the Catholic Church also contributed to the decline of these communities. A few lasted through the 20th century, with the last member dying as recently as 2012. At one point there were 96 begijnhofs in Flanders alone, though less than a third that number still exist there today. Common uses now in the remaining communities include retirement homes, schools, university student housing, and artists colonies; some have been taken over as convents.

The remaining thirty or so begijnhofs that remained standing and are reused in Belgium are typically urban in their settings. Sizes range from about 5 to 20 acres. They include residences in the form of small cottages and dormitories, as well as a church or chapel; originally workspaces for weaving, brewing, and the like were included in the program. They are typically arranged around a small green park or cobbled plaza. While most remain walled, and occasionally moated or adjacent to a water feature, they are normally fully integrated into the street pattern of the surrounding city, accessible through gates in the walls.

Today, the beguinage provides an excellent physical model for the redevelopment and infill of existing cities. Numerous building typologies can take advantage of such a secure and accessible format, particularly small footprint affordable housing. The "compound housing" concept recently advocated by Andres Duany fits into this model very well. It provides a level of both design and administration smaller than a neighborhood, allowing for more flexible response in community decision-making and change over time. As a physically bounded yet porous retreat, in the center of a larger active community, a Begijnhof provides both peaceful security and accessibility to the wider opportunities of the city as a whole.

Cities Built as Spiritual Metaphor

The places we build reflect the values we hold. Our furthest city-building ancestors often built their cities with a sense that they were reflecting some sort of heavenly order upon the land. There are innumerable examples of urbanism based on spiritual, symbolic, or metaphorical intentions. This was typically manifested in the location and orientation of a main temple and central square with the astronomical alignment of a main street or avenue. However, this is normally limited to a precinct, compound, or individual building. Rarely has an entire city been planned and designed as a symbolic whole.

Various capital cities of empires in the Americas display elements of cosmological or spiritual intentions in their layout. Cities of the Mayan civilization, and Tenochtitlan, capital of the Aztec Empire, illustrate this. An amazing deviation is the layout of Cusco, the capital of the Inca Empire. Its shape was in the form of a Puma, a sacred animal totem symbolic of the power of the earth.

In European traditions, we typically consider Rome the most spiritually inspired city, although this physical manifestation is somewhat haphazard and uncoordinated. After the fall of the Roman Empire, the city shrank from a peak population of over one million to perhaps as little as 17,000 by the mid-1500s. Under Pope Sixtus V, a series of streets began to give the remaining city some coherence. These were intended to connect the seven churches within the city as a method of improving transportation and the routes of religious pilgrims. This was essentially to connect preexisting spiritual centers; it was largely a transportation effort rather than any reflection of fully spiritual intentions.

A more intentionally geometric, if not overtly spiritual, European city design can also be found in Italy – that of Grammichele. This small Sicilian city bears a superficial resemblance to the better-known example of Palmanova. But whereas Palmanova's geometry was intentionally military and defensive in nature, Grammichele's hexagonal shape has no defensive wall nor any military purpose. It was built in 1693 after an earthquake destroyed much of the surrounding settlements. It follows the design concepts of ideal cities that were in play during the Renaissance, led by designers such as Alberti. It mimics Palmanova's radial street system but without military defenses, meeting the countryside directly. A hierarchy of street and plaza dimensions is employed. While no particular spiritual or symbolic intention is attached to the design, Grammichele provides an early model of a town fully designed with intention according to artistic values.

The ancient Vedic practice of Vaastu Shastra in India is a form of geomancy. Geomancy is used here as an umbrella term for a variety of different approaches to divination and creating design on the land. These include Vaastu Shastra in India and Feng Shui in China. It is a collection of principles in the service of architecture, interior design, and urbanism. These principles focus on relationship of the built environment to the cardinal directions, the five fundamental elements of nature (air, water, earth, fire, space), and astronomy. It also takes into account localized conditions of the natural environment. It is a method of creating living spaces replicating the divine cosmos. The most well-known city built upon its principles is Jaipur in India. It was established in 1727 as a fully planned city, spiritually ruled by the deity Govind Dev Ji, and laid out as a mandala of nine sections, corresponding to the nine planets.

Perhaps the most intriguing example of cities fully laid out to reflect a cosmological order is to be found in China. Several villages and small cities are laid out in the pattern of a "bagua." The bagua is a symbol in the Taoist spiritual tradition of the cosmology of the Tao and the eight fundamental principles of reality or forces of nature.

These are shown as the eight trigrams of the I Ching arranged octagonally around the classic yin-yang symbol. A bagua is also a tool used in feng shui, a Chinese form of geomancy or design on the land.

The largest and most complete of the communities laid out in this manner is Tekes, completed in 1936 in far western China. Each of the eight main streets is 1200 meters long. Four ring roads shape the octagon, with eight radial streets within the first ring, sixteen in the second ring, thirty-two in the third, and sixty-four in the outer ring.

Walking these streets, one is fully immersed in a setting of spiritual reflection.

The cities of medieval Europe were often designed, and certainly understood, in terms of spiritual metaphor. The geographer Keith Lilley, in an article entitled "Cities of God: Medieval Urban Forms and Christian Symbolism," shows how such symbolic form is to be found in the circle and the cross. From the 12th through the 14th century, cities were often laid out in general terms in order to reflect the heavenly City of God. A circular wall pierced by gates located at the four cardinal points was understood as an imitation of the heavenly City of God.

The German architect Klaus Humpert has researched the layout of various medieval cities, particularly Freiburg. His findings seem to debunk the idea that the maze-like streets were "organic," natural and unplanned. Rather, such streets were highly intentional in their use of precise geometric lines and curves. Designers of the time were completely fascinated by numbers and used geometry as a way of being in accord with God's rules.

The Importance of Non-Existent Places

In the highly nebulous field of dream interpretation, it is generally acknowledged that an image of a house symbolizes the interior life of the dreamer. Various rooms might represent aspects of the personality or character, for instance. Jung had such a dream, described in an earlier chapter, of a house of multiple levels, each representing stages of history. My dreams too are often dominated by the setting of a house, either mine or that of a person who appears in the dream.

A second dream of Jung's included not merely a house but an entire city. What is referred to as his "Liverpool" dream shaped his understanding of both his personal and professional situation at the time (1927); it redirected his efforts in both as a result. In the dream, he found himself in the city of Liverpool, traveling with several other Swiss. The city was quite dirty and sooty but arranged radially with all the streets converging on a small island at the center. On that central island were found a tree and bright streetlamp – light and life at the center of an otherwise dismal city. He knew upon reflection that this image represented his own life, and what lay at the center of it. It marked a transition point in both his life and professional research.

Having stumbled across this story a couple of years ago, I

determined to make use of my own fantasy story of a city in an intentional manner. Since childhood I have carried with me a fantasy world, a small town which I named Harton. It is a relatively small, leafy suburb of a larger city which has gone by various names over the years. Much like a novelist might do in creating a setting for a story, I populated my Harton with imaginary friends and favorite locations. Harton has a history and a map, as does the larger city just up the trolley line. I put the world of Harton aside decades ago, but the idea revived itself after reading Jung's dream.

In my practice of shamanism, I often make use of what is known as "journeying," which is quite similar if not equivalent to Jung's method of "active imagination." Both are essentially approaches to interacting with the "other world," whether that be understood as the spirit world of a shaman or the personal unconscious as Jung described it. The methods for all appearances are similar to a meditative state but on the contrary, journeying and active imagination are quite participatory. The intention is to interact with the various characters one might meet, as might occur in a lucid dream, for instance. In this way, Jung sought to externalize various character traits or aspects of the personality, personify them, name them, and interact with them, in order to learn from and manage them when necessary.

I determined to develop my own method of "journeying," for private self-discovery and development, which involves the design and exploration of a more intentional vision of Harton, or rather its larger adjacent city. It has morphed as a city into a collection of islands in a lake, divided by natural creeks and formal canals, each a neighborhood unto itself with its own mood and feel. It includes all the elements one expects of a thriving city: stadiums and theaters, industrial works, hotels for temporary visitors, more than one fairly squalid district, a university, hospital, markets, musty old bookstores, a hall of records, on and on. At its heart lies a ceremonial tower which is only accessed by way of a deep watery grotto.

I am now a flaneur of my own imaginary city, my own inner world, my own soul, wandering the streets populated with characters and archetypes of my own unconscious Self. I have no hope of getting to know the entire population, and am surprised by the range of citizens who inhabit it. There are ordinary and conventional men and women, as well as strange characters including an old crone and her protege, a young goddess; mermaids living in the canals; dwarf-like workers; a magical boat on which I travel; and a shadowy thug and secretive enemy. Every visit includes some small lesson at least, sometimes a shocking adventure and revelation.

These visits most often take place while I sit under my special tree, a Linden or Basswood, along the Potomac River just south of Alexandria. I may meditate prior to beginning, to settle myself into the right frame of openness, but the visits themselves are not meditative or calming at all. While meditation is intended to empty and calm oneself, these journeys are intended to be active, filling and nourishing, like a multi-course meal with friends.

My journeys begin and end in the same manner and place, on one particular small island to the side of the city, with a particular group of nonhuman companions, my "welcoming committee." The city is at this point far from fully built; early journeys were to a series of dense woods and wetlands with no development at all, a primeval place with only one ancient inhabitant. A series of small villages emerged and have gradually grown together to form a metropolis. It is always under redevelopment, as is any city ... or soul.

The highest task of personal development is what Jung defined as "individuation." Aniela Jaffé, one of Jung's closest associates, describes individuation as the process of making "what fate intends to do with us entirely our own intention." In my own words, it is the process of bringing my conscious intentions for my life into alignment with what my higher Self has planned for me. My conscious ego which I define as "me" is not truly the author of my life; I am rather an actor on stage, riffing or ad-libbing off a script that I can only partially see. I need to coordinate my role in this play of life with the director, stage manager, and script writer – my soul, my higher Self. This check-in is part of what I do on my journeys.

This has become a regular, intimate way to discover the complexity that lies within me, my relations, and the world around me. What the various characters and situations share with me might be direct and blunt words of advice, or subtle and rather oblique insights, usually confusing and occasionally horrifying. We typically think of the spiritual path as a lonely place to be. I have found that my inner life is by no means lonely; I am filled with innumerable invisible characters with whom I may interact. While psychic and spiritual work is private, it is by no means isolated. I am not one being, but a multitude.

So too are you. Each of us is a city, packed with residents making up various aspects of our personalities and inner psychic lives. We are never truly alone; we travel with our inner demons and angels. The entity we each think of as "me" is truly made up of characters and characteristics so independent of our control that we can think of ourselves as inhabited by a multitude of other beings. Today we tend to name these as various psychological traits and emotional conditions; our ancient ancestors named them as gods and demons. One way to manage and interact with them is to personify them. When finding myself becoming angry, I might imagine meeting a character on a street in my "city" – "Oh, here is Mr. Jones again. Hello, listen, I don't have much time to spend with you at the moment, but I'll listen to what you have to say for a bit, so thanks for stopping by, good day." And with that acknowledgment of a fellow resident of my interior community, I dispense with my interaction with angry resentment. Or joy comes to us – "How delightful to see you, Ms. Smith! Please join me and tell me your story as we walk." And so, we interact and learn from the many sides of ourselves that we may not know well enough or even acknowledge.

CHAPTER XIII
The Search for New Metaphors

"Believe those who seek the truth. Doubt those who find it."
– Andre Gide

It is well understood that whenever western culture (that is, European and American) has interacted with traditional native and tribal cultures, a fundamental and violent aspect of the inevitable conquest has involved the destruction of the traditional mythical values and structures of the society. The loss of that foundational mythology of a people results in their psychological destruction. Take away the operating myth of a society and it will die.

What is less recognized is that the same process is happening to western civilization as well. The contemporary West believes it has thrown off the ignorance of unnecessary, even problematic religion, and replaced it with the clearer truth of science and rational technocracy. With this thinking, we are doing to ourselves what we once did to the tribal cultures we dominated. We have destroyed our own mythology. We see the results today in our political and cultural divide, our psychic chaos, planetary destruction, and loss of direction, both personal and societal. The political history of the 20th century, with its defining two world wars and the resulting death of hundreds of millions of people, is the great case study in this. Those societies which intentionally sought to replace a traditional religious foundation with a strictly technocratic political approach – the Soviet Union and Maoist China as the largest examples – ended up murdering tens of millions of their own people.

In his last work, *Man and His Symbols*, Jung stated that our world today does not realize the extent to which the overly rational mind of our civilization is destroying our capacity to understand symbols and symbolic ideas. The attempt to free our culture from superstition has reduced our respect for spiritual values so fully that we are at the mercy of our psychic shadow, those psychological forces that act upon us without our awareness. This is why the atheist tends to make the same mistake as the fundamentalist; they misunderstand the role of myth, and thus perceive "god" as merely a large and judgmental ego.

Again, this is not to say that religion is by any means free from guilt; rather that religious *institutions* are just as easily manipulated by the psychological shadow as any other cultural or political entity. Popular opinion seems to rest on the idea that religion is the root cause of divisiveness, hatred, and war. Yet *The Encyclopedia of War* reveals that, of all 1,763 known wars recorded throughout history, only 7%, or 123, have had religion as their primary cause. Rather, religion seems to be easily and regularly hijacked by the collective psychic shadow. The fear of cultural differences and the lust for security, power, and gold are the more universal drivers of conflict, though religious language is used for justification.

As noted in Chapter II, the city of Venice was essentially founded as a refuge from the danger and chaos brought by invading hordes as the Roman Empire collapsed. More broadly, the Christian church has acted for centuries in the same role, as a psychological and spiritual refuge. Western society also adapted and incorporated the ancient mythic stories of Greece and Rome into its culture, alongside the Church. Together, these two strands of myth and religion have combined to provide an authoritative source of calm, safe, secure community, ethical standards, and moral direction. This is not to downplay the many shortcomings the Christian church has to answer for, its prejudices and violence; but its role in western society has been to provide an operating system of cultural and spiritual values. From this place of psychological safety and security, individuals have been enabled, as much as they are willing and able, to jump out from culturally sanctioned religion into the dangerous and very insecure waters of a transformative private spirituality, from which much of true personal, and thus societal, growth occurs.

This solid metaphysical foundation that the western world has rested upon for centuries is now, to all appearances, in its death spiral. The Christian faith is not always respected or even understood, and the classical myths of the Greek and Roman worlds are virtually unknown, kept alive only in rough form via occasional Hollywood movies of heroic adventure. I would even venture to say that the Christian church is no longer the sole repository of Christian values. Yet no civilization seems able to sustain itself without some mythic foundation from which its operational principles can grow. Christianity has for centuries made available to us all the lessons it holds, and these have been incorporated into society as much as could be hoped. In that process of incorporation, the Enlightenment can be seen as a means of translating religious values into secular values of basic human dignity. In that process, however, an understanding of the original source has been lost. But it seems time to move on to larger lessons, whether we are ready or not, much like a schoolchild must move on, ready or not, to larger lessons after the elementary years have passed. As both Joseph Campbell and C.G. Jung stated, something of a larger and more inclusive and contemporary vision needs to incorporate, carry forward, and expand upon the lessons of Christianity and its predecessors.

We need to reclaim a civilization which respects the fundamental psychological need of symbolic and metaphorical myth. They naturally emerge out of the collective unconscious of humanity and develop over the course of thousands of years. It is not reasonable to dispense wholesale with the psychological foundations that we have relied upon for millennia without significant negative consequence. We flounder without them.

In acknowledging the fundamental value that mythological symbols and metaphor provide, we must respect and utilize the old while making ourselves open to new symbols, new mythologies. What might that look like, and where might the new come from? After delving into what I see as the trouble we are facing as a civilization – a crisis of faith is one way of phrasing it – I'll explore some possible sources of renewal that seem most likely. The challenging question for a book such as this is what possible relationship such questions hold for urban planning and the shape of cities; and what, in turn, cities can contribute to this as well.

Conventional Paradigms

Like the sinking of Venice, our historic trust in the safety and security of the Christian religion is, by and large, fading away. Or rather, we have outgrown it. We have incorporated most of its fundamental tenets into our cultural institutions; its moral and ethical teachings no longer seem transcendent but obvious. And as rationality and logic have come to dominate our culture, with science expanding our horizons at every scale, our ancient stories no longer suffice. Mythologies written thousands of years ago remain metaphorically true, yet at the same time no longer match our understanding of the physical universe, cultural landscape, or personal psychic lives. Our language no longer matches theirs, and we misunderstand the messages because the images and metaphors don't resonate. Too, we must now take into account cultures and civilizations that were unheard of by the writers of our ancient texts, which have their own mythic stories of creation and morality.

We can think of the Biblical Old Testament as an evolutionary series of biographies where over time, these individuals came slightly closer to the image of an ideal person. Moses, Jonah, David, Job … these were not perfect humans by any stretch, but their attempts to grow and develop were told in story form to provide examples and inspiration. The New Testament continued that progression, revealing in Jesus Christ the highest level of spiritual development and showing how such a life is conducted. But Jesus himself implied that others after him would rise to even greater achievements.

We can trace the history of such development and transition. The teachings of Hinduism, for example, hold enormous ancient truth and wisdom, though they remain strongly tied to a particular cultural history. Buddhism grew out of the tradition by transcending that particular culture to make its teachings more widely available. In the West, the roots trace back to Mesopotamia, which influenced Egypt, both of which nurtured the thinking of Judaism. Judaism in turn holds enormous wisdom to share with the world but remains culturally bound. Christianity then used that foundation to grow beyond its cultural foundation to share its story with the wider world.

What will grow out of this 2,000 year old Christian narrative? What will incorporate its truths and yet transcend it? There is no reason to believe that humanity has reached a final stage of moral or psychic development. Humans have always needed some sort of psychological operating system in the form of symbol and myth. This has not changed, nor will it ever. The failure of contemporary rational thinking is that it believes it knows enough to banish everything from the past that it does not know or understand. Yet as Jung said, "Two thousand years of Christianity must be replaced by something at least as powerful." The idea of an "end of times" seems a given these days;

many believe that we have reached a historical dead-end. Not limited by any means to an Apocalypse as envisioned by evangelical Christians, such an expectant air is everywhere, from New Age hippies to political commentaries on our shared geopolitical situation to the environmental crisis of climate change. But "apocalypse" refers not to the physical destruction of the world so much as the destruction of a paradigm, a way of thinking; the end of a psycho/spiritual ordering system, in order to make way for a larger and more whole visionary system to take its place. This can be – should be – fundamentally a personal as well as cultural process.

Foundational spiritual stories cannot be pulled out of thin air; they emerge over time of their own accord, organically. While it is easy to observe the breakdown of the old stories, what will replace them remains obscure and takes decades, maybe centuries, to emerge. How does a hyper-rationalized civilization which no longer arranges itself upon mythical and metaphorical ideas, and has little poetic vision, develop a new mythology and the guiding principles accompanying it? It cannot do so, since mythology and accompanying symbols emerge spontaneously from the unconscious. Yet with this awareness of our place in history arises an opportunity to prepare ourselves in some small fashion for what is to come. This era of history is perhaps the first time in human experience when such a dramatic shift of the underlying cosmological foundation can be seen with conscious awareness and thus prepared for. What *can* be contributed consciously is the setting of the stage and an openness of the heart. A safe assumption though is that the new will make use of and include the old stories, not merely discard them. Let's consider some sources from which a new set of stories might emerge. There are many; I briefly discuss a few below, those I'm most familiar with and seem foundational in their perspective. The reader will no doubt see others as well.

Evolution

One of the most powerful ideas to upend traditional religious views in the western world has been Darwin's theory of evolution. Evolution's only goal is to find the best fit for a species to survive in its given environment. Beyond this, though, functioning simply as a process, evolution does seem clearly to trend toward two qualities: ever-increasing complexity, and interconnectedness. It does not move us merely from amoeba to ape to human, but more generally from the simple and isolated to the complex and connected.

For all his various shortcomings and prejudices, Darwin does seem to have, if I may say, evolved in his thinking. This is seen in *Descent of Man*, the lesser-known follow-up to his *Origin of Species*. One of the points emphasized in *Descent* is the emotion of sympathy as an evolved trait. In this we see more clearly that the popular but misunderstood phrase "survival of the fittest" is better understood to mean "fitness" as the most appropriate, not the strongest or most aggressive.

This holds true not only in biology but in human civilization as well. In his work *Nonzero,* journalist and author Robert Wright describes how both cultural and civilizational evolution trend over time toward ever-increasing complexity and connection … and cooperation. Win-win solutions, rather than win-lose confrontations, have driven more positive change over time. Evolution in this light seems a natural fit for an emerging global mindset.

Gaia

The Gaia Principle was developed by James Lovelock and Lynn Margulis as an outcome of Lovelock's research for NASA into the possibility of life on Mars. The essential idea is that the various forms of life and the elements of the environment interact to form a stable and hospitable setting for the continuation of life. Living species and their environment interact as a single unified process. As Margulis phrases it, "Life on earth does not exist *on* the earth's surface, it *is* the earth's surface." Together, the variety of species and various environmental systems of hydrology, geology, and climate operate in an evolutionary spiral, and act in a sense as the organs of a living meta-being known as earth, intent on maintaining a balance appropriate for the continuation of life.

For instance, even though the intensity of solar radiation has increased significantly since life first appeared here billions of years ago, the self-regulating elements of earth have continued to create conditions appropriate for the maintenance of life, though the forms of life themselves change significantly in response.

Since emerging as a scientific theory in the late 1960s, the concept quickly became a mythic spiritual story as well. The Gaia Principle operates now as a metaphor of the Mother Goddess. We are all of us dependent upon, and indeed a part of, this feminine foundation of creation. In this way, humanity may once again learn to have a respectful relationship with the earth as a being.

Shamanism

What can shamanism contribute to a vision of a modern scientific urban spirituality? As the world's oldest known form of spiritual practice, with evidence going back an estimated 30,000 years, it can be thought of as the foundation of all subsequent spiritual traditions.

Shamans play the role for their tribe of priests, medical healers, psychotherapists, seers, storytellers, and wisdom-keepers. When called to the work, traditional shamans undergo ritualized training that is typically extremely difficult, even dangerous, both physically and psychologically. They have a particularly intimate connection to the spiritual world, and are able to move about it and relate to its inhabitants easily. A shaman inhabits and travels to three spiritual realms: this world on earth, a lower world under the earth, and an upper world among the sky and stars. Each of these three plays a particular role, inhabited by specific characters and entities, some friendly, some not.

Shamanic societies understand that every species of plant and animal, and the stones and rivers and mountains as well, have some form of spirit in them, with which we can build a connection to and learn from. A fundamental principle of shamanism is that we are here temporarily, as incarnated spirits, to learn, grow, and experience. It is often assumed that shamans use some sort of plant-based drug such as peyote or ayahuasca to assist or induce spiritual trance. This is not universal by any means; the majority of shamanic ceremony makes use of rhythmic drumming as the basis for the psychic journey, not drugs.

Phil Borges is a professional photographer and human rights worker who traveled the globe in his career. In this capacity he has encountered and interviewed dozens of tribal shamans in Asia, South America, and Africa. The similarities he sees among them are astonishing. Various practices seem universal, including the ecstatic traveling to the three worlds, drumming to induce ecstatic trance, interaction with spiritual beings, etc. He describes three types of relationships that shamanic societies value that the modern world seems to have a tenuous hold on at best. These are: relationship to each other; relationship to and knowledge of the local landscape; and relationship to the spiritual world.

We no longer live in small tribal societies, however. Our world is larger, global, interconnected, and complex, founded on science, unlike anything our deep ancestors could imagine. How could a spirituality that preceded the organized religions of civilization by thousands of years act as a type of universal metaphor in an urban world at a time when religion and spirituality no longer hold their power over us? We must understand that every society has always had such spiritual teachers, even today, though going by different names. Shamans are by no means limited to ancient or tribal cultures. The word "shaman" is specific to the Tungus tribe in Siberia but has come to be applied universally, most typically for the western imagination in the people of the Peruvian Andes. And yet the West has its shamanic traditions as well, most notably in the ancient Celtic world of Europe. The foundation of Greek philosophy is shamanic in nature, specifically in the pre-Socratic world of Parmenides, Empedocles, and the Oracles. The West does not need to look to other traditions to find spiritual strength; it has its own, which has been forgotten and overlooked.

Integral Spirituality

As the name implies, and as I've defined it in earlier chapters, Integral Spirituality simply refers to an approach seeking to include as many fundamental truths from as many disciplines as possible – from East as well as the West, from premodern and modern and postmodern, from the hard science of physics to the softer approaches of psychology and spirituality. The intent is to find the similarities and shared religious and mythological concepts throughout the world and in all history, and integrate them into a deeper and more universal understanding; to make such an evolutionary perspective an intentional, conscious effort of spiritual development.

Philosophers and spiritual thinkers leading the integral theory movement include Ken Wilbur, Craig Hamilton, Brian Swimme, and Don Beck, among others. The idea of evolutionary development is basic to all their thinking. As Wilbur outlines the evolution of humanity in history, over the course of tens of thousands of years there have been five stages of psychic development: archaic, magical/warrior, traditional mythic, modern rational, and the current information stage in which we find ourselves today, that of postmodern pluralism.

All these previous stages of human development were marked, according to Wilbur, by a deeply held belief that their values were the only true ones; all others were seen as wrong, sometimes dangerously so.

A new and more broadly inclusive stage seems to be emerging now. This new state accepts that truth and value are found in all stages and perspectives. Integral makes room for all; it is radically inclusive yet acknowledges that each view is limited in perspective, revealing only partial truth.

An associated line of thinking is that of Spiral Dynamics. Spiral echoes these various levels of psychological development, using color-coded stages of mature development. It is quite possible – even typical – for both individuals and entire societies to move up and down, to advance and recede, among these various levels.

For the Integral philosopher Steve McIntosh, the evolutionary process is not random but has a clear direction. The impulse of evolution reveals the direction of the Universe. Its goal is the great triad of Goodness, Truth, and Beauty. Humans and their free will are the agents of the Universe to achieve this.

As a theology of sorts, there are a number of basic tenets which Integral holds to be true. First and fundamentally, the evolving Universe had a distinct and dramatic beginning. This initial creative act, the uncaused Cause, is transcendent of time, space, energy, and evolution. This Cause is infinite, eternal, universal, and perfect. The initial creative act was an act of separation of some aspects or parts of the Whole, into discreet and limited elements, which remain in some manner a part of the original Whole. Evolution – physical, biological, cultural, and psychological – is the operational way these parts interact in a process of dialectical development, a slow but creative return to Unity. In this way, each person can connect with the intrinsic value of truth, goodness, and beauty found in each other, as aspects of the purpose of the First Cause (god).

Jung's Alchemical Psychology

To summarize the thinking of psychologist C.G. Jung is no easy task; his was one of the most wide-ranging intellectual and insightful minds in history. It has been said of his genius that he not only asked questions no one had ever conceived of before, but he also provided the answers. He was able not merely to see into the psyche of an individual client, but to trace the evolutionary psychology of civilizations over the course of thousands of years, and the impact of millions of years of biological evolution upon the psyche of humanity. His bringing together of rational conscious inquiry and the more "irrational" aspect of the human psyche marked a high point of 20th century thinking. Some who knew him place him alongside such spiritual teachers Lao Tzu, The Buddha, and Christ.

In developing my own understanding of Jung, I arrange his thinking into three categories: his theory of the elements and structure of the individual psyche; the process of "individuation"; and the evolutionary history of psychic development. Professionals and more experienced students will perhaps have a more subtle perspective.

The general public is most familiar with Jung's theories relating to the structure and elements of the individual psyche. Many of his theoretical terms have entered into public awareness such as the shadow, synchronicity, anima/animus, archetypes, persona, projection, and the collective unconscious, among others. Most familiar to the public is his personality typology regarding introversion and extroversion and the four modes of operating in the world: thinking, feeling, sensing, and intuition. These make up the basis of the Myers-Briggs personality test, though he had nothing to do with creating any such test. He also developed methods of therapeutic introspection and dream analysis.

Jung's theories of the individual psyche describe the stages of the process of "individuation" which can be described simply as becoming what one is intended to be. This happens naturally in the course of life; just as an acorn grows into a tree, so humans have the opportunity to develop into their truer self. Individuation requires a conscious, intentional, and quite painful effort involving the development of a relationship between the conscious ego and the larger Self, or soul. Individuation is the conscious attempt to bring the universal program of human existence to its fullest possible expression in the life of each individual. Just as we desire to understand this psychic realm of our lives, so too does the larger unconscious aspect of ourselves seek to know and interact with the conscious ego. Dreams are the basic tool used by the unconscious to interact and communicate with us in order to help us balance the opposite aspects and tensions inherent in life. For full and healthy psychic development, an individual must learn and conform to social norms to develop healthy relationships and contribute to society; but at the same time they must transcend social norms through individuation to achieve their full private potential.

The more complex and difficult aspects of Jung's teaching begin here. Over the course of his career, he moved on from focusing on the healing of neurosis in individual patients, though he continued seeing patients occasionally. His research and writing began to delve almost exclusively on what might be termed the "numinous," that is the spiritual or divine presence which seems to guide human history. His studies and travels ranged so widely as to cover ancient mythology, evolution, particle physics, shamanism, the Tibetan art of the mandala, the tribal wisdom found in Africa and southwestern America, Gnosticism, and alchemy. He discovered repeating themes and patterns of development across cultures and thousands of years of history; the evolution of psychological understanding as displayed in myth and religion; and the emergence of consciousness in our most distant ancestry. This heritage of psychic inquiry reaches back from prehistoric shamans to the Greek Oracles, through the early Christian Gnostics, the Jewish kabbalah, and medieval alchemy. Jungian psychology translates that mythological, religious, and spiritual heritage into contemporary language for the modern, rational West. Jung equated this repeating pattern of the numinous irrupting into the world to a rhizome; while a plant may grow and blossom for a time only to wither and die, the underlying root remains, waiting for another day. The metaphor of the rhizome helps us understand the repeating patterns of history.

In all this, he was quite clear that we are controlled and made use of by powers larger than ourselves. This not only includes the unconscious and instinctual elements of ourselves that we have inherited through thousands and millions of years of biological evolution (what the ancients understood as "the gods" we now think of as aspects of our psychological and emotional make-up), but also the emergence of consciousness itself, the desire to grow out of simple animal instinct into ever-increasing conscious awareness. Laurens van der Post, a South African storyteller and associate of Jung, reported in the documentary about Jung called *Matter of Heart* that a deeply fundamental core concept of Jung's thinking was in accordance with the Zulu teaching that god or the creator has given over some tasks to humans; that is, humans have god-like tasks to perform in the world. To the extent we find our own personal contribution to that task, we derive meaning and purpose.

Regarding the spiritual and mystical traditions of the West, Jung viewed alchemy as the penultimate expression of the Christian experience. Alchemy carried the Christian story further by the inclusion of both the feminine and the dark side. Its goal was not merely an early attempt at experimental chemistry – the attempt to turn lead into gold – but was more metaphorical. The lead was the leaden material of the individual psyche to be transmuted into the gold of mystical enlightenment. The methods and processes of alchemy turn out to mirror Jung's methods of individuation. The alchemists' methodology included the projection of psychological elements into matter, chemicals, stones, etc. The alchemist and his psyche (there were few female alchemists) used chemical substances and processes in the same way an artist uses color to give shape to the images in his soul. An astonishing perspective of alchemy is that it sought not only the redemption and healing of the person, but the healing of God as well. It intended the release of God from imprisonment inside matter, and thus the redemption of matter in which God is trapped and sleeping.

By no means is the current psychological state of humanity a culmination of history, as Jung saw it. The cycles of history continue, and we are on the cusp of yet another dramatic evolutionary shift. The whole of human history can be seen, in this light, as a never-ending desire of the Deity to become manifest in the world. Without a religious or mythological grounding, however, our civilization has lost the ability to fulfill such a task. The need is too large for words, so it always comes to us in mythical stories, images, and symbols. Lacking much of a symbolic life today, we now rely on psychology to muddle through.

The ancient world relied on myths, symbols, and ritual to make sense of the structure of the outer world and its events and determine the right response. In contrast, today we need myth, symbol, and ritual to determine our inner psycho-spiritual worlds. Myth-making is a fundamental aspect of humanity, tracing back to the emergence of consciousness tens of thousands of years ago. It is so fundamental to us as a species that Joseph Campbell said in his introduction to *The Portable Jung*, "One could almost say that if all the world's traditions were cut off at a single blow, the whole of mythology and the whole history of religion would start all over again with the next generation."

This aspect of Jung's thought is best expressed in the books *Aion* and *Answer to Job*, the implications of which are quite frightening in their own way, best suited to more experienced students of psychology, history, and myth. Nevertheless, they are foundational to understanding what Jung wanted to express.

The most significant source of Jung's insights, psychological writings, and therapeutic methods are all traced to a series of intense, even traumatic, dreams and visions experienced over a number of years, as he recorded in *The Black Books*, elaborated in *The Red Book* (or as he termed it, *Liber Novus*), and then translated into the prose that makes up his body of psychological understanding. These writings have a wildly dramatic, poetic, and mystical feel to them; they read as if written by an Old Testament prophet or a shaman in trance. Indeed, the process by which these experiences took place, which he called "active imagination," was shamanic at its essence. His task required that he translate very difficult mystical language into something that our overly-rational, scientifically-oriented world could understand and accept. The resulting gift is the body of work we can now more readily utilize.

He operated like the classic shaman, traveling to the spirit world to bring back insight and healing for his people. Can we think of Jung as the ultimate shaman for the contemporary, rationally-minded West? Indeed, Sonu Shamdasani, editor of Jung's The *Red Book* wrote of just this. In his article, "Is Analytical Psychology a Religion?" published in the *Journal of Analytical Psychology*, he states that Jung described his psychotherapy as "religion in statu nascendi" – that is to say, a religion in the process of being born. Jung went on to say that the disappearance of Christian dominance in western thought formed the basis for the emergence of psychology – indeed the very need for it.

The several paradigms discussed so briefly above may or may not form a new foundation of some new cosmological mythology to lead the West. Yet we are clearly at a point in history in which the old ways of thinking, the old values and institutions, no longer suffice, and we are awaiting something larger and more inspiring to establish itself. This is not new in human experience; there are historic precedents we can explore.

It is said that when the religions of the ancient Roman world began to fade in their power, it became fashionable for citizens of Rome to make a pilgrimage to Egypt. The even more ancient religion found there was fascinating in its unfamiliar and exotic forms and ideas. Those Romans romanticized the world of the Pharoah, of Ra and Isis, Thoth and Horus; its very unfamiliarity gave it an air of power and wisdom to the uninitiated, whereas the myths of their own gods, of Jupiter and Minerva, with their constant petty squabbling and domestic drama, had become stale and unbelievable in their familiarity.

As we in the West experience the decline of the Christian tradition today, the same story seems to be playing out. Tired of the shallow hypocrisy exhibited in much of the church – particularly to the extent it is now dominated by conservative evangelicals – and having already absorbed and integrated into social norms the basic moral lessons that the faith has provided, many Americans and Europeans are looking abroad for something of greater depth. For them, Buddhism, Hinduism, and other traditions such as Andean shamanism hold the same draw that Egypt did for those ancient Romans.

Yet while so many romanticize and seek to learn from and honor the deep wisdom of Asian spirituality, South American shamanism, and so forth, many do so specifically in rejection of their own western traditions of which they are deeply ignorant. Many reject the Bible without having ever bothered to read most of it, let alone understand it. The other Eurocentric traditions, those of Celtic, Roman, and particularly Greek origin, are hardly even known anymore. The deepest origins of western philosophy, logic, and rational science have at their core a mysticism that is essentially that of shamanism, as found in the pre-Socratic seer Parmenides. The West holds as much unknown mystery to be explored as what more exotic and unfamiliar cultures have to offer.

The psychic need for a soulful life has not diminished in us, but it has been increasingly ignored in favor of a more quantitative rationality. But rational thought is inadequate to fully manage human complexity. It is an extremely useful and essential toolset, yet remains incomplete. Civilization requires a living mythology. Entertainment and consumption, our current economic and cultural foundations, are hardly adequate substitutes for the foundation of a culture of urbanism; they are mere distractions from the higher goals of meaning and purpose.

We cannot discard a fundamental aspect of human psychological makeup and cultural experience, utilized for tens and hundreds of thousands of years, arrogantly thinking that we know so much better than all previous generations. Religion, myth, and symbolic imagery are so ancient as to be practically embedded in our DNA. Indeed, our morality had its beginnings in our prehuman animal instincts. We acted out of pure instinct in our primate beginnings and before, to create social habits that worked. As early humans, we started to ask why we did such things, and then told stories as a way of understanding our actions. Those stories were further elaborated over the centuries and developed into myths. They evolved further into ritual as a way of re-enacting the myths. Formal religion refined this further as a way of abstracting the myth and ritual into shared belief. This is the process of human awakening as a species, out of instinct and into greater consciousness and intentionality.

The Urban Design of an Unknown Metaphor

We are historical creatures – the past matters. We cannot understand ourselves personally or as a civilization unless we know and integrate this past – historically, psychologically, and biologically. This is partially what the desire for an inner life of the soul is, and to ignore it is deeply unhealthy, both for individuals and society. We cannot discard the gifts of western civilization, the ancient Greeks, the Christian heritage, or science. Better to make use of their strengths by integrating and transcending them. But to renew them is not a conscious effort only. Myths and symbols, or for that matter a true religion, cannot be intentionally created by rational thought. They spring unbidden from the unconscious, of their own accord and in their own time. How then can we even consider designing the physical layout of place with them in mind?

Again I must ask, what is the connection between some new cosmology or mythology – or those now existing, for that matter – and the design of urban places? It involves, I think, the interplay of ego and soul, of rational and conscious intentionality guided by the unknown spirit of the irrational unconscious. I have said repeatedly that the places we design reflect the values we hold; but conversely, design can promote, intentionally or not, a set of values. Whatever emerging global mythology might take hold for our descendants, it will almost certainly have at its foundation the concepts of complexity, interconnection, interdependency, and change, all as elements of personal psychic or spiritual exploration. There are a few ways in which urban design can reflect and support this.

A primary aspect of the soulful design of place can be found in the process used to create place. A classic method of publicly inclusive and participatory design is known as the "charrette," a public design method pioneered by, and made use of, the New Urbanist movement. Design on a grand scale, at the site plan level, provides for the insertion of memory and meaning at a cultural scale. Design at a smaller and more personal intimate scale brings in beauty and playfulness. The flexibility of design assumes change will occur in both use and form. It institutes policies of inclusiveness and variety, nurture, play, inciting curiosity – finding ways of turning problems into opportunities. Take water, for instance. Our conventional thinking, as reflected in the standards of municipal engineers, is that water is a nuisance to get rid of instead of a resource to respect and opportunity to celebrate.

Such a mindset, focused on creating a place of soulfulness as a primary intent, may seem superfluous given the overwhelming crises we face today. Responding to climate change, inequality, and the myriad of other large systemic troubles facing our civilization through technical/scientific/political solutions is tactical and perhaps even strategic in nature. This is all necessary, but not primary; a higher visionary approach is more fundamental. This is driven by a combination of individual psychic and spiritual development and the emergence of a larger, more integrated cosmological myth.

One of the highest transcendent values is the ability to bring order out of chaos. The bedrock vision of western civilization is that each individual has this potential. This is what the city represents; the bringing of order while accepting the element of individuality. An enduring task of a city is the storage, dissemination, and creation of information, as Louis Mumford reminds us. The ages shift and change throughout history, passing their accumulated knowledge and wisdom on to a new civilization.

The urban design of an unknown metaphor therefore involves a return to mythic symbolism. The planning and design of cities must become an effort of a profession that honors its practical poets and intellectually and spiritually reflective generalists who have the vision of history-minded therapists, rather than only those specialized bureaucratic technicians. As Socrates reminds us, "By far the greatest and most admirable form of wisdom is that needed to plan and beautify cities and human communities."

After all this, the question still remains: what does the physical design of a city, the urban morphology, have to do with myth and metaphor? I contend that the pattern and layout of a community can awaken and support a deepening relationship between the ego and soul. Let's turn to the story of L'Enfant's design of Washington, DC to begin to learn how.

CHAPTER XIV

L'Enfant and Washington, DC:
Designing the City of Metaphor

"The life of a city is rich in poetic and marvelous subjects. We are enveloped and steeped as though in an atmosphere of the marvelous; but we do not notice it"
– Charles Baudelaire

The story of the founding and design of Washington, DC makes it one of the most inspirational cities anywhere on earth. Its physical manifestation, as designed by one man and changed and implemented by many others over the decades, is clearly intended to act as both a political and spiritual metaphor.

To the extent anyone thinks about the layout and pattern of streets in Washington, DC (and really, who doesn't?), the common perception is that there are two systems at work. First, a basic grid arrangement of streets running north-south and east-west, and a second wheel-and-spoke pattern of avenues layered on top, connecting significant architectural or topographical features around the city. And for visitors, how confusing that can all be! But aside from the obvious look of the city with its grand avenues set at angles to the underlying grid, the grid itself has always struck me as unusual. The gridded streets are not uniformly arranged, resulting in a variety of block sizes and shapes; large and small, square and rectangular, oriented either vertically or horizontally. Ah! I thought to myself, Pierre L'Enfant intended to create so much variety! I was fascinated by this syncopated street pattern and imagined the design intended to create a variety of opportunities for the development of large or small buildings, on larger or smaller parcels of land, for all the unknown uses and activities that the future of the city might require. Who can truly know what the future might bring? As the designer of the city, L'Enfant showed great foresight in this, I imagined; by contrast, our conventional suburbia of today lacks this sort of versatility. And I saw a metaphor in this for us all, as we go about planning our personal lives for our individual unknown futures. I was to find out how wrong I was regarding L'Enfant's intentions; he was very precise in what he planned.

During the economic downturn of 1992-93, I lived in Old Town Alexandria, just outside of Washington, and paying work was thin. Consequently, I wandered the streets of Washington with a lot of spare time on my hands. I observed so much, and one of the things that stood out to me as an urban planner interested in history (aside from that syncopated street pattern – I hear the rhythm of jazz when I think about it) was the location of the Supreme Court. Grand though the building is, the location seems like an afterthought, stuck behind the Capitol building. How could this be when L'Enfant was so thoughtful about everything else? Disappointed in the outcome, I decided I'd redraw the city plan with my own ideas and make it right. It seemed obvious to me that a capital city hosting a government of three parts – executive, legislative, judicial – needed three excellent buildings in three prominent locations. Since the area of downtown that houses so many federal offices is known as the "Federal Triangle," there really should be a triangle represented in the city, with the Capitol, White House, and Supreme Court anchoring each corner. The White House and Capitol seem appropriately located, so the obvious location for the Supreme Court, to my mind, was at Buzzard's Point, now the home of Fort McNair at the confluence of the Anacostia and Potomac Rivers. Thus a true federal triangle would be defined, with each branch of government keeping an eye on the other. I spent over a year working on my idea, finishing in 1994, but my naive ignorance of what L'Enfant created shows through easily in the plan I produced, in retrospect.

As it turns out, L'Enfant had other ideas for the Supreme Court and Washington, DC. His was a much more grand and integrated vision, his process and methods far more subtle and sophisticated than what I conjured. The intent of his design was for the city pattern to act as the physical embodiment of the ideals found in the Constitution, the Declaration of Independence, and the heavens above.

My research to discover the story of L'Enfant and his design of Washington took me down many rabbit holes of history and conspiracy theories. Among the sources of websites, documentaries, and books, none seem to agree and generally offer wildly divergent ideas regarding what L'Enfant intended. An excellent starting point, though, on the historical context and biographical background is Scott Berg's book *Grand Avenues: The Story of Pierre L'Enfant.* Oddly, since I understand that he is a trained architect, Berg virtually ignores the actual plan and design that L'Enfant produced, focusing instead on the personal story and political machinations. Regarding the design, Berg offers that L'Enfant was inspired by Versailles and perhaps London and leaves it at that. For a deeper historical background on the story of the land's design, I turned to *Proof* by Amir Alexander. *Proof* tells the history of how concepts of geometrical order developed through royal garden design and became the basis of both physicality and political order. This culminated in the royal gardens of Versailles, a metaphorical setting of political power which L'Enfant became familiar with as a child and art student.

Two other writers have focused on the urban morphology of Washington, the street and block pattern L'Enfant created for the city, and the methods he employed. Each has come to starkly different conclusions regarding the methods and meaning of L'Enfant's work. One finds that L'Enfant's design of the city is firmly rooted in the ancient traditions of "sacred geometry." The other is fully convinced that the stars and zodiac directed the design of Washington. I discuss each in separate sections of this chapter. First, a little background.

The Founding of the City

Most capital cities begin their story long before their designation as a center of political or cultural power. London, for instance, existed for hundreds of years before becoming the capital of a kingdom and empire. So too it could have been for the capital city of the newly created nation of the United States.

Choosing the location for the seat of government was an enormous difficulty for the early Congress, and hotly debated nationally. Several dozen options were presented and promoted. New York and Philadelphia each felt they were the logical choice, since they were already established influential cities and Congress had met extensively, though temporarily, in each. But southern states felt they were too far north. A compromise was needed, and the decision was finally left to President George Washington via the Residence Act, passed by Congress in July 1790.

In January 1791 he selected, to no one's surprise, a site just a few miles upriver from his home of Mount Vernon, along the banks of the Potomac River. This worked as a satisfactory political compromise and held promise as a financial investment and transportation hub as well. Washington was an investor and partner in the Potomac Canal Company; he envisioned the future city to act as a hub of a wide transportation network west to the Ohio River and had significant real estate holdings in the area.

In the ensuing weeks of early 1791, Washington appointed Andrew Ellicott to survey the area and set the boundaries of the 100-square mile federal district, comprising land on both the Virginia and Maryland sides of the Potomac. Thomas Jefferson had suggested that the area be laid out as a diamond, a square resting on a point; Ellicott suggested Jones Point in Alexandria, VA, a well-known riverside navigational marker at the mouth of Hunting Creek for Potomac sailors, as the starting point. Ellicott assembled a team to begin work, including the mathematician and astronomer Benjamin Banneker, a free black man. It was Banneker, according to reports, who set the precise location of the point of beginning, lying on the ground at night to observe six stars as reference points.

Once this point of beginning was located, the first boundary stone was set. On April 15th, 1791, a formal ceremony was held to commemorate the event, in full Masonic ritual. Then the forty-mile (ten miles to a side) boundary work would begin, with the initial line running northwest through Virginia, and stone markers placed every mile. It took Ellicott until December of 1792 to complete this task. Almost all these stones remain in place today, to be found in the middle of roadways, parking lots, and private backyards.

The ritualized marking of the boundaries of a city is an extremely ancient practice, and Ellicott's task and the Masonic ceremony were very much in keeping with this tradition. For instance, the founding of Rome is said to have occurred when Romulus plowed the original line around the city on April 21st, 753 BC, physically setting its spiritual demarcation. The Masons who held their boundary-setting ceremony on April 15th may have been fully aware of their re-enactment of the Roman Pomerium, as the ceremony was known; certainly, they were very precise in their coordination with astrological configurations.

At about the same time that Ellicott was beginning his boundary survey, President Washington assigned the task of designing the city within those boundaries to Pierre L'Enfant. Who was L'Enfant, and why did Washington have so much faith in his ability to pull off such an extraordinary design effort?

The Story of L'Enfant

Pierre Charles L'Enfant was born in Paris in August 1754, the son of a court artist employed by King Louis XV of France. As a Parisian, the child of a royal painter, and a student at the Royal Academy, L'Enfant was acquainted with concepts of city design, geometry, civil and military engineering, proportion, and perspective, and particularly for our story, with the gardens at the Tuileries and Versailles.

For unknown reasons, though no doubt related to youthful idealism and desire for adventure and glory, he chose to leave for America and join the fight for colonial independence. His wartime service focused on military engineering, leaving him wounded during battle in Savannah. As a young officer, he served under George Washington at Valley Forge, where he met many long-time friends and patrons, including Baron von Steuben and Alexander Hamilton.

After the war, he established himself in New York as an architect and artist. His most prominent work prior to his commission to design the US capitol city was as the architect of the transformation of New York City Hall into Federal Hall in order to accommodate Congress. However, his true desire was to design the new federal city; he straightforwardly asked for such an appointment in a letter to George Washington in a letter in September 1789.

He got his wish. In early March 1791, just after Ellicott began his boundary survey, Washington appointed L'Enfant as the designer for a new federal city. Washington was fully confident in his selection, believing that no one else in America had the ability to accomplish such a task. Wasting no time, L'Enfant dropped everything and left for Maryland, arriving at Suter's Tavern in Georgetown on March 10th, 1791. He began work the very next day.

L'Enfant's Design Process

The precise location of the Fountain Inn, also known as Suter's Tavern, has been lost to history. Some speculate it was located near what is now 31st and K Streets in Georgetown. During the year 1791, however, it was quite well known. George Washington held numerous meetings there with local landowners, and L'Enfant used it as his base of operations during his design of the future city.

Thomas Jefferson had supplied L'Enfant with numerous maps of various European cities to use as inspirational resources. These were graciously accepted and immediately ignored. Washington and L'Enfant both held a strong belief in the future of the United States as an unprecedented opportunity to create an empire of ideals; *Novus Ordo Seclorum* (A New World Order) was taken quite seriously. Thus, L'Enfant intended a city on a very grand scale worthy of such aspirations. He stated to President Washington that his design intention was to create a place wholly new and without precedent. What this required was a method and process wholly new as well. Not only what L'Enfant accomplished, but the way he went about it, was of unprecedented elegance. The conventional assumption is that he overlaid a series of diagonals over a gridded street system, after identifying important topographical features. What I wish to share here is the possibility that he took a radically different approach.

Much has been made of the secretive influence of the Masons on the design of Washington, which will be considered later. But what L'Enfant held in his toolkit was nothing particularly secretive nor limited to the Masons. Trained in the design values of the Baroque period, many, if not all, educated artists and architects at that time made use of the tricks L'Enfant employed – the ancient techniques of geometry, mathematics, and the symbolism they held. These included basic artistic methods such as perspective and proportion; but also the golden mean (the ratio of 1 to 1.618) the Fibonacci Sequence, pi, and so forth. Again, these are not secrets but universal patterns found in all sorts of natural structures: a honeycomb, the pattern of pinecone bristles, the arrangement of petals on a flower, and the structure of DNA itself. The golden mean is a foundational pattern that the ancients knew, understood, and made use of for thousands of years in art and architecture. This was the common and shared cultural landscape of the time.

L'Enfant employed these techniques in a way never before seen; the layout and structure of an entire city, in a method all his own.

Like any land planner, the very first task L'Enfant undertook was to walk the land he was responsible for. This, too, was unprecedented, in scale; the thousands of acres he was designing were equivalent in size, during his day, to New York, Boston, and Philadelphia *combined*. The weather made the task that much harder; icy winter rain and fog dominated his first weeks of work. After becoming familiar with the topography, vistas, wetlands, and slopes of the land, he began work at the drafting table. Despite the cliché, by the way, the city was *not* built on a swamp.

During his initial site visits, he quickly identified two major points, locations for what were to become the Capitol and the White House, each of which sat atop high ground overlooking the area. He would eventually connect them with what we now know as Pennsylvania Avenue, roughly following an existing trail extending from the Anacostia River to Georgetown. But he did not merely arrange angled avenues overtop a basic street grid. He likely sensed that would be too ordinary and simple-minded, not grand enough for the task at hand. He might have started with that fairly conventional process of design layout but then had some sort of insight or inspiration and started again. This is typical in the urban design process; insight is gained over time by weaving together the project's program with the land's opportunities, and the personal experience and knowledge of the designer. Additionally, numerous changes were made after his initial private presentation to President Washington.

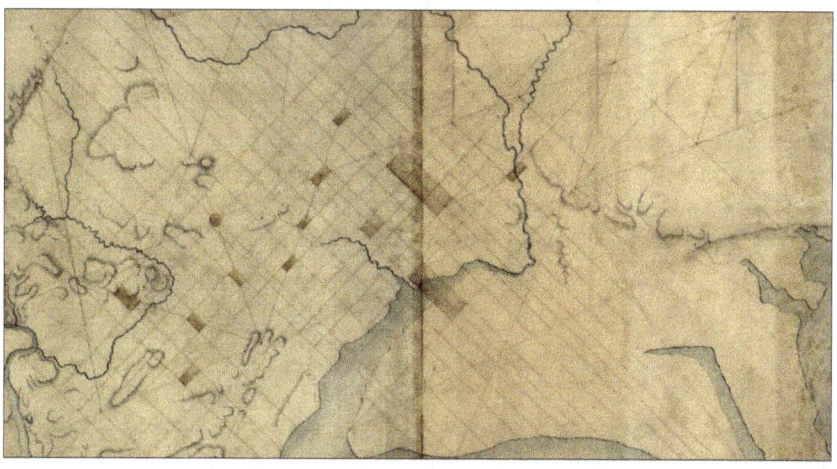

An inset of L'Enfant's early unfinished draft plan, known as the "Dotted Line Plan," which he shared with President Washington during their private meeting at Mount Vernon in August 1791. Note how streets and avenues radiate out from both the Capitol, to the right, and the White House, lower left, yet do not meet. L'Enfant left room for these two buildings and intended for streets to visually terminate at the entrances, not the centers of the buildings; hence the avenues offset as they pass through the area. Tiber Creek, lying below the White House and running up toward the Capitol, was filled in during the 19th century and is now part of the Mall.

L'Enfant kept his intentions and methods secret, leading to much confusion and misunderstanding about his work. Nothing of this was known until quite recently, as uncovered by Nicholas Mann and his astonishing book *The Sacred Geometry of Washington, DC*. After reading it multiple times, I realized what an astounding feat L'Enfant had pulled off. If Mann's hypothesis is correct, and I strongly suspect it is, his book should be required reading for every urban planner, as well as for those interested in American history and democracy, and perhaps surprisingly, ancient spiritual wisdom.

In a letter to President Washington dated June 22nd, 1791, L'Enfant provided a status update and draft plan. His language is extremely difficult to follow, his spelling and grammar riddled with errors, and in the end says very little. He gives almost no information regarding process, except to say:

> "Having first determined some principal points to which I wished making the rest subordinate I next made the distribution regular with streets at right angle *north-south* & *East-west* but after wards I opened other on various directions as avenues to & from every principal places, wishing by this not mearly to contrast with the general regulariety nor to afford a greater variety of pleasant seats and prospect as will be obtained from the advantageous ground over the which these avenues are mostly directed but principally to connect each part of the city with more efficacy by, if I may so Express, making the real distance less from place to place in menaging on them a reciprocity of sight and making them thus seemingly Connected...."

In other words, three phases made up his design process: identifying and connecting principal points, laying down the gridded streets, and then adding several other additional avenues, which appear to me to be those mostly to the north and west – New Hampshire Avenue, for instance. Mann puts much effort into reverse-engineering L'Enfant's process, discovering and understanding what was done, how and why, by long trial and error.

From what Mann uncovered, L'Enfant clearly did not begin by laying out streets over the land. First in the process was the creation of an underlying conceptual geometric "trellis" based on ancient principles of sacred geometry, upon which the city's plan could then grow. Identifying the locations of the Capitol and White House were fundamental to this, but they began as geometric points in the landscape, not locations on a street plan. What L'Enfant did foremost was to create a conceptual "map of meaning" first; the plan of the city of streets and squares then grew out of this.

He employed roughly a dozen steps in his design process, laying these geometric concepts over the land he had come to know. I outline them below as best as I can understand them. It should be noted that this is the work of Nicholas Mann; I merely summarize it here.

1. Choose a point of beginning, from which all other work of the design would grow. L'Enfant chose Jenkin's Hill as his starting point, the highest elevation in the area; we now know this as Capitol Hill. This makes the Capitol Building the centerpiece – pointedly, not the White House. This location symbolically reflected the central place of the citizen in the new democracy.

2. Create two streets emanating from this central point; one running north-south, another running east-west. Today we know these as North and South Capitol Streets, East Capitol Street, and the Mall. This process follows the method of the ancient Romans, who as city planners used a central point to create what was known as the *Cardo*, the main street running north-south, and its companion known as the *Decumanus*, running east-west.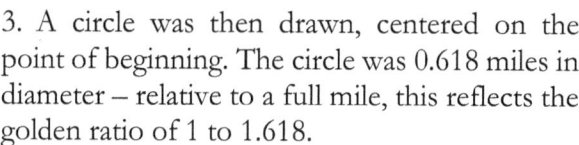

3. A circle was then drawn, centered on the point of beginning. The circle was 0.618 miles in diameter – relative to a full mile, this reflects the golden ratio of 1 to 1.618.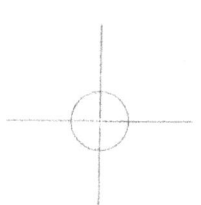

4. A second circle was then drawn, its center one-mile due east of the beginning, with a one-mile radius so that its edge touched the point of beginning.

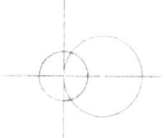

5. A third circle was drawn, centered again on the point of beginning, with a diameter of 1.618 miles. This gives three circles with diameters of 0.618, 1.0, and 1.618 miles, reflecting the golden ratio.

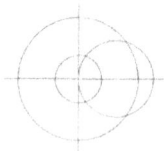

6. A five-pointed star was drawn within the one-mile circle, with a point facing east. Symbolically, east faces the sunrise, the point of beginning.

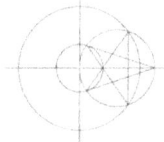

7. Two more circles for stars were drawn to the north and south sides of the point of beginning – these three stars determine angles of avenues on the east side of the city and connect the principal points L'Enfant had identified or created.

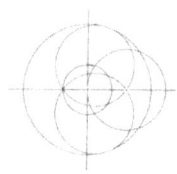

8. A final star was placed within the largest circle, its orientation reversed so that its point faced west, emanating from what would become the location of the Washington Monument. This gave orientation to several avenues to the west of the Capitol.

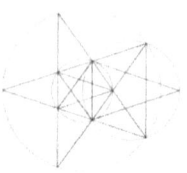

9. A network of triangles was drawn to the west of the point of beginning. These grow out from the angles of two stars: the original star with its point furthest east, and another with its tip at the point of beginning. These triangles determine the alignment of most avenues on the western side of the city.

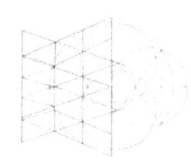

10. The grid of streets running north-south and east-west was then drawn. Their locations were determined by intersections and points of the stars and triangles.

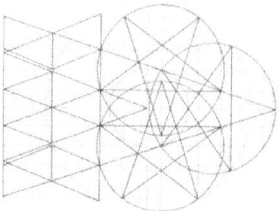

11. Two avenues were drawn emanating from the White House at 60-degree angles (today's Connecticut and Vermont Avenues). Using today's S Street as the third side, these form an equilateral triangle above the White House. They are distinct from the other avenues to the west since they do not grow out of the triangular network.

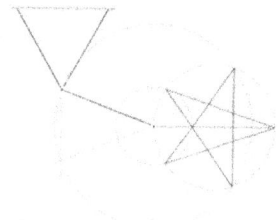

Other angled avenues were also placed throughout the city, which do not correspond to the underlying triangular pattern. These I assume were those L'Enfant mentioned in his memo to the president as the last avenues intended to connect the rest of the city to the whole, including today's New Hampshire Avenue and several others (unbuilt) found around today's Dupont Circle.

Various buildings and institutions were placed at significant intersections and points of the underlying geometric trellis. These include the Supreme Court, city hall, a national church, and various squares, circles, plazas, and markets. Each state was to receive control of a square, to be designed for its own purposes, and acting as the centerpiece of its own neighborhood.

The result is a trellis-like geometric pattern upon which the street plan of the living city could grow. Once this trellis was produced, then the actual city plan was created from it. Of utmost importance to L'Enfant was the "reciprocity of sight" between the various resulting points, the visual connections between one place and another.

L'Enfant's Plan for Washington, DC, 1791

Drawing of L'Enfant's geometric "trellis" and partial street grid, courtesy of Nicholas Mann

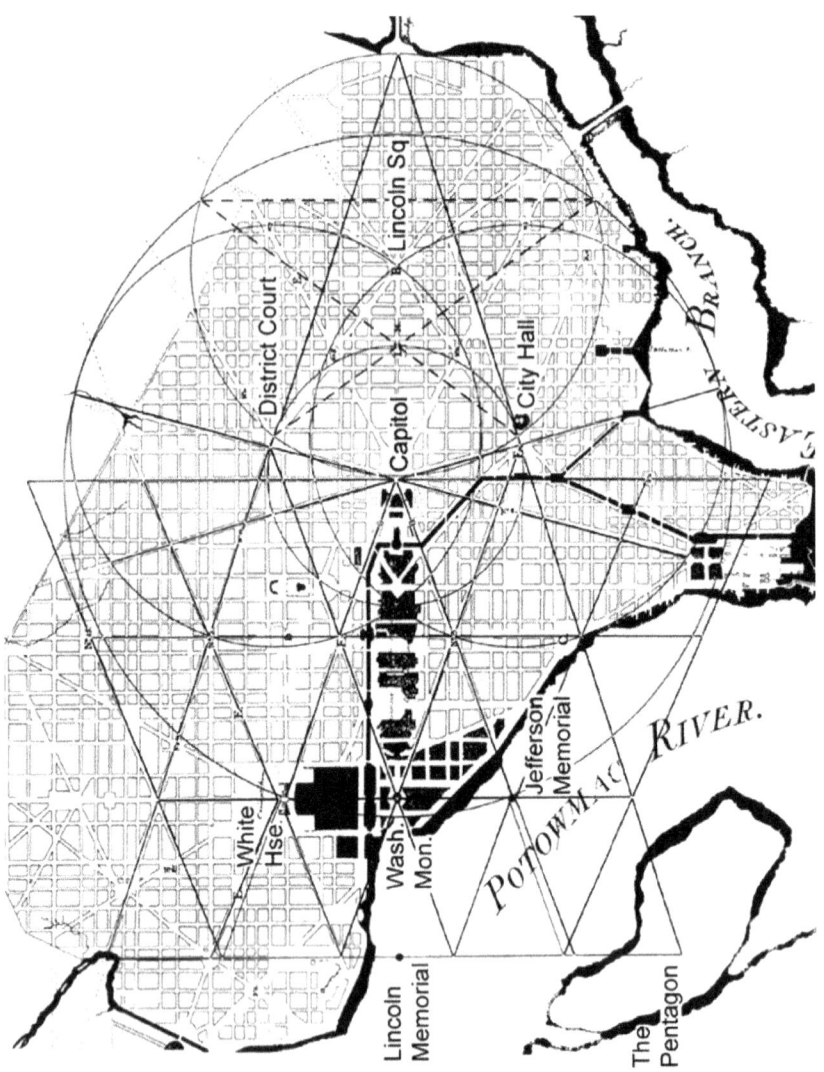

The conceptual geometric trellis laid atop L'Enfant's *final street plan, showing the highly accurate relationship between the two, courtesy of Nicholas Mann*

A great deal of misunderstanding and secretive conspiracy thinking surrounds the math and geometry involved, with observers and critics seeing nefarious intent in it all. This is the sort of thing that worries various denominations of Christians, but it needn't; these are the same principles used in the design of Solomon's Temple, for instance.

L'Enfant wanted to symbolically represent the uniting of heaven and earth, that American ideal of democracy. According to Mann, the numbers five and six hold the key based on their symbolic meaning in the ancient world. The number five, displayed in the pentacle stars expanding out from the Capitol, represented in the ancient world the spiritual power of the earth and its people. The number six, represented by the triangle formed by the two avenues angled at 60 degrees extending out from the White House (Connecticut and Vermont Avenues), held the spiritual power of the king and the gods in the heavens or in this case, the presidency. L'Enfant apparently intended to symbolize a reconciliation of heavenly and earthly powers; the geometry itself was to reflect the union of spiritual aspirations and the political processes used to manifest them.

When simply walking down the streets, a pedestrian becomes an actor on a stage, set in an immersive environment of political and spiritual symbolism. The question the city poses to both the individual pedestrian and the nation as a whole is, *What are the conflicting intentions in our lives, earthly and spiritually, personally and politically, and how will we reconcile them?*

The design's brilliance is that the geometry fits so well with the given landscape. Jenkin's Hill, for instance, turns out to have been precisely the right distance from the Anacostia River for the initial two circles to span accurately, and thus the golden ratio to operate effectively given that starting point.

The location of both the Capitol and White House give further evidence of the unity of the landscape and geometry. Each was intentionally located on prominent high ground offering wide vistas. The site of the White House was chosen not only for its prominent elevation, its relation to the Capitol, and the connection between the two via Pennsylvania Avenue, but also that it was located along one side of a geometric star, at a point 1.618 miles from the Capitol – where the angle of the star meets the circle 1.618 miles in diameter. The trellis of symbolic geometry combines with topography in a beautiful synergy.

While the city today is weighted to the west in its intensity and activity, L'Enfant intended the city to emphasize the east. What is now called Lincoln Park, the center of the one-mile circle and halfway between the Capitol and the Anacostia River, was intended to be the great American gathering spot, equivalent to the Roman Forum, with arcaded shops lining East Capitol Street. In fact, if L'Enfant had his way, Lincoln Park would be the location for a new international meridian line, forming a new 0-degree point. Thus, we would measure by Washington Mean Time, instead of the current Greenwich Mean Time established outside London. *Novus Ordo Seclorum*, indeed. Instead, the area became a pleasant but quiet residential neighborhood. At the Anacostia, a large market was intended as a port for the city of commerce. Today this is roughly where the District General Hospital and Jail are found, and Congressional Cemetery. Remember, George Washington had already started organizing the Potomac Canal Company with the intention that the city would become a crucial transportation and commercial hub to the west. For a number of reasons, this never blossomed, but the original design held that intent.

By the way, that concern of mine about the location of the Supreme Court was not lost on Major L'Enfant. He had a very specific location for the Court, much different than mine, and with vastly different reasoning as well. He located the Supreme Court a bit off the beaten path, so to speak, where today we find instead the District of Columbia Court of Appeals. This would have been a somewhat discreet spot, and intentionally so. While the White House and Capitol are highly visible and political, it seems L'Enfant understood that the Supreme Court is emphatically *not* political, and therefore downplaying its prominence is appropriate. Yet, located roughly halfway between the executive and legislative branches, its location would allow it to symbolically keep an impartial eye on both.

I have to concede that what all this comes down to relies on very well-researched speculation. The conceptual foundation of the design, based on geometrical and mathematical principles used by the ancients, had remained a complete unknown until Mann uncovered it. But the case he presents is so logical and internally consistent, going far beyond what any other author has uncovered.

There is no indication that L'Enfant operated personally from any spiritual motivation, yet the design clearly indicates his understanding of the ancient symbolic and spiritual meaning held by geometry and its associated numbers. My strong sense is that the design process of sacred geometry that Mann ascribes to L'Enfant is precisely right. Having reproduced it myself, the geometric trellis uncovered by Mann fits almost perfectly when overlaid on the subsequent plan of the city, matching the avenues, the street grid, and the location of significant points.

Conflict, Dismissal, and Ellicott's Revisions

The city that is so well known today clearly remains L'Enfant's, yet his grand vision was not at all fully realized. What actually transpired is something of a tragedy, instigated mostly by L'Enfant's own arrogance, naivete, and difficult personality. As a child of the Old World, he very much felt that he was operating directly under the patronage of President Washington, much as a European artist would have received patronage dispensed by a king. Everyone else involved, however, understood that he was under the supervision of the three city commissioners Washington had appointed to oversee the development process. Refusing to accept their authority (along with his controversial demolition of a landowner's house), he left Washington no option but to release him from service in February 1792. The brilliant plan he offered was never fully realized and was later significantly changed against his will.

L'Enfant not only had drawn the plan of the city but also elaborated a subtle approach to the sale of lots, including the designation of various squares to each state (so as to spur development via the competitive pride of each state), negotiations with foreign embassies regarding their locations in the city, and a highly detailed construction and work plan. So much detail required that all plans be precise, but the commissioners needed to raise money immediately for construction to begin and moved ahead with a land auction months before L'Enfant recommended; he went so far as to refuse to allow his map to be shown at the land auction. The sale proved a complete failure, as L'Enfant predicted. Perhaps L'Enfant was more than a design genius. In any case, Washington himself deeply respected L'Enfant's talents and was worried at the loss of L'Enfant's services. In a letter to the city commissioners dated December 18th, 1791, Washington stated, "If ... he should take miff and leave the business, I have no scruple in telling you (though I do not want him to know it) that I know not where another is to be found who could take his place."

Those individuals who took over the work, which is to say Ellicott and Dermott later, had absolutely no feel for any grand vision, but were simply technical engineers and surveyors, who did not hesitate to compromise the design for the sake of expediency and practicality. One of the reasons so many current critics have failed to see the geometric concept L'Enfant created is because they look at the current layout of streets for clues, which varies considerably from what was intended, rather than the original design which was never fully carried out. Additionally, many today confuse L'Enfant's plan with the later version by Ellicott, and the eventual officially adopted Dermott Plan of 1797. By the way, while Ellicott was appointed to take over from L'Enfant, Ellicott too was eventually dismissed by the Commissioners after only a couple of years. While he did good precise and timely work surveying the 100-square mile district boundary, his professional habits in continuing L'Enfant's design of the city were marred by cost overruns, slow work, significant inaccuracies, and a regular pattern of lying to his superiors. James Dermott, Ellicott's assistant, took over; although known as a serious alcoholic, he operated honestly and accurately. His work was used as the official street plan for the development of the city in the 1800s.

After L'Enfant was dismissed, his plan was altered in numerous ways. He became heartbroken at the way his symbolic design was disfigured by changes made by both Ellicott and Thomas Jefferson, who knew nothing of nor likely would have cared for the original grand intentions. His plan was altered in at least eighteen ways, which essentially erased the visionary layout and the sacred geometry employed to create it.

1. The alignment of Massachusetts Avenue was straightened.
2. The alignment of Pennsylvania Avenue was shifted.
3. The equilateral triangle above the White House was effectively eliminated by reducing the angles of Connecticut and Vermont Avenues from 60 to 50 degrees.
4. The Supreme Court was not located in its assigned neutral place.
5. The site reserved for a national nondenominational church was erased by Thomas Jefferson.
6. Ellicott reduced the number of squares from 20 to 11.
7. The Capitol building was shifted slightly west, right to the edge of the bluff of Jenkin's Hill, misaligning it to the surrounding streets, and its orientation reversed so that the plaza and entrance faced east, not west.
8. The location of the White House also shifted a bit to the south. L'Enfant had designed the building and streets as an

ensemble, so that the streets focused not on the center of the building but on particular doors and entrances. This is true of the Capitol as well. This accounts for the intentional misalignment of Pennsylvania and New York Avenues for instance, on either side of the White House, most easily seen in an early working draft plan.

9. The square at the east end of East Capitol Street was eliminated.
10. The dock and commercial plaza along the Anacostia River was reconfigured to a park (today's hospital and jail).
11. The Mile Column (at Lincoln Square) was eliminated; Jefferson later moved it close by the White House, placing it at the same location as the original spot reserved for the Washington Monument.
12. City Hall was not located in its designated spot.
13. The canal to replace Tiber Creek was never properly implemented and was eventually paved over (it now lies buried under Constitution Avenue).
14. The commercial center of the city was not focused east of the Capitol, thus "Square B" (today's Lincoln Park) did not develop as the great American commercial hub or Roman style "Forum."
15. Worst of all, L'Enfant's name was left off the adopted plan, replaced with Ellicott's.
16. After Ellicott, changes continued with the relocation of the Washington Monument (more on this in a moment).
17. The location of the Treasury Building blocked the reciprocal view of the White House and Capitol, at the direction of President Jackson.
18. The McMillan Commission of 1901 was formed with the stated intention of reinstituting L'Enfant's vision, yet it did no such thing. While it did gift us with the Mall as we now know it, the Commission furthered the destruction of his plan, eliminating Ohio Avenue and numerous other streets and squares, and completely ignored L'Enfant's plan east of the Capitol.

Another major reason the plan was not fully implemented was that L'Enfant never shared with anyone his methods and intentions. The entire concept – the manner in which the geometric ratios were employed and why; the use of the golden mean as the foundation; why the major buildings were located and oriented in precise fashion relative to streets and terminated vistas – he kept it all in his head. Perhaps he had written something of his methods, but at his dismissal, his rooms were ransacked and much of his work was stolen; evidence seems to point to Ellicott as perpetrator. Otherwise, he shared with no one the theoretical concept. His letters to Washington give no indication; perhaps in their private conversations he may have explained the symbolism to the president. Yet if the president had known, perhaps he would have intervened to stop the design changes, on behalf of the plan, if not for L'Enfant. Once he was dismissed from service, L'Enfant complained about the changes but simply kept quiet regarding his technique and intentions while his design was compromised by Ellicott and others, practical men who had no inkling of the underlying vision: Jefferson in particular seems to have despised L'Enfant personally. In the end, L'Enfant died penniless and forgotten, living off the kindness of friends. His remains were eventually re-interred at Arlington National Cemetery after lying in state at the Capitol.

It seems most likely, as Mann indicates, that L'Enfant did not share the intentions and methods of his symbolic design because he was aware that his work did not align well with the mood of the new nation. His symbolism may have smacked too much of an authoritarian Old World monarchy for a newly emerging Protestant democracy, and been summarily rejected. Certainly, Jefferson had a strong distaste for cities in general. Nevertheless, it was accepted by Washington and Congress as a city plan, perhaps because they were not aware of the metaphorical meaning underlying the design. It was both too esoteric for those of a conservative mindset, and too religious for the anti-church faction. The members of the Masons among the Founding Fathers – and there were many, including Washington himself – may have sensed the inherent scheme L'Enfant was after, but it was not obvious. Most of the geometric trellis created by L'Enfant remained implied rather than visibly drawn on the final map; he inferred the stars, laying them out partially, and downplayed the equilateral triangle above the White House, keeping them hidden from direct view. In any case, for more than 200 years the true inspiration of the plan lay obscured until Mr. Mann's astonishing detective work uncovered it.

For all the changes that mar the original plan, it still holds the ability to inspire. Prominent locations still attract prominent buildings and uses. The site intended for the national church is now occupied by the National Portrait Gallery for instance; what was reserved for the Supreme Court is instead made use of by the DC Court of Appeals. The intended location for a district court is now Union Station. Both the Lincoln and Jefferson Memorials are located on points of L'Enfant's geometric trellis, even though they were under the waters of the Potomac in his day and not built until the 20th century. But the drama of how the city was designed and built does not end with L'Enfant, by any means. He set the stage for others to play with ideas equally grand as the years went by.

Calling in the Patron Goddess of Washington, DC

Many if not most significant cities of the ancient world had patron deities to watch over them, granting power and protection. The Mesopotamian city of Babylon, for instance, had the god Marduk as founder and protector. Athens had Athena, Corinth had Poseidon. In fact, the Greek city-states were always founded on some mythic story in which the local topography often figured prominently.

The zodiac too usually played a foundational role. In his *Tetrabiblos*, Ptolemy wrote "…with regard to cities, it is necessary to state that those points or degrees of the zodiac, over which the sun or moon are in transit at the time when the construction of any such city was first undertaken and commenced, are to be considered as sympathizing with that city in an especial manner." The Greek root for the word "zodiac" means "living being" – the gods were truly alive in the stars to our ancestors. In his work to discover L'Enfant's geometric design, Mann references this call to both local myth and the zodiac in seeking the approval of the gods. The local myth of the Widow's Mite and the Goddess Columbia fulfill this role for the City of Washington, he says. David Ovason, an author specializing in astrology and the zodiac, goes much further than this, however. His book, *The Secret Architecture of Our Nation's Capital*, argues that the entire design of Washington is an elaborate and intentional call, led by members of the Masonic community, to bring in Virgo as the patron goddess of Washington, DC. Ovason's idea seems to rest on five pieces of evidence.

1. The ceremonies for the placing of foundational cornerstones for the Capitol Building, White House, Washington Monument,

and the first boundary stone at Jones Point, were all conducted in full Masonic ritual and precisely timed so that Virgo was prominent in the zodiac.
2. A series of zodiacs emphasizing Virgo are to be found in the Capitol Building itself, the Library of Congress, all along Constitution Avenue from the Dirksen Senate Office Building, the Mellon Fountain at the National Gallery, through Federal Triangle, and then west to the Federal Reserve Building, and finally to the Einstein statue at the National Academy of Sciences. In fact, he has identified 23 zodiacs in the city, and at least 1,000 zodiacal symbols, far more than in any other city.
3. The triangle formed by the White House, Washington Monument, and the Capitol Building are, according to Ovason, equivalent to the stars Arcturus, Spica, and Regulus respectively; these first-order stars surround the constellation Virgo.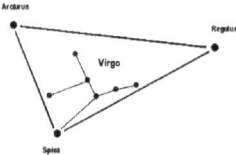
4. These three stars do not form a precise right triangle in the sky. Thus, the right triangle formed by the three structures needed to be adjusted to match that in the heavens. The location for the Washington Monument happens to have been moved from L'Enfant's designated location, roughly 371 feet east and 123 feet south; this new location approximates the angle of the stars.
5. The alignment of Pennsylvania Avenue is such that it points to the spot where these three stars set on August 10th when viewed from a certain spot of the Capitol Building.

Ovason connects these dots and sees a long history of coordinated efforts over many decades by members of the Masonic community to implement the call to Virgo. In fact, he states explicitly that the entire design of the city comes down to one feature – the alignment of Pennsylvania Avenue to the setting of the three stars surrounding the constellation Virgo on August 10th. "This truth – and this truth alone – explains the structure of the city."

I find this farfetched to say the least. As an urban planner and occasional designer of place, I can state that what L'Enfant produced and the amount of effort it required, covering thousands of acres in a span of well under one year, 6 months really, is astonishing.

L'ENFANT AND WASHINGTON, DC

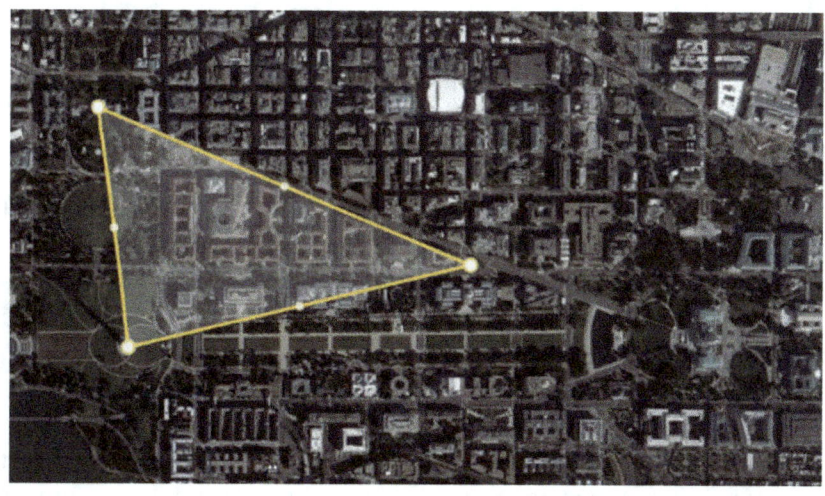

The triangle of stars surrounding Virgo is recreated here in the Federal Triangle of downtown Washington: Arcturus is represented by the White House, upper left; the Washington Monument representing Spica, lower; and to the right, the Mellon Fountain in place of Regulus

To state that the only features of note are the alignment of one avenue and three structures is absurd; there is too much complexity and subtlety in the city's pattern and urban morphology to think so.

Additionally, Ovason seems to argue against his own position at times. For instance, he speaks of two federal triangles – the Capitol/White House/Washington Monument, and then also the smaller Federal Triangle downtown district formed by Constitution Avenue/15th Street/Pennsylvania Avenue – with the Mellon Fountain acting as a pivot point. Neither actually seems to match at all his stellar triangle in the sky. My own sketching indicates that the triangle formed by the White House, the relocated Washington Monument, and the Mellon Fountain matches much more closely to the stellar triangle. I'm not sure even that is correct (a trained astronomer might know), but perhaps close enough to operate as a metaphor. He is very precise regarding the coordinated timing of ceremony with the zodiac, but not at all with the geometry. Finally, if the call to Virgo was the original intent, requiring the arrangement of the three structures to align with the arrangement of the stars, the Washington Monument would have been placed appropriately from the beginning, without needing to be moved.

Even so, it is clear to me that Ovason has uncovered something of real significance and value in his research. But he conflates original intent with later subsequent embellishment, thus coming to wildly inaccurate conclusions. The original and intentional design of the city was based on L'Enfant's knowledge of symbolic geometry and mathematics, not astrological mythology. Later generations of Masons had enough insight and knowledge to recognize the possibilities inherent in the plan and made use of it for their own mythic purposes. Masons were regularly active in the development of the city for many generations: George Washington, two of the original city commissioners, numerous presidents and artists involved the development of the city, and Daniel Suter, the owner of the Fountain Inn, even Senator McMillan of the famed Commission was a Mason. But Ellicott was certainly not; he was a confirmed Quaker. L'Enfant was in fact a Mason, but only nominally. According to the Scottish Rite website, L'Enfant was initiated into the Holland Lodge #8 in New York City on 17th April 1789. No further mention of him is ever made and he apparently did not advance at all; it's speculated that he was not encouraged because of his reputation of being a very difficult personality. In any case, the knowledge he used in the design of the city was not gained as a result of his brief Masonic connection; his skills and insight had been gained much earlier as a student in Paris.

The Intentional Misalignment of the Washington Monument

Probably the most iconic structure in Washington is the Washington Monument. It is known as an obelisk, a four-sided column topped with a pyramid. Traditionally, obelisks are made of a single stone, so while the Monument may not pass that test, it certainly remains the world's tallest freestanding masonry structure. In its own way, it fulfills L'Enfant's intentions regarding the symbolic unification of the numbers five and six all by itself, precisely because it is *not* where it was planned to be.

Years before George Washington died, the nation already agreed that some sort of memorial statue was needed to honor him. L'Enfant's design gave this a place of high prominence – the intersection of the north-south line running through the White House (now 16th Street) and the east-west line running from the Capitol along the Mall.

In L'Enfant's scheme, and most thinking at the time, it would be an equestrian statue, large and prominent, but not massively overwhelming as the obelisk we know today.

By the 1830s, Congress had not seen fit to appropriate funds for any memorial, however. A private effort began, led by prominent Masons, to gather funds and begin construction. A design competition was held as well, and the winner was Robert Mills of South Carolina. At that time, ancient Egypt had gained a fascinating appeal in the public imagination, so the entries tended toward pyramids and obelisks. Mill's winning proposal was so massive and therefore heavy that the ground beneath could not support it; at the time, the spot was on the mouth of Tiber Creek where it flowed  into the Potomac. The final weight of the obelisk is somewhere above 80,000 tons (the Lincoln Memorial is comparatively light at 38,000 tons, yet its location was completely under the Potomac River in L'Enfant's day and is built entirely on landfill.) As mentioned earlier, the location was moved about 370 feet east and 120 feet south. The originally intended location is marked today by the Jefferson Pier. The visual offset is glaringly obvious when viewed from 16th Street, with the Monument well to the left of the White House; from the Capitol, the misalignment was hidden through artful design of the Mall as per the McMillan Plan of 1901.

The misalignment of the Monument is easily noted when looking south from 16th Street NW, as it was intended to center on the White House

Mill's design changed over time. Its original 1845 look was a 600-foot shaft surrounded by a colonnade complete with horses and chariot. Within three years, however, a quite different structure was dedicated in a Masonic ceremony in 1848.

By then, a much less ornate design had come about, focused on precise and significant dimensions rather than visual complexity. The design of the Monument reflects the numerical, rather than geometric reconciliation of the numbers five and six used by L'Enfant. Including the pyramid on top of the shaft, the height of the Monument is just over 555 feet, 5 inches. The reconciliation of five and six? When measured in inches, this translates to just shy of 6,666. The pair, the five of the earth and the six of the heavens, united in one.

This discovery, and additional subtle dimensions of the Monument provided by Mann, convince me of his, rather than Ovason's story of the inherent symbolism. Mann provides very precise numbers and angles regarding the design of the Monument, while Ovason provides none regarding his concept of matching celestial and earthly triangles. I have no evidence that Mills was a Mason, but his clients seem to have been, and clearly a Masonic understanding of symbolic geometry and numerology was at play. An equestrian Washington Monument, or an obelisk of reduced size, could have been placed at its reserved location but was not, precisely because the massive size of the desired obelisk was needed to accommodate specific symbolic dimensions.

The Jefferson Pier marks the original intended location

The Legacy and Opportunity

I believe it is safe to say that the original design of the city was based on L'Enfant's visionary understanding of sacred geometry and the symbolic opportunities it holds. The later implementation of the urban morphology in the city as we know it today is a combination of engineering expediency and ignorance on the part of Ellicott, the anti-urban and anti-religious views of Jefferson, and later insight and opportunistic embellishment of a Masonic and zodiacal nature.

The National Capital Planning Commission, the agency charged with overseeing the federal built presence in urban Washington, published a long-term vision plan, "Extending the Legacy," in 1997. This plan seeks to return to some principles L'Enfant established, including an emphasis beyond the Mall, looking east and south toward the waterfront, and locating significant institutions throughout the city.

Discussion continues regarding the fate of the now defunct and soon to be demolished RFK stadium, which sits at the peak of L'Enfant's large star by the Anacostia.

Beyond the city of Washington itself, the influence that the L'Enfant Plan has had on future urban design appears quite limited. The plan for the city of Detroit, for example, seems to have originally taken some inspiration from Washington, though without much insightful intention beyond the use of radial avenues. It is also possible that it had some impact on Baron Hausmann as he laid out the new boulevards of Paris during the 1860s. That is just speculation, however.

At the end of his book, Mann reemphasizes the feminine aspects inherent in the grand power of the golden mean. This is perhaps the most useful lesson for us to take away from L'Enfant's plan today – a new perspective on the natural and feminine aspects of the plan. We so rarely find ourselves able to design from scratch here in the 21st century. What is very pressing, however, is the need to redevelop the fabric of community by healing the wounds that we as individuals and citizens have suffered and must begin to face – economic and political inequality, global climate change, neglect of the oppressed, the challenge of sea level rise for our coastal cities, etc. The places we build reflect the values we hold; neither our values nor the places we build seem to work any longer.

L'Enfant's use of sacred and symbolic geometry as described by Mann, and the call to Virgo through the zodiac discovered by Ovason, may seem improbable, naive, and even a bit ridiculous to our contemporary thinking. We do not think in those same metaphorical or poetic terms any longer. But our ancestors most certainly did, and their methods and ideals produced an artistry of grace, elegance, and meaning that we still admire, desperately need, and must recover.

What can city design take from the legacy of L'Enfant? Elegance, memory, and harmony of our political and spiritual aspirations must infuse our thinking, on both a personal and communal level. The current political and cultural divide across the nation needs all manner of healing and reconciliation, and L'Enfant showed us clearly how the built environment can symbolically support this. Can his methods apply to our built environment today? Taken together, the application of sacred geometry as uncovered by Mann, and the later embellishment of mythic symbolism revealed by Ovason, can provide an excellent source of design inspiration in the creation of places of meaning. The next chapters will explore this possibility.

Where is the Center?

One final little oddity appeared as I wrapped up my research on L'Enfant. Having worked as a surveyor in Alexandria for a few years in my youth, I wanted to understand a bit more regarding the boundary survey that Ellicott completed. I noted a lack of any connection between L'Enfant's design of the city and the district boundaries laid out by Ellicott. The city lay well inside those boundaries by several miles. The Capitol Building, lying at the cross of the "Cardo" and "Decumanus" operates as the center of the city – and the heart of the nation — symbolically if not geographically; but what is the geographic center of the 100-square mile diamond of the original federal District of Columbia? When drawing a line from the western boundary stone in Falls Church, VA to the eastern stone, and from the first and southernmost stone at Jones Point to the northernmost in Silver Spring, where is the proverbial "X" that marks the spot?

X marks the spot: Google Earth identifying the approximate center of the District of Columbia in the garden of the Organization of American States

Since the land on the Virginia side was returned to Virginia by the federal government in 1847 (which today comprises Arlington County and Alexandria, Virginia), few seem to have ever cared to consider it. Given his obvious desire to infuse symbolic geometric meaning into the city pattern, it is surprising that L'Enfant did not take it into account. Mann, however, notes it in passing. What he describes in his book is close, according to my own investigation – perhaps close enough to provide metaphorical inspiration – but not precisely accurate. He states in his book that the intersection of the north-south and east-west lines is just off 17th Street and Constitution Avenue, in the rear courtyard of the Organization of American States (OAS). Even more specifically, he identifies the spot as being marked by a statue of the Aztec god Xōchipilli, known as the playful lord of springtime, dance, and flowers. What a lovely image!

The truth is slightly different, but perhaps even more inspiring in its own unexpected way.

Wanting to assure myself of this amazing find, I visited the site twice, and spoke with the curator of the adjacent Art Museum of the Americas (who knew nothing of such a story). I then conducted a little online research. Making use of measurement tools on Google Earth, I determined after quadruple-checking that the actual crossing point, the more precise geographic center of the original federal district, is about 180 feet to the northeast of our Aztec friend. As far as I could make out, the center of the district lies underneath a line of shrubbery, next to an overhanging catalpa tree and adjacent to the retaining wall of a driveway. Not memorable in the least – unmarked, completely forgotten and unknown as a special site. Looking back toward Xōchipilli, sitting serenely by the museum overlooking a pool of water, I felt that he certainly is seated close enough to play an inspirational role, keeping a bemused eye on the center of the most powerful city in the Americas.

Then just by chance, I glanced in the opposite direction, and a statue caught my eye; it's near C Street but still on the OAS property and about the same distance away from the forlorn center. The three spots, Xōchipilli, the district center point, and the statue form a straight line, running southwest to northeast. A memorial statue of Amerigo Vespucci.

How much should I read into this? The two statues were erected more than 100 years apart, Xōchipilli in 1910, Vespucci not arriving until 2012. Could any of this have been intentional; the center merely implied between these two points, in the same way L'Enfant left his stars hidden rather than obvious? Is it mere random and meaningless chance; or is this the way the unconscious soul emerges from the earth through synchronicity? Vespucci, the namesake of America, represents the civilization of the Old World north of the equator and east to Europe, and a more rational way of viewing the world. Playful Xōchipilli of the New World south of the equator and to the west, provides a more soulful perspective.

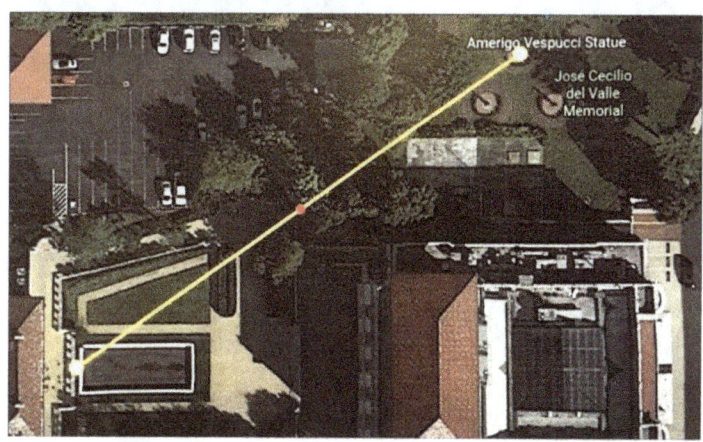

Xochipilli seated to the lower left, Vespucci to the upper right, equidistant to the district center marked by the red dot

Each of them not quite 180 feet away from the center, together adding up almost to a full circle of 360, encompassing the world. A balancing act? The center we seek is so often hidden, and perhaps not always in the middle we expect.

CHAPTER XV

Sacred Geometry and Mythic Symbolism:
A New Foundation for Urban Design

"The task is to bring the ancient back to life in a new way" – C.G. Jung

The previous chapter described L'Enfant's design of Washington, DC, his use of "sacred geometry," and the infusion of mythic symbols of the zodiac throughout the city by others over the course of many decades. But just what is this sacred geometry, which I did not define; and what are myths and symbols in general, and the role they play for us?

Our souls, the unconscious, and the Creator, all want to communicate with us and our rational egos, but they don't always speak any rational language we can understand. Rather, they often speak to us in images through symbols, dreams, visions, and myths. The natural world easily accommodates this process as a setting, providing all sorts of material for symbolic imagery: plants, animals, rocks, wind, water, the whole of the natural landscape. We have been interacting with the natural world for hundreds of thousands of years since our biological beginnings, so these images are deeply embedded in us, down to our DNA. The human urban environment, which we construct for ourselves, also has a history, though not nearly as long. Over a period extending back thousands of years, our ancestors created a built environment of cities as their most significant places, with symbolic meaning designed directly into the architecture, an immersive environment of their cultural aspirations and cosmological understanding. This continued even up to the 1700s through many different visions and philosophies. Starting in the 1800s at the latest, however, this came to a slow halt, so that our cities today reflect nothing of any spiritual meaning. Efficient engineering is the only apparent goal now, leaving our surroundings with the harsh look of mere infrastructure. Occasionally, a scrim of playful decoration is overlayed to soften the calluses but often remains bereft of any psychic meaning.

Increasingly we spend our time disconnected from natural settings, living only within the built environment. Historically, when civilization held myth and symbol in high regard, there was urban "material" that the creative spiritual forces could use to speak to us in dreams and so forth.

Today, with our almost purely technological and engineered approach, almost no newly created symbolic material can speak to us. We now build places that have nothing of value to communicate or teach. Rectifying this situation is the intention of what I have coined "symbolic urbanism."

The laying out of a town or city is nothing if not geometric. The word "geometry "simply means "measurement of the earth." Its study is assumed to have originated, as we understand geometry in the West, with the ancient Egyptians, though its roots are certainly older. The Egyptians had a practical need to measure the earth on an ongoing basis due to the regular flooding of the Nile River into the farmland along its valley. The Greeks, however, who learned from the Egyptians, were the first to formalize it as a field of study. Pythagoras (circa 500 BC) is said to be the father of geometry, while Euclid (circa 300 BC) was the first to organize its principles. Eratosthenes was the first to measure the circumference of the earth in about 200 BC. Geometry involved much more than the measurement of the earth, however, and included the mapping of the stars in the night sky and its vision of music as geometry that can be heard. The step-by-step logic of geometry is the basis of the modern scientific method. Most of us today have at least some basic education regarding the principals of geometry, which have remained essentially unchanged for all these centuries. Most high school students will admit to only a mild interest in it, to be sure.

So, what makes it so special, and what could possibly be "sacred" about it? And what too, are the symbols and mythologies that are so often embedded within it? For our purposes here, how can sacred geometry, myths, and symbols be made use of as sources for the experience and design of place? The question must be asked too, what is the need for all this? What problem is a "symbolic urbanism" intended to address? What follows is a very cursory overview of sacred

SACRED GEOMETRY AND MYTHIC SYMBOLISM

geometry, signs, symbols, and myth; more significantly, I propose a method by which sacred geometry can be used to create the "skeleton" upon which a mythic and symbolic life can be expressed as a fundamental ordering principle of urbanism.

What is Sacred Geometry?

The ancient world thought of geometry as much more than mere angles and shapes. Geometry was deeply infused with a spiritual vision. Legend has it that the entry to Plato's school of philosophy in Athens 2500 years ago was inscribed with the words, "Let no one enter who does not first understand geometry."

What moves geometry away from dry, dull formulas toward the "sacred" is its ability to make visible that which is invisible, to reveal the repeating patterns and forms found throughout the universe and natural world. Geometry becomes sacred because it represents and codifies the hidden structure behind physical matter – it is the instrument used to create the world. Geometry thus is the blueprint which God used in the creation of the physical universe.

The flower of life is a fundamental pattern of sacred geometry which grows out of the golden mean (the ratio of 1 to 1.618). It can be considered a sort of "DNA structure" containing all the patterns and shapes of the universe. The structure of DNA itself, by the way, also follows very definitive geometric patterns. It is symbolic of the connection of all sentient beings to each other. It has been found in locations around the world, going back several thousand years, including the Egyptian Temple of Osiris and the Forbidden City in Beijing. Leonardo da Vinci studied it deeply and included it in his creations. Sacred geometry is thus both a practical tool of engineering and a contemplative process of spiritual understanding. This symbolic value supports the evolution of the soul, the reconciliation of the rational and the intuitive, giving satisfaction to both left brain and right brain ways of thinking. Only with the coming of modernist values in the 20th century did sacred geometry fall out of general knowledge and use.

Sacred geometry ascribes certain symbolic values to specific geometric shapes, patterns, and numbers. A fundamental starting point is the golden mean, or phi – the ratio of 1 to 1.618. Phi, along with the square root of two and three for example, is an example of dynamic symmetry, the idea that spaces can be divided in a way so that the parts reflect the same proportions as the whole. Fractals are a more recent addition to our understanding of sacred geometry. They are objects which do not lose their detail or proportion at any scale, whether magnified or diminished.

Numbers too were ascribed particular symbolic meaning. One, to no surprise, represents unity, wholeness, and the initial act of creation. Two represents duality, opposites, and polarity. No action can take place in the physical realm without opposites (nor, according to Jung, can there be any consciousness without opposites). Three holds divinity and is required to make a plane. Four is made up of two pairs of opposites (which Jung describes psychologically as a "quaternary") and is the first number in which a solid object can be created. The number 10, being the sum of 1+2+3+4, is considered the number of wholeness and completion.

Perhaps we can we think of geometric shapes as archetypes, just as Jung thought of numbers as archetypes holding their own specific symbolic meaning.

Sacred geometry is a very hands-on study, in which one spends a great deal of time in contemplative drawing, much in the manner of working a mandala, seeking to understand physical and spiritual connection and relationship. While geometry held very practical uses for the ancient world, its sacred aspect was fundamentally developed to ensure that human affairs were kept in alignment with the "divine order." Thus, it is the point at which the visible and invisible meet in service to one another.

The Creation Story

Sacred geometry is so all-encompassing that it is impossible to gain a deep understanding of its entirety. It is so all-encompassing in fact that it should be no surprise that it includes its own version of a creation story. The story in Genesis closely follows what is described below, although the creation of the world according to sacred geometry is far older than Genesis, pre-dating the Old Testament and likely having its roots in ancient Egyptian mystery schools. Its steps roughly correspond to the first seven days of creation as told in Genesis.

In the beginning, there were no dimensions of space or time. There was only an eternal void. God (or the Creator, the Universe, Spirit, Nature … choose your own term) was essentially indistinguishable from this void and had the choice to either remain in this state of static unity or begin creating. The choice was made (thank goodness!) to create a canvas on which the universe could be painted, or a trellis established upon which the material world could grow.

The Creator began by acting as a single point of beginning, from which the three physical dimensions emanated or were projected conceptually: up and down, left and right, forward and behind. Because the pre-existing void is infinite, boundaries needed to be established. This is accomplished by connecting the end of each line of dimension to the end of every other. This results in an octahedron, a shape that is depicted in the Star of David. Consciousness – God, the Creator, etc. – can now move about, since there are points that are relative to each other.

This shape is of course linear, made up purely of straight lines. To the ancient world, straight lines were considered male, while curves were considered female. The next step involved rotating the octahedron around its points. This act traces a sphere. A sphere is thus purely female. This may be the source of Eve being born out of Adam's rib, as described in Genesis.

The Creator then had another choice to make: to remain static or repeat the process. This time, however, the first sphere or circle acts as an original reference. In the next act, the Creator moved from the center of the circle or sphere to the edge and projected a duplicate. The result is two equally sized spheres (or circles) with the edge of each touching the center of the other. The area of overlap is known as a vesica piscis, or mandorla. The process was then continued, the only rule being that the point of intersection of the previous circles act as the beginning center point of the next circle. Each circle/sphere added brings new information, patterns, and complexity. After seven such circles, we see what is known as the "seed of life," which corresponds metaphorically to the Seven Days of Creation in the Book of Genesis. This is the foundation for the physical patterning of the entire Universe. Viewed in three dimensions, it creates a "tube torus" which is a shape that folds back upon itself.

An additional six circles are placed around the original seed and known as the second vortex motion, and then a third group of six in a third vortex motion, creates what is known as the flower of life. Two more such vortices give the fruit of life. The process produces the template for the entire physical universe. The Creator and the patterns created as described here, provide the two essentials of all reality:

structure and consciousness.

Sacred Geometry in the Natural World

We see various principles of geometry repeating in natural structures constantly, from the microscopically small to the incomprehensible vastness of galactic structures.

At the very small scale, crystals organize their structure according to only seven arrangements, from the simple cube to the complex rhombohedral. Frozen water – snow! – is well known to arrange itself in a myriad of beautiful hexagonal shapes. Snowflakes have the ability to grow, but never beyond 1.6 times their original size, which reflects the golden ratio of 1.618. The foundational molecule of our bodily being, DNA, is arranged in a double helix arrangement, with two intertwined strands similar to the intertwining snakes of a caduceus. Ten "ladder rungs" make up one complete turn of a DNA strand; when viewed from atop its axis, a pentagon shape is visible.

Moving to the largest scale, the structure of spiral galaxies reveals a pattern similar to the golden spiral. This is also reflected in the storm pattern of a hurricane.

The more accessible ways nature makes use of sacred geometry is at the middle scale, visible to us. The structure and shape of leaves and their arrangement is revealing. In many plant species, smaller branches and particularly leaves will grow out of their stem in a spiral arrangement, rotated roughly 137.5 degrees around the stem relative to the preceding one. This provides greater opportunity for each leaf to access sunlight. Flower petals also are typically found on plants according to the Fibonacci Sequence; they typically number 3, 5, 8, 13, 21, and so on. Seed patterns display this too, particularly in that of a sunflower. Counting the spirals of seeds, there are 34 clockwise spirals and 21 counter-clockwise spirals. These two numbers, 21 and 34, are sequential in the Fibonacci Series.

Sea creatures display sacred geometry in their structure. Perhaps most famous is the nautilus shell and its well-known example of a spiral. As the nautilus grows and moves forward in its shell to a larger chamber, the outer shell spirals up and out in accordance with the golden spiral.

The human body also displays the Fibonacci Sequence. This is easily observed in the fingers, in which each bone is roughly 1.618 times longer than the previous, moving back from the tip.

As a phenomenon of nature, music has traditionally been considered geometry for the ear. The rational and mathematical foundation of music was deeply explored by the composers of the Baroque period, particularly Bach. A contemporary alignment of the geometry of music and stories of creation is to be found in the Middle Earth writings of Tolkien. Far more than a mere adventure tale of Bilbo, Frodo, and Gandalf, Tolkien included a creation story. In it, the creator-god, Iluvatar, teaches the angels, known as the Ainur, to sing. The vibrational harmonies of the Ainur gave shape to the physical universe.

Sacred Geometry in Art and Architecture

Artists including Leonardo da Vinci used sacred geometry in their search for composition and structure in their creations. It is fundamental to the use of perspective in painting. We can see this in the image of *The Vetruvian Man*, and the well-known *Last Supper*.

In the architecture of ancient civilizations, aligning structures and constructing buildings with certain proportions was universal practice. The ancients tended to use ratios of whole numbers; 9/8 for instance, instead of decimals like 1.618, for their ease of use in construction. The Parthenon in Athens is based on the ratio of 9 to 4, not on the golden mean of 1.618, although they are closely proximate.

An early and familiar application of sacred geometry is found in the Pyramids of Giza. For the Egyptian builders, the angle of the slope held the greatest significance. The distance around the base is equal to the circumference of a circle with a radius equal to the height of the pyramid. To achieve this, the ratio of 7:11 was often used.

The dimensions of the Temple of Solomon in Jerusalem are also significant in the world of sacred geometry. When measured in cubits, its dimensions were 120 long by 60 wide, and 20 cubits tall (roughly 206 feet long by 103 feet wide, and 34 feet high). When multiplied together, these dimensions equal 144,000, a well-known sacred number in itself. These reveal that not simply area, but the volume of a building was also important to the ancient world.

Gothic cathedrals, from Notre Dame in Paris to the National Cathedral in Washington, DC are completely based on proportions and dimensions of sacred geometry, but come with a fascinating twist. The story, perhaps true, perhaps only apocryphal, is related to the Knights Templar and their escapades of the early Crusades around the year 1200. The Templars established their headquarters on the ruins of the Temple of Solomon and took back with them the dimensions of those ruins to be used as a basis for new churches and cathedrals in Europe. Somehow, those dimensions became scrambled, so that the structures seemed to stand on their side; rather than 103 feet wide and 34 feet tall, they were misinterpreted as 34 feet wide and 103 feet tall! Such a tall structure was inherently unstable, given the technology of the time. The solution came in the form of flying buttresses to hold up the extremely high walls and weight of the roof, and large stained-glass windows helped lighten the load. The resulting interior spaces are a marvel but based on a simple misinterpretation. Not a bad approach to one's life, using mistakes as a source of growth! It is said that creativity is allowing oneself to make mistakes, but art is knowing which mistakes to keep.

The layout and site planning of structures such as Stonehenge and the Pyramids are found to align in accordance with solar and lunar events, star patterns and constellations. Such ceremonial sites and complexes have long been laid out and aligned with reference to significant geomorphic or astronomical features. A more foundational and directly influential story of geometrical place-making for us today is Versailles, the royal palace and gardens outside Paris. What led to the garden design of Versailles, and its intentions, is wonderfully described by Amir Alexander in his book *Proof*. The book describes how, over the course of several centuries, the design of royal gardens in France became increasingly complex, geometrically, in their patterns and layout. These gardens were intended to function as displays of the king's power over all of France. The level to which King Louis XIV took this was far beyond anything before. The layout was such that all the major avenues converged on one point, the King's bed-chamber, symbolizing that all political power emanated from there. It represents a strong and clear intent to display power and control over politics, culture, and nature. Overwhelming public spectacle equaled the display of uncontested power. The entire 37,000 acres as designed by Le Notre functioned as an immersive propaganda machine, reflecting not just a rigid political hierarchy but the embodiment of a universal truth of nature.

In this view, nature is not messy, random, or unsymmetrical, as we might assume when walking through a forest. Order and symmetry were not being imposed on nature because nature is in itself already ordered and symmetrical. This simply needs to be exposed, revealed to the human eye, so the thinking went. The purpose of a garden was to make visible the preexisting order of nature. Such an understanding of nature easily and usefully fit into the hierarchical control desired by the king. A rational, orderly, and bureaucratic state under the king therefore operates in the same manner as nature itself.

Numerous attempts at translating geometry into urbanism both preceded and followed Versailles, including Rome under Pope Sixtus VI, Evelyn and Wren's unbuilt plans for London, St. Petersburg Russia, the Ringstasse in Vienna, and most notably Paris under the hand of Baron Hausmann. None of these, however, match the achievement of L'Enfant and his plan for Washington, DC, directly influenced by his childhood spent at Versailles, explored in the previous chapter.

Alexander's final chapter concludes with what would appear an enormous let-down to the proponents of any symbolic geometric design. He essentially argues that the discovery of non-Euclidean geometry by a Hungarian named János Bolyai in 1823 removes any pretense of meaning from geometry of any sort. Bolyai created – or discovered – a series of geometries, each of which is internally consistent but cannot be reconciled with the others mathematically. There are a perhaps infinite number of incompatible, irreconcilable truths coexisting together.

Alexander perhaps rightly argues that because of this non-Euclidean geometry, it is pointless to try to animate any specific political structure through geometric symbolism. What he does not consider is the psycho-spiritual, rather than political, possibilities this brings up. While there may be multiple incompatible geometries in existence, our felt experience is Euclidean. This strikes me as a cue pointing to a spiritual, rather than political, role for a symbolic geometry. While political structures require certitude, the spiritual life is nothing if not ambiguous. As Jung points out, a fundamental aspect of psychological growth is learning to manage, cope, live with, and hopefully transcend irreconcilable opposites. Can an urban pattern intentionally reflect this concept of opposites and their reconciliation?

Time and the Zodiac

Any understanding of the implications of sacred geometry regarding urbanism must include all dimensions, including that of time. Specialists in theoretical physics are now hotly debating whether time is real or not. We do experience it as such though, living in the here and now, and so must take it into account here.

Our experience of time is essentially cyclical, even though our western minds assume it to be more linear. There are so many cycles which affect us, both small and large. Those which have the most immediate impact on us are, of course, more short and frequent. The spinning of the earth gives us the daily experience of day and night; the moon affects the twice-daily tidal surges of the seas. The calendar of weeks, the monthly lunar cycles, and the annual cycle around the sun gives us the four seasons. These are the most familiar to us, and for the ancient world, a good understanding of them was a matter of life and death.

The cycles that move most quickly and that we can most readily perceive are kept track of through clocks. They have become more precise as we have developed a perceived need for more accuracy in the hectic contemporary world. Calendars are put to use for those slightly longer cycles of months and years. They don't always hang on our kitchen walls, however. The well-known Mayan and Aztec calendars were often displayed as public works, carved into stone wheels up to 10 feet in diameter and probably set atop their pyramids for all to see. Some clocks keep track of more specific events such as the solstice and equinox. Stonehenge is a well-known example; it is aligned to track the solstices and likely served religious and ceremonial roles as well.

Less well-known but equally intriguing and more accessible is the series of 21 Spanish mission churches along the central and southern California coast, and others continuing down south to Peru. Those in California were established between 1769-1823 by Spanish Franciscan missionaries. These mission complexes were laid on an east-west axis, but intriguingly, their sanctuaries often were not. Research by Ruben Mendoza has shown that they were not aligned perpendicularly but instead canted by a few degrees. The result is that on the winter solstice, the rising sun enters the sanctuary door and travels up the center aisle to the main altar, illuminating the central crucifix in brilliant light. The spiritual symbolism is clear and memorable.

A more contemporary example is found at the Salk Institute in San Diego. The campus is a 60s-era Brutalist design by the architect Louis Kahn. The iconic design centers on a narrow water channel running to a fountain and pool in the center of a plaza. The plaza overlooks the Pacific Ocean, facing west. The water channel, known

SACRED GEOMETRY AND MYTHIC SYMBOLISM

as "The River of Life," is aligned precisely with the setting sun on the spring equinox, turning the channel into a river of fire.

There are other cycles which move so slowly that we do not really experience them though they do impact us; in some instances, we have not even known of their existence until quite recently. These include such occurrences as climatic ice ages, which come roughly every 100,000 years, and the precession of the zodiac caused by the wobble in the earth's axial spin. This precession takes about 25,700 years to complete one rotation through the stars of the zodiac. Each of the twelve signs of the zodiac thus lasts roughly 2,160 years, far longer than most civilizations.

Ruins and the crumbling remains of abandoned buildings can also play a connecting spiritual role in helping us locate ourselves in the flowing stream of time. Old structures abandoned but not rebuilt or re-used, but simply left in a stable state of disrepair, can provide us the valuable lesson that nothing we create truly lasts forever, yet our task is to carry on the work of our ancestors. Often, abandoned ruins are located in significant or prominent locations, adding to their evocative power and the value of their presence. Historic preservation approaches this but I would say that the impetus for the preservation of significant structures is less a desire for spiritual and ancestral memory found in ancient ruins and more a response to the utter lack of harmony and beauty in our contemporary designs.

Poets and spiritual teachers throughout the ages have reminded us that our calling as humans is to expand our conscious awareness – to know ourselves more fully. We cannot know ourselves without a sense of context and history. Such a contextual history expands well beyond our personal inner life and family legends. We must understand the story of the cultures from which we sprang; the story of western civilization going back 3,000 years; the development of the human psyche going back almost 300,000 years; and our biological evolution that has shaped us over tens of millions of years.

To the ancient world, to know oneself was to know the gods and their stories. What the gods represented to ancient peoples we now view as the various aspects of our psychological makeup. Humans remain the same in essence across thousands of years, and the stories that moved our ancestors still move and inspire us today. We can still learn of ourselves from those ancient stories. They are stored for us to be viewed at any time in the zodiac. Think of the constellations of the zodiac as a reference library of stories and lessons; they functioned as an early storage device for accumulated knowledge and wisdom, used by pre-literate people in the same way we use books and online resources. An epic tale, tragedy, or metaphorical story of the human condition could be passed down through the generations by placing it in connection to the stars where the gods dwelt. Virtually every ancient civilization created systems of the zodiac – our own western heritage beginning with the Greeks, Egyptians, and Mesopotamians, as well as Chinese, Hindu, Celtic, Mayan, on and on. Just as the ancients embedded their stories into the stars above, can we not design those universal myths and symbols into our cities and towns?

Symbols, Signs, and Myths

We have discussed sacred geometry as a possible foundation for a new symbolic urbanism. Before we look at what that might involve, the question must be answered; just what is a symbol and what does it provide for us?

There are a number of ways to think about symbols, but the essential quality is that they are visual images conveying a meaning beyond our current ability to comprehend. Thus, they have a spiritual, religious, and psychological core. When something is understood as symbolic, it means that a person senses a hidden and ungraspable essence and cannot capture in words the elusive secret. As Jung phrased it, "There are not many truths; there are very few. Their meaning is so deep that they cannot be grasped except by symbols." Symbols serve a specific purpose. It seems that the unconscious – god, spirit, or soul – rarely speaks the language of our conscious minds. It thus uses symbols to communicate with us in dreams and visions, with "primitive analogies" that speak to both our unconscious and the intuitions of our consciousness. Symbols have their source in our unconscious. They are rooted deep in our ancient ancestry and biological experience tracing back tens of thousands of years and more, so far as to long precede written language, even spoken language. Our interactions with the natural world provide the essential source catalog.

Symbolic behavior by humans is seen as far back as 120,000 years ago. Evidence of music, mathematics, and art – the ability to envision things that do not exist, so to speak – goes back at least 50,000 years. The anthropologist Genevieve von Petzinger has made a study of the earliest pre-literate signs and symbols of the Paleolithic age. There are images of animals of specific geographic regions that humans may have interacted with. Additionally, she has found geometric shapes which appear to be located in widely different parts of the world and thus seem to be universal – beasts, the process of birth, the delicate grace of an emerging flower bud. The variety is unending. A symbolic life seems to have been part of our experience as humans for an extremely long time.

Symbols are deeply embedded in our unconscious and cannot be ignored. We must therefore be firmly connected to history. Yet the emergence of symbols is not reserved to the deeply ancient past; they continue to emerge from the unconscious even now, as our experience of the world expands. Think of the double helix structure of DNA, or the system of electrons around an atomic nucleus, deeply embedded in the public imagination even before they were developed during the 20th century. A most famous instance of a symbolic dream is that of James Watson, who dreamed of a spiral staircase, which led to his discovery of the double helix shape we now know as DNA, a basic building block of life.

Symbols can be categorized in various ways, coming to us in all sorts of images, depictions, and shapes. Each holds meaning, sometimes collective to all humanity, or a specific culture, often deeply private and personal. Animals, plants, the human form, astronomical configurations, and simple to more complex geometric shapes all have been ascribed meaning by humans. To give just one example, one which acts as a guide to my own life; consider the mandorla, or vesica piscis as it is more typically known. I've mentioned the mandorla before – it's made of two overlapping circles with the edge of each touching the center of the other, and it symbolically represents the resolution or reconciliation of two opposites. This might be the conscious and unconscious, spirit and matter, male and female, or the divide between two people or entities. The overlap is the place in which the two communicate and reach healing. The vesica piscis is an element of the flower of life, discussed above, a more complex symbolic shape that has been found around the globe at sites going back at least 6,000 years.

Symbolic life is so deeply ingrained in our history that it's essentially an instinct for humans. To quote Jung from his work *The Dynamics of the Self*: "There is a thinking in primordial images, in symbols which are older than historical man, which are inborn in him from earliest times, eternally living, outlasting all generations, still making up the groundwork of the human psyche. *It is only possible to live the fullest life when we are in harmony with these symbols: wisdom is a return to them*" [emphasis mine].

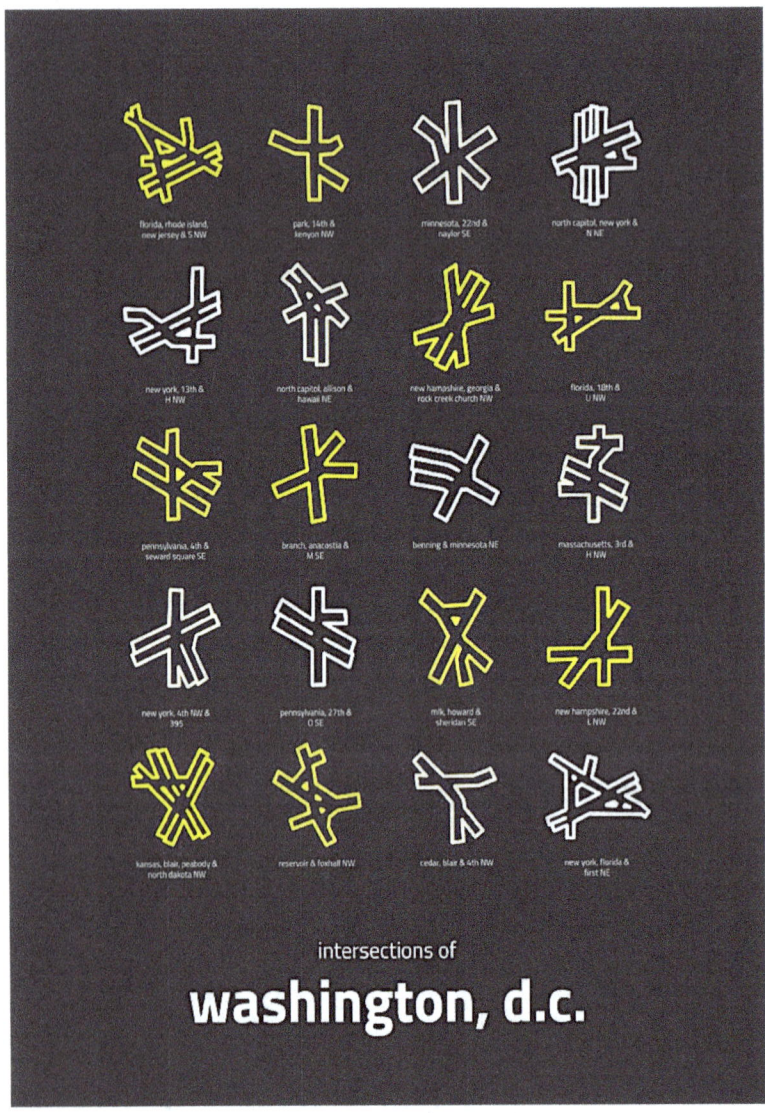

Intersections of DC: A playful rendering of the intersections of various streets in the city of Washington, by Peter Gorman. A fabulous poem by Zoe Ravenwood interprets them as ancient Celtic runes, playing off a Nordic myth:

SACRED GEOMETRY AND MYTHIC SYMBOLISM

> The Seidkonur speak in hushed tones of
> strange sights seen
> Upon their journeys to the Well at Yggdrasil's
> Mighty root
>
> Shown them by the three ancient women of
> The Wyrd who there reside. She who spins
> The DC intersections into being, She who
> Weaves them together, and She who cuts
> Them short
>
> It is believed that if one can divine the meaning
> Held within DC intersections
>
> That they too, might attain knowledge of all
> Things past and future
>
> And become as wise as great Odin himself
> Who once gave of himself, to himself upon
> Yggdrasil,
>
> That he could retrieve the shapes of DC
> Streets and know the secrets they contain

In an enormous effort to support such a large human undertaking, a fabulous resource has been compiled over the past several decades by the Archive for Research in Archetypal Symbolism. ARAS was founded by a group of Jungian scholars who sought to further his research into the archetypal and mythic symbolism which lives unconsciously in the human psyche. Hundreds of symbols from around the world and through all history are cataloged and presented visually along with poetic essays describing each.

We do not experience the world so much as a collection of objects but rather live in the world as if it is a story or narrative. To that end, a basic way we incorporate the message of a symbol is through ritual. A ritual is basically the acting out of a symbol and is thus perhaps the foundational source of religion – the theatrical playing out of unconscious ideas which we only dimly understand. As the Gospel of Philip reminds us, "Truth did not come into the world naked, but it came in symbols and images. We do not receive it any other way."

And what of myths? These are the stories that make symbols and archetypes understandable to us. Mythology and mythic storytelling have come to be viewed as mere entertainment, perhaps holding some valuable lesson but generally regarded as a fiction: "that's nothing but a myth," we say dismissively. But each of our individual lives can be understood as such a story, a grand mythic adventure. As Joseph Campbell relates, there are four essential tasks that a myth can take on – I discussed these in Chapter III but will return to them again in this context. First, a myth has a mystical role to play; to open us up to a transcendent mystery beyond the ordinary everyday experience of the world. Second, myth has a cosmological task; to provide a vision of how the world is structured. This can change dramatically over time, as a culture's knowledge and horizons expand. This is particularly significant for us today, because a major reason we no longer trust our old myths is that our science has expanded our horizons so dramatically that the old stories of 2,000 years ago are no longer capable of garnering our respect. Third, a myth has a sociological role; that is to construct and validate a particular culture and social order. Finally, a myth plays a pedagogical role in the lives of individuals; how to manage the unending everyday crises we face through the various stages of life. The relationship between myth and symbol is of course deeply intertwined; a symbol may contain a whole mythic story.

The Alchemical City
A small, obscure, and largely forgotten corner of world history has made use of symbols as a fundamental tool for spiritual exploration and growth, that of alchemy. Entire libraries have been devoted to the subject of alchemy, and I cannot hope to add anything to such a deeply complex and ornate subject. Yet any attempt to consider urbanism from a symbolic perspective must take it into account, even if only briefly. I began a discussion of alchemy in Chapter VIII, but will return to it in more depth here.

Far from the conventional image of alchemy as an amateurish attempt to turn lead into gold, or even an early attempt at developing the scientific method, alchemy was at its core a spiritual discipline. The cliché of trying to turn lead into gold speaks to a psychological metaphor, not a chemistry experiment. Alchemists were attempting to turn the leaden human life into the golden light of spiritual wisdom. Each alchemist seemed to have developed their own symbolic and metaphorical language to describe the process, but there were essentially between five to seven stages of transformation, including the dissolution and re-integration of various aspects of the soul.

More pertinent to the study of urbanism, however, is also an almost completely unknown and astonishing assumption of alchemy, shared by the medieval European, Chinese, and Arabic traditions alike. Not only the human was to be transformed and elevated, but the Divine must also be freed. Alchemy sought not simply the development and healing of the person; but the Creator too was asleep and locked inside physical matter and in need of release. Alchemy was a search for release of both the human soul and Divine matter. God the Creator is to be found in physical matter itself, which is in need of redemption.

Alchemy was very much a study in process. Sometimes five, but generally seven separate steps are taken in the alchemical process of soul development, from the breaking apart of the old to identify the parts, through transformation of those parts, and on to the union of the components. These are sometimes identified as calcination (the breaking down of ego and attachment), dissolution (exploration of the unconscious), separation (review of psychic elements), conjunction (merging of the conscious and unconscious), fermentation (psychological testing through suffering), distillation (purification of the spirit), and coagulation (union of the duality of matter and spirit). One does not transform the soul all at once.

Just as an individual grows and develops as a process over time, so do lovable places. We cannot expect to create urban places of meaning that are deeply loved through large-scale, all-at-once corporate development. A small-scale process of intimate, "bite-sized" projects tend to create the places we love, as shown through history. Perhaps the alchemical analogy for urbanism can be found in the New Urbanist approach of Incremental Development as advocated by John Anderson and illustrated in Christopher Alexander's sequential design and the Sky Method of Steve Mouzon. As the landscape architect Douglas Duany reminds us, "Relearning vernacular processes consciously is a responsibility given to our era if one wishes to create rich environments and mitigate the alienation inflicted by the modern mind."

C.G. Jung viewed the process of alchemy as a culmination of Christianity and western thinking, and at least procedurally, the equivalent of his process of psychological individuation. Marie-Louise von Franz, one of Jung's greatest students and collaborators, put all this in more contemporary psychological phrasing for us: "As physics is a mental reconstruction of material processes, perhaps a physical reconstruction of psychic processes is possible in nature itself." This implies to my mind the possibility – even the necessity – of redeeming the city through a process of symbolic design.

CHAPTER XVI

The Principles and Practice Of Symbolic Urbanism:
Myth and Meaning in the Design of Place

"He who moves with familiarity in this world of the street has Hermes as his god" – Károly Kerényi

To paraphrase the spiritual writer and psychotherapist Thomas Moore, a community best serves itself when it promotes the awakening of the distinctive story emerging in the life of each person. Generally, when we consider what a community might offer its members, we picture support in terms of social programming and structures like libraries, life skills training, food and financial aid to the poor, and the like. These can be useful and appropriate responses to those in immediate need, but to Moore's point, how does a community support the distinctive story of each person? We have a psychological need for an expanding spiritual depth, not only the maintenance of our more daily needs.

In order to respond to Moore's call, we must expand our understanding of the role of urbanism to that of an intentional educational setting – the city as classroom. If our incarnated life on earth is analogous to being sent to a "spiritual boarding school," our cities are thus extremely important classrooms. We must outfit them as such, with all the potential educational tools we can muster. A basic aim of this school to which we are sent is, in my Jungian perspective, to bring the contents of the unconscious into conscious awareness. As Jung has described in *Aion: Researches into the Phenomenology of the Self,* a link can easily be found between symbol and city: "From the circle and quaternary motif is derived the symbol of the geometrically formed crystal … From here, analogy formation leads on to the city, castle, church, house, and vessel." This too is what sacred geometry intends, the revealing of the hidden order of the universe, the manifestation of the underlying universal principles. This makes it a fundamental application to the design of place. Modernity has done away with meaning, leaving us to live in meaningless places. Our cities and towns have essentially become mere collections of engineered mechanical infrastructure, operational in nature and efficient to some degree, but little else.

What is a Symbolic Urbanism?

There is no way we can anticipate what new mythological or psycho-spiritual tradition awaits us in the future, nor is there a need to, I suppose. We are living in the "in between times," as James Hollis reminds us. However, my working assumption is that the new tradition will have a strong emphasis on the reconciliation of opposites, in the Jungian sense. A spiritual science or a scientific spirituality for instance; one which does not discard the past but incorporates it and transcends it with a wider, more inclusive vision. Our understanding of what our cities and towns are meant to be must take this into account. The working out of this results in an urban morphology of mythological narrative.

What an odd thing to ask from the design of the built environment. But we have seen the ability to imbue a place with physically manifested spiritual dynamism in the example of L'Enfant's Washington, DC. Even if vanishingly few people recognized the symbolic plan, its power could still be felt and inspired others to build upon it. The way in which successive generations continued to overlay spiritual symbolism into the city confirms this.

Regarding real estate development, the conventional understanding of amenities is that they respond to leisure-time recreation and entertainment. Certainly, this can remain as one aspect of Symbolic Urbanism, but its intent is to rise beyond such entertainment to support residents and visitors who seek lives of deeper meaning and intention. The conscious awareness of our need for mythic and symbolic meaning is largely lost on us now, yet it remains hidden in our unconscious lives. The ancient world viewed myths, symbols, and rituals to make sense of the structure and events of the outer world and determine the correct response. In contrast, today we need mythic symbols and rituals to determine our *inner* vision, without which we cannot operate properly in the outer world. No reform of political or economic systems will suffice without this grounding. Thus, a Symbolic Urbanism must have the ability to support both formalized public religion or cosmology and individual, private spiritual quest. That is, it must create physical space for a secure and comforting social foundation, and at the same time hint at a way for the private and nonsocial, thus dangerous, individual quest of spiritual and psychic development.

Is this really a role that urbanism can or should play? It certainly has in the past, though at a much smaller scale. Think of the Stations of the Cross found in many Catholic and mainline Protestant churches. The Stations of the Cross are narrative images located around a sanctuary that depict events of Christ's final earthly days – his sufferings set in motion at the Last Supper, his death on the cross, and his burial. Customarily, they are arranged in chronological order around the interior walls of a church. In following the Way of the Cross, as the Stations are also called, devout Christians make a symbolic pilgrimage. Stops are made at each successive Station along the route for a devotion appropriate to the incident commemorated.

Just as we furnish our homes with sentimental nick-nacks and spiritual tokens as reminders and sources of inspiration, so too can we do so with our cities, towns, and neighborhoods. This is the role of statuary, memorials, and monuments, after all. Using sacred geometry as a foundation for symbolic urbanism makes space available for symbols to arise in selected locations of cultural, energetic, or geographic significance. This "skeleton of meaning" becomes the trellis upon which organic form can grow. That trellis might be founded on a geometric pattern, numbers, symbol, an aspect of the zodiac, ancient text of any religious tradition, the myths of any appropriate culture, or any combination thereof. The story may be told in any number of ways. One value of emphasizing civic space as the initial formative skeleton of placemaking is the sense of (relative) permanence it can provide. Land uses can change, families move away, shops and favorite entertainment haunts may come and go, but civic activities and structures tend to outlast others. They also emphasize the unified public essence of physical community, while making room for individual experience.

The selection of terms is a bit tricky. Regarding geometry, the conventional term is "sacred," and developing a sense of the sacred is a core intention of Symbolic Urbanism. The general public does not think in such terms though. Nor could any planning commission or governmental agency in the US, at any level, be seen as promoting anything resembling a religious attitude, and would do a disastrous job of it in any case. Thus I choose the term "Symbolic." This term carries its own complexities, however. A symbol is more than a sign, which is never more than the idea it represents. A symbol always stands for something more than its obvious meaning. Further, symbols are not really invented; they appear spontaneously as collective representations or manifestations that imply a vague, unknown, or hidden meaning which nevertheless is intuitively understood as somehow significant. How then does a Symbolic Urbanism emerge?

Principles

What follows is an incomplete set of general principles which guide the concept of Symbolic Urbanism. These are not final nor complete, and not presented in any required order.

> *Intent* – Symbolic Urbanism is a process of urban design and placemaking with the explicit intent of creating an immersive environment infused with a sense of psychic or spiritual meaning and participation in a story of higher purpose of the spiritual history of humanity. A fundamental inquiry in this process is how a site can participate in the larger spiritual story of the ongoing and evolving psychic development of humanity. This is accomplished through the use of sacred geometry and mythic symbolism as foundational elements of the public realm. The general intent of this approach is the creation of lovable places of meaning and memory which can promote not only greater civic community but an immersive environment which acts to enhance psychological well-being, and potentially spiritual development.
>
> *The City as "Psycho/Spiritual Classroom"* – It is an attempt to urbanistically symbolize the individual and collective process of psychic and spiritual development. A fundamental psychological law as described by Jung is the need to become whole by including and balancing opposites. Structured geometry might be thought of as representing rational consciousness, with the intuitive, irrational unconscious manifesting in flowing organic form in the interstices. Each plays a necessary role.

Grounding – The major alignments, points, and vertices of a geometric pattern must coincide with at least one actual point, line, or intersection pre-existing on the land, or else any resulting site plan is mere nonsense. These may include a street crossing, hilltop or other topographical feature, water course, a significant historic building which shall remain and not be demolished, or other similar feature.

Foundation – The history, form, and energy of the land itself, and the cultural story of the people having used or inhabited the place, will determine which pattern of sacred geometry is to be applied, and what symbols and mythic stories are to be expressed.

Structure – Symbolic Urbanism provides the foundational trellis upon which traditional urbanism, best exemplified in the Charter of the New Urbanism, can be structured.

Layers – Two levels of experience are built into Symbolic Urbanism. First, the skeletal arrangement for the street pattern and block layout seen in plan-view, and also the eye-level experience of the pedestrian. In general, the application of sacred geometry is more appropriate at the plan view. The direct human experience of urbanism is enhanced best through symbol, mythic references, and visual metaphor. These two layers interact in a manner so that the more intimate and detailed experience helps reveal the larger pattern.

Unification – These two layers, of geometric patterning and eye-level experiential embellishment, present a set of symbols and metaphors which are coordinated and relate a single theme of story or related stories drawn from a single or closely related sources. In other words, a mixing of traditions and metaphors is discouraged unless they reveal complementary narratives.

Commingling – Symbolic Urbanism is the coming together and commingling of the rational and intuitive.

Scale – Symbolic Urbanism functions at all scales, from the larger vision of multi-acre site planning, the intermediate scale of street dimensions, block size and dimensions, park and plaza layout, and the smaller scale of decorative building façade design and street furnishings.

Mutuality – In its task of promoting a public realm of deeper meaning and intention, Symbolic Urbanism explicitly supports both the realms of shared public religious expression in *all* its forms and traditions, and of privately conducted interior spiritual quest.

Hierarchy – A hierarchy of values and service is understood as follows:
- Technology is accepted as a useful tool but only in the service of efficiency;
- Efficiency is essential but gives way to the higher good of sustainability;
- Sustainability is fundamental but is best achieved when in the service of lovability;
- Lovable places are fundamentally those holding the emotional content of mythic symbolism, and function in serving lives of higher meaning and purpose.

Pattern – Creative design emerges out of the appropriately chosen pattern, based upon what is kept and what is erased, what is emphasized or diminished, and what is explicitly drawn or only implied.

Dimensions – All dimensions, not only those on a flat 2D site plan, may be used as expressions; this includes both elevation (the use of a hill, valley, or grotto for instance), and time (night/day, moon cycles, sunrise/set, seasons, tides, zodiac, etc.)

Action – The process of design on the land, as well as its ongoing habitation, includes an appropriately chosen ritual(s) of meaning, memory, and intention.

Points of Memory and Meaning – Significant locations are found in the intersections, angles, centers, edges, or other features of the geometry. They may function as a dispersed civic commons recognized through art, statuary, civic structures, and natural features. Such points may be used to determine street alignments, locations of significant structures, civic amenities, building entrances, architectural features such as towers, or public open spaces. They are intended as locations that ground the community in its civic, cultural, artistic, and environmental heritage, including recent traditions and ancient history. They act as sources of inspiration and learning.

Immersive Environment – Beyond simply creating and locating specific points, the overall goal is the creation of an immersive environment of psycho/spiritual uplift, emphasizing the essential element of the civic commons.

Visibility – Such points should be visually connected to the greatest extent possible, via street alignments, pedestrian paths, waterways, building alignments, or even through windows and doorways. This reciprocity of sight should connect at least two points if not more. The geometry can be intuitively understood as well as visually observed and experienced.

Educational – The chosen patterns, myths, and symbols should generally reflect culturally shared or known symbols and myths expressing aspirational truths, not merely a personal or private image of the designer's own conscious effort, in keeping with the intent of creating an immersive psychic experience.

Change and Local Expression – Accommodations should be made for ad hoc, temporary, and local grass-roots artistic expressions. A Symbolic Urbanism thus acknowledges impermanence and makes room for change over time, at least in one location.

Formal and Informal Structure – The fundamental pattern of place may be rigidly linear or informally curved in nature, or some combination of the two. A more structured geometry might represent the conscious ego, while a more free-flowing organic form represents the unconscious soul.

Precedent – Local traditions of design and materials are to be respectfully considered and incorporated, but need not be strictly adhered to.

Process

Every designer will bring their own methods to the process, and every project will ask for a little variation in how it is brought into being. Standard practices of site planning are fundamental, but creating spaces of deep meaning out of seemingly nothing requires extra depth in the process. Creativity, however, does not come *from* the individual but *through* the individual; we don't possess creativity as much as we are possessed by it. Sacred geometry as a foundation for urbanism makes space available for symbols and signs to arise in selected locations of cultural, energetic, or geographic significance. How does a designer allow for the spontaneous to emerge from the unconscious?

Not in the design alone but in the process. In a true sense then, designing for a Symbolic Urbanism of psycho/spiritual meaning must intentionally include meditation, what Jung would describe as active imagination (for others this might be identified in some other way such as a shamanic journey), and ritual. The designer of urban space thus begins to play the role of shaman for the community. Some essential steps in the process are described below.

> ***Become Familiar With the Land*** – This includes becoming intimate with the land and its story. Walk the property with a knowledgeable person; walk the property alone and meditate on what is seen and intuited. Conduct deed research and other history of the land, its former owners and uses, as well as whatever history can be gained of the ancient and indigenous stories and traditions associated with the place. Identify features on the land as well as on adjacent properties which might act as significant points of energy and geometry.
>
> ***Perform a Healing Ceremony*** – Ask forgiveness and reclaim lost energy due to past wounds inflicted on both the land itself and previous users/inhabitants.
>
> ***Determine Various Potential Design Approaches*** – Using a preferred combination of intuition, meditation, shamanic journeying, and so forth, explore what aspect of sacred geometry, symbolism, and myth is most appropriate for the basis of the site's design. This is best conducted quietly on a prominent location on the land. What story is asking to be told? Design sources might include the mandorla, seed/flower of life, the golden spiral or ratio, a hexagon, pentagon, triangle, and so forth; an aspect of the zodiac; sacred numbers or ratios (in addition to the golden mean are the silver, bronze, and copper ratios, for instance); or more conventional and accessible sources such as Biblical scripture, Greek mythology, or local indigenous narrative.
>
> ***Develop/Sketch Initial Options*** – Using identified features on the land and any on adjacent properties that may be advantageous (geomorphology, topography, water, wetlands, historic or significant structures, and other existing built features), develop and draw an initial series of options.
>
> ***Spiritual Insight*** – Return to the land to ask Spirit/Unconscious

for input on the chosen approach.

Test the Chosen Pattern – Does the design on paper resonate when experienced on the land itself? Ensure that the emerging geometric trellis is in strong alignment with features on the land as well as those offsite. An excellent method for this is described by Christopher Alexander in his book *The Battle for the Life and Beauty of the Earth*. Using string, stakes, and flags, lay out the site plan on the land to give an initial sense of how the design relates to the land and whether the geometry and symbolism will activate together.

Design Transition – Using the skeletal foundation of sacred geometry, transition to the design and layout of the full site according to the patterns of traditional town planning as understood by New Urbanist conventions. This is the appropriate stage for a charrette if one is to be conducted.

Test the Layout and Pattern – This is a repetition of the previous step, but including the emerging site plan as well as the underlying geometry. Does the design on paper resonate when experienced on the land itself? Ensure that the underlying geometric skeleton and emerging urban pattern are both in strong alignment with features on the land as well as those offsite, and are in harmony with each other. With the design staked out in this manner, once again invite the spirit of the land for any further insight.

Adjustments – Make any refinements and revisions as necessary.

Blessing – Conduct a ritual ceremony of commencement at ground-breaking. This is not unlike the ancient ritualized "topping out" ceremonies conducted on large architectural construction projects such as skyscrapers, or the Roman tradition of the Pomerium.

Implementation at Scales

Symbolic Urbanism can be understood and implemented at every scale, from a large site plan of many acres, to intimate half-block infill. To the extent that symbolic geometry can be tied into and coordinated at various scales, deeper intentions can be developed. For instance, perhaps a larger cultural story is to be built into the site plan, an intention for the specific community embedded in the architecture and arrangement of blocks and lots, while a more intimate personal mythical story is communicated through decorative detail. Let's look at how this can be implemented on various scales.

- *Regional* – At the scale of the region, Symbolic Urbanism remains at its most "symbolic," as it is least able to be experienced or understood visually. At this scale, it functions similarly to certain ancient ley lines in England. These lines connect various natural and man-made features on the landscape across many miles. While many people view them as lines of energetic connection and part of a larger "earth chakra system," no evidence of this is confirmed. The lines do, however, play a symbolic role of connection between significant places; beyond that, they seem to have acted as roads and lines of communication in the ancient past.
- *Site Plan* – At this scale, the possibilities for creating a truly immersive environment are strongest. This is focused on issues such as the arrangement and orientation of streets, paths, and buildings, and creating linkages and connections to outside/off-site community features.
- *Street and Block Layout* – This scale concerns the relationship between structures, street width and profile, building setbacks, dimensions and materials of sidewalks and pathways, staircases, vertical shifts, lot arrangements within the block, etc.
- *Architecture* – Here we look at building proportion and elements (doors, windows, roof slope, etc.). This scale also includes the various elements of landscape design and decisions regarding plantings and greenery, as well as statuary, memorials, and fountain and waterworks design.
- *Decorative Detail* – Here we find possibilities for symbolic and mythical artwork; such as images of symbols, and decorative designs on buildings, street furniture, sidewalks, etc.

On Ritual as an Aspect of Placemaking

The places we build today, and even re-build and renovate, rarely have a deep sense of authenticity. Even new development that intentionally focuses on "place-making" often feel contrived and fake. To a large degree this is due to a lack of history; most development projects seeking to create a "sense of place" are built all at once by large corporate entities. History rarely enters the mix except as a gesture to note its existence.

This lack of a "sense of place" has to do not only with poor design or materials, but a lack of underlying meaning. History, of course, can supply this; when this too is lacking, meaning can sometimes be created even when not received from the past. Meaning can be infused into a place through ritual. Ritual is of course the re-enactment of a myth or symbol.

We have seen examples the use of ritual to infuse memory and meaning into a place in the story of Washington, DC – the foundational ritual of laying the boundary stones, and the corner stones for the Capitol Building, White House, and Washington Monument. Such foundational rituals not only memorialize an event but help create the myth of a place; the foundation of Rome by Romulus where he is purported to have plowed the land around the land that was to become the city is still celebrated 2,500 years later. This intentional creation of meaning is crucial today; there are so many places littering our suburban landscapes with no remaining sense of history. A forlorn place may begin to gain meaning, however; a place can be infused with meaning because we choose it to be so. This is our gift to an otherwise unloved place. Such a ritual is one of forgiveness, healing, and hope for a renewed relationship to the land and to history, and as a legacy for the future.

Healing is a central aspect of ritual. There is a distinction between healing and curing. To cure someone is to bring them back to their earlier level of health prior to a wounding or illness. Healing is much more; it advances the health of the person above and beyond where they were prior to the wounding. With this in mind, we cannot heal the wounds we have inflicted on the earth, only cure them. However, we have the ability to heal the wounds we continue to inflict on our cities and towns, and thus our civilization.

Ancient rituals have not disappeared. One very ancient ritual in the world of placemaking remains the world of construction. Known as "topping out," this ritual is the practice of placing a tree on the highest point of a building when its construction nears completion. There are numerous histories regarding the source of this practice, some going back to ancient Egypt, when a tree was placed atop a pyramid to honor the deaths of construction workers. Such a ceremony was typically intended to appease the gods or spirits of a place after disturbing their land. This practice continues today; fir trees can be spotted atop skyscrapers in larger cities, though perhaps not with quite the same intention to make peace with the spiritual realm.

Another ancient construction ritual can be found in China. Prior to laying the foundation of a house, a priest and feng shui practitioner would be called in to provide ritual protection to the new home. This involved driving a long iron spike into the ground, symbolically nailing the demons of chaos below, preventing them from rising up out of the underworld.

A more ordinary ritual for the beginning of a construction project is the ceremonial groundbreaking celebration, in which various project and community leaders gather to turn the first soil, marking the beginning of work with ritual shovels. Such practices serve to advertise and create interest and excitement for the project, and also to offer thanks to those who made it possible and those who will undertake the construction itself. Both the beginning and end of construction are times for the expression of gratitude and remembrance.

The medieval city was understood by its inhabitants, according to geography professor Keith Lilley, via the role of ritual and procession in civic life. Both local and Christian liturgical celebrations often involved parades and processions, whose routes would include stops at various locations of special significance for ritualized celebration and remembrance.

The Task

There is no political, bureaucratic, or technological salvation for our flawed urbanism without a renewed sense of a larger cultural meaning and purpose. Any effort to create a vision of Symbolic Urbanism must be made in a fairly blunt and obvious fashion; contemporary western culture, particularly here in the US, no longer naturally thinks in terms of mythic symbols. Our educational system has done little to nothing in recent decades regarding the teaching of traditional western culture, its mythology, art, civics, or history in general for that matter. As a result, we have lost touch with the foundations of our own civilization. While myth and symbols emanate from our unconscious and resonate with us naturally, there must be some fairly straightforward effort toward public education in any project founded upon Symbolic Urbanism. This is not a new issue for urban planners; as long ago as 1960, the urbanist Kevin Lynch understood the concern, as he outlined in his book *The Image of the City*: "True enough, we

THE PRACTICE OF SYMBOLIC URBANISM

need an environment that is not simply well organized, but poetic and symbolic as well ... in the development of the image, education in seeing will be quite as important as the reshaping of what is being seen ... *A highly developed art of urban design is linked to the creation of a critical and attentive audience"* [emphasis mine]. In other words, the value of urban design lies at least in part in its ability to teach a lesson.

It is not the role of Symbolic Urbanism to promote any particular new or existing religious, mythological, or political agenda. Its intention is to re-invigorate, expand, communicate, and make more readily available to the general public those stories and myths already developed, creating a setting of receptivity to whatever new mythic vision might present itself to us of its own accord. It is intended to help manifest the ongoing process of psychological awakening and spiritual development that seems to be the fundamental call of humanity throughout the ages. If a new mythic story develops over time, an event of which I have no doubt will come naturally, then a mindset of urbanism will be ready to make supportive space for it.

The designer aspiring to Symbolic Urbanism must therefore possess a wide and deep base of understanding, grounded not only in the techniques of traditional urban design, but steeped in art, poetry, history, psychology, and mythology. The role of the urban planner thus becomes aligned with that of the shaman, a healer of both the land and soul, a bringer of insight and wisdom to the community. This is an enormous task, requiring a range of knowledge very few of us possess today. Our furthest ancestors understood the enormous effort required though; Socrates is credited with the intimidating quote, "By far the greatest and most admirable form of wisdom is that needed to plan and beautify cities and human communities."

The more complex life becomes, the more it seems defined by impermanence. Or rather, its inherent impermanence becomes more obvious. People come into our lives and then leave, jobs come and go, homes are traded for newer places, old ideas, beliefs, and values grow and develop into new perspectives. So too do our places change. A Symbolic Urbanism must honor this while at the same time give a sense of stability and continuity. The value of emphasizing civic space through Symbolic Urbanism as the initial formative skeleton of place-making is the sense of (admittedly relative) permanence it can provide. Civic institutions and activities tend to outlast residential, commercial, and other uses and structures. They emphasize the unified public essence of physical community, while making room for private individual experience.

The role that mythic symbolism has developed over thousands of years is the set of possibilities for human societies and individuals to discover the resolution between chaos and order. It may seem that the goal of Symbolic Urbanism – to develop a foundational role for myth and symbolic geometry in the design of urbanism – involves wildly complex goals that seem completely beyond the conventional realm that cities have played for at least the last several hundred years. The example provided earlier, that of the waking and dreaming experience of the streets of Paris, helps make the possibilities more clear. Creating the experience of movement from dreamscape to awakening and back again is necessary. We need to attend to both sides of that conversation, of soul and ego.

The shift from aesthetic town planning to mere engineered problem-solving can be traced back to the European Baroque period as an aspect of military defense. The resulting city started to become an afterthought, subsumed to the primary needs of defense. This was greatly accelerated under the modernist approach begun under Corbusier. Today, the city itself in the US is subsumed by the needs of cars and their engineered highways. This was no mere metaphorical shift away from the intuitive to the rational, but an intentionally radical unbalancing that must be realigned. This reconciliation of opposites between the soulful and the technical, between the masculine and the feminine, is a larger cultural shift taking place with which the design of cities must engage. The design and management of cities have been the exclusive domain of the "patriarchy" for too long – by that I mean technology, engineering, rational quantitative problem-solving, and finance. We need a fundamental rebalance of values to give equal respect to what the "matriarchy" provides – poetry, art, the whole of the "irrational" world of the unconscious – the two sides of the same spiritual coin that is our embodied life on earth.

This book has traced the intentional inclusion of symbolic geometry in the design on the land, and the evolution of its purposes. Le Notre made use of geometric design at Versailles in order to promote a very specific cosmological and political order, in support of a unified and unambiguous monarchy. L'Enfant made more refined use of the same techniques for a very different political order, that of the dispersed power of participatory American democracy and its moral aspirations. The proposed Symbolic Urbanism described here seeks to make use of sacred geometry and mythical symbolism in service of an even more amorphous vision, that of an unknown spiritual expression that brings together the rational and the irrational, the conscious and the unconscious, the public and private, and the body and the soul.

Symbolic Urbanism, using the tools of sacred geometry and mythological symbolism, seeks to provide an outlet for the psychic contents of our unconscious back into the world so that we can better acknowledge and interact with them. The urban pattern is the canvas upon which this work takes place. Our ancestors operated in this way in their designs upon the landscape; we have the opportunity – the fundamental need – to renew and expand upon this history. We can view the city then not merely as a repository of art, but as an enormous and immersive work of art in itself, doing the work always intended of art – to give expression to the highest aspirations of civilization.

CHAPTER XVII

Sacred Redevelopment:
Testing Symbolic Urbanism

"The creation of the world did not take place once and for all time, but takes place every day" – Samuel Beckett

To paraphrase C.G. Jung, there is no coming to full psychological maturity without a relationship to place. How can we create places that intentionally support this maturation process which he termed "individuation"? Is this even a role for the built environment? We have severely constrained our creativity by giving unyielding primacy to the engineering requirements of traffic and sewer systems and an architecture of machinery; we do not like the results. Perhaps we should expect more from our cities.

Certain places on earth have always given humans a sense of spiritual and energetic power. These are well known to most of us, even working their way into the imagination of pop culture – places like Machu Picchu and Stonehenge, to name just two. Furthermore, some see that they may be connected across the globe by a network of energetic "lei lines," not unlike the chakra system of the human body. These geographic concentrations of energy and their network might be considered the chakra system for Planet Earth. They tend to be found where geologic formations allow for natural energy to become exposed, such as particular rock and crystal formations, fault lines, or volcanoes, wherever the planetary geomagnetic field becomes more directly accessible to us. Since before recorded history, humans have revered these places, erecting monuments and temples, conducting ceremonies, and founding cities. This is alluded to in the quote from G.K. Chesterton: "This … is how cities did grow great. Go back to the darkest roots of civilization, and you will find them knotted around some sacred stone or encircling some sacred well…. [People] did not love Rome because she was great, she was great because [people] loved her."

The question for us today is whether such energetic centers can be created intentionally by us through design, activated by love. Can spiritual energy be gathered together in a place, not through the power of nature, but the intentional and loving human use of geometry and design? In his book *The Battle for the Life and Beauty of the Earth*, Christopher Alexander answers in the affirmative. The process he describes in the design and construction of Eishin, an educational village Tokyo, Japan, resulted in what he describes as a "living being."

The example of L'Enfant's design of Washington, DC gives us an excellent model to draw from as we think about bringing them together and infusing urbanism with a sense of the spiritual. The opportunity rarely arises now, however, to design from a blank slate as L'Enfant was able to do. More important for our time is the effort to heal, renew, and transform the wounds we have inflicted on both natural systems and urban structures. Can the principles used by L'Enfant two hundred years ago help us today in our very different set of issues, including the creation of spiritually energetic centers? Can the mythic symbolism, and geometry L'Enfant used in the design of Washington, DC help us today in the process of urban renewal and suburban sprawl repair? Let's try an experiment.

For about twelve years, during the late 1990s and early 2000s, I served as a member of the Lancaster City Planning Commission in southeastern Pennsylvania, including a couple of terms as chair. During that period, the owners of the regional mall, Park City Center, approached the Commission with a desire to undertake some expansion and exterior improvements. I recall posing the question to the owner's representatives about whether they might consider a full conversion to a walkable town center at some indeterminate point in the future. The conversation went no further, but for years I held onto the idea of reworking the entire mall in some pattern of walkable mixed-use. Years later, after studying L'Enfant's process for Washington, the idea reemerged for me. First, a little background.

Park City Center Mall and Downtown Lancaster

One of the more infamous names in mid-century urbanism and modernist design is Victor Gruen. Few will recognize the man who "invented" the design concept now known as the enclosed suburban shopping mall. In 1965, he was hired to redesign an entire city block of downtown Lancaster, which had been razed in order to create a new office and retail center, in a desperate attempt to make the decaying downtown competitive with growing suburbanization.

The problem was the ribbon-cutting ceremony of the downtown Lancaster Square project took place within months of the opening of Park City Center. Almost immediately, the downtown effort failed. Aside from that terrible timing, fault can be placed at the feet of some terribly bad design decisions – it seems Gruen forgot his own design principles when reworking the downtown block. Market forces played a hand as well.

Today however, the tables have turned. As of the summer of 2021, the retail world of regional indoor shopping malls continues a long and steady implosion. At least 3,800 stores were anticipated to close in 2018, and it is estimated that nationwide, 25% of indoor shopping malls will close by the year 2022, according to an article in *Time* magazine. Our nation is severely oversupplied with shopping; nationwide, the US has about 24 square feet of retail space per person; comparatively, Europe has only 2.5 square feet of retail per person. Despite the enormous upheaval, the shuttering of malls gives an enormous opportunity for a community to reassess and re-form itself. Not all malls are closing by any means, and indications are that Park City Center in Lancaster remains economically viable for the time being. Several of its major tenants, however, are by no means strong. Sears, JCPenney, Foot Locker, Payless Shoes, and GNC, among others, are all anticipated to experience bankruptcy in the next year or two.

An Experiment in Redevelopment

To begin this unpaid experiment in the redesign of Park City Mall, I sought the appropriate geometric pattern to drawn upon for inspiration. Various aspects of sacred geometry present themselves for this purpose: the golden mean, mandorla, pi, the flower of life, and the attendant hexagonal honeycombs. Additionally, development work should always take into account local precedent and tradition. The local precedents appropriate to this locality include the Amish "hex" signs one often sees in the area. These have no real history other than decorative art. Although they occasionally include patterns reflective of sacred geometry, no meaning is ascribed to them by the Amish themselves. However, Lancaster County is known as the "Garden

Spot" famed for its agriculture; while several approaches are possible, it seems appropriate to focus on the geometry of the flower of life and thus the hexagonal pattern of the beehive honeycomb.

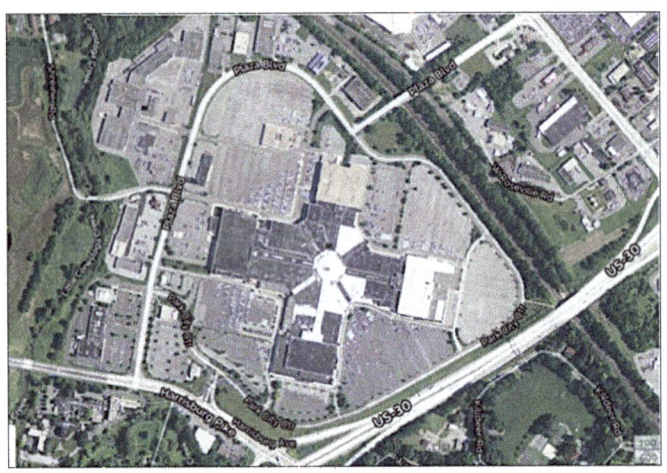

Park City Center Mall, Lancaster, PA

Once this decision was made, I created a series of steps similar to those L'Enfant took, as outlined in *The Sacred Geometry of Washington, DC* by Nicholas Mann. (**Note:** The experiment as I undertook it encompasses land beyond the Park City Mall property, including commercial land across Plaza Boulevard, both within Lancaster City and Manheim Township.)

Step 1: Determine a central point of beginning. The obvious choice was the crossing point of the two existing axes of the shopping mall. The four existing "big box" stores will remain for re-use, while all other built elements on the site may (or may not) be demolished.

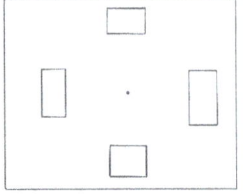

Step 2: Draw a circle 618 feet in diameter. This represents the golden ratio of 1:1.618. This circle roughly arcs through the center of each of the four big box stores.

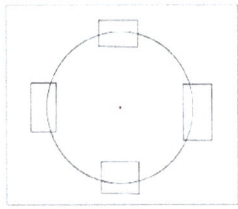

Step 3: Draw a second circle of equal size so that the edge of each touches the center of the other. This creates a football-shaped overlap, known as the vesica piscis, or a mandorla. Psychologically and spiritually, the crossing of two entities, between their centers and edges, speaks to universal connection with others and all of creation. Where the two meet and cross into one another, transformation occurs.

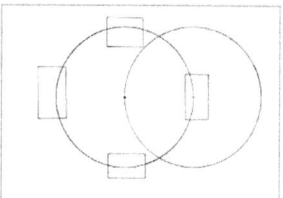

Step 4: Continue drawing such circles until a pattern known as the seed of life emerges. This is a pattern of seven circles, which forms the basis of the flower of life. Some consider the seven circles to represent the seven days of the Biblical creation story.

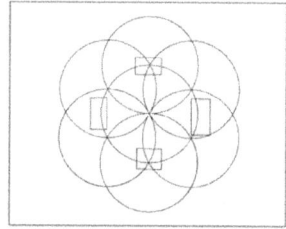

Step 5: Continue the pattern until a field of flowers appears. This larger pattern is known as the flower of life, described earlier as a foundational pattern of universal geometry.

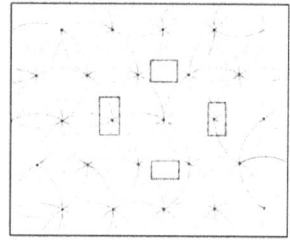

Step 6: Within each flower, a hexagon can be drawn, using the tips of each petal as an angle for the hexagon. Significantly for this project, the initial central hexagon fits amazingly well within the area formed by the four big box stores. Two sides of the hexagon align almost precisely with two building facades, while two angles of the hexagon are located at the approximate center of the other two buildings. This result, an unexpected synchronicity, confirmed to me the appropriateness of this pattern for the redesign of the site, in much the same way L'Enfant must have felt when seeing the circles of his geometry and circles spanning precisely from Capitol Hill to the Anacostia River.

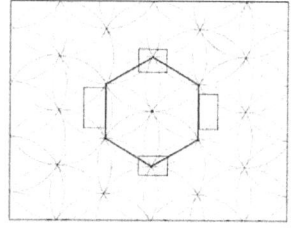

Step 7: Continue drawing hexagons. A beehive pattern emerges. Bees use a hexagonal arrangement in building hives, as this shape is both strong and efficient. As mentioned earlier, Lancaster County, with its strong agricultural heritage, is known as "The Garden Spot," making the beehive an appropriate symbol and pattern for this project. Moreover, each hexagonal cell can be considered as the basis for individual neighborhoods within the town center as a whole.

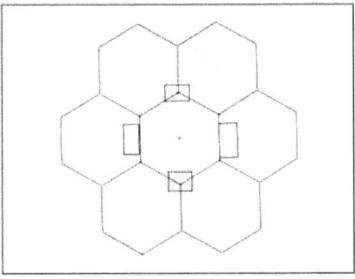

Step 8: The points and intersections of the hexagons and the centers of the flowers, shown here as red dots, are then overlaid on the site. They designate potential locations of significant elements of the design or "points of memory and inspiration," such as squares, fountains, sculptures, monuments and significant buildings, the alignment of streets and pathways, terminated vistas, and prominent sites for civic structures and activities. A skeleton of sacred geometry is now prepared, around which the body of a town center can be laid out. At this point, I transition to fleshing out this skeleton with a set of New Urbanist design and policy tools. These include emphasizing compact pedestrian life, street design, and fine-grained mixed uses.

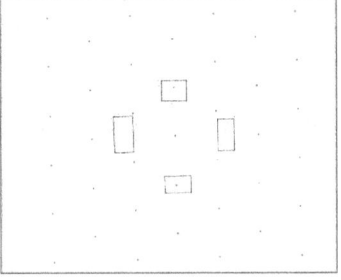

Step 9: The site plan emerges. The street pattern and arrangement of blocks are based upon the location of the geometric points. Some pre-existing elements in addition to the four big box structures are preserved, including the approximate locations of entrances onto the site, and the alignment of the loop road. To the greatest extent possible, visual lines of sight are to be maintained between the points, both for ease of orientation and so

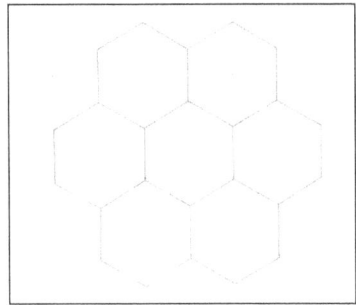

that a sense of an immersive environment can be created; that is, one feels a sense of being in a central place of special significance, surrounded by memory and meaning.

Mixed use projects such as this have long included residential, shopping, and office space. Today, there is a societal shift away from shopping to "acquire things" toward a desire for "experience," adding a new element to the mix, that of entertainment. Yet the inclusion of meaningful cultural and civic life is still almost nonexistent other than parks and open space. Providing a civic heart, places that can evoke meaning and memory, remains the missing amenity. The "points" that the geometry provides are meant to fill that gap; not to promote any particular approach to religion or spirituality, but to express those elements of civilization that find their source there. This comes in the form of celebrating local history and environment, writers, poets, artists, musicians, inventors, etc. These are designated in a number of ways – parks, small fountains, trees, sculptures, monuments, outdoor stages, cultural institutions, etc. – places where we can share our personal and collective stories and create new ones.

The final site plan shown below reveals a full community. This includes a variety of residential types, large and small retail space, offices, artisan workshops, parks and open space, and provisions for civic uses. The four remaining big box outlets are imagined to be reused in the historic mixed-use pattern of classic multi-story arcade buildings such as Westminster Arcade in Providence, RI or The Arcade in Cleveland, OH. Each is topped with green roof gardens, solar electric and hot water generation, and other elements of sustainable technology. Two of the points of meaning and memory are located with these mixed-use arcade buildings.

The central area surrounded by the big boxes – what currently constitutes the indoor mall – is envisioned as a mixed area of small buildings fronting onto intimate pedestrian streets. Examples of such spaces are seen in the images shown here. On the east side of the site, currently a parking field, I envision a small senior living community, patterned after the "begijnhof," a semi-cloistered medieval urban form.

Civic life, as expressed in the various points of memory and meaning, can be found in a number of ways in this plan. They are included both as larger places of public gathering and more quiet spots of private reflection.

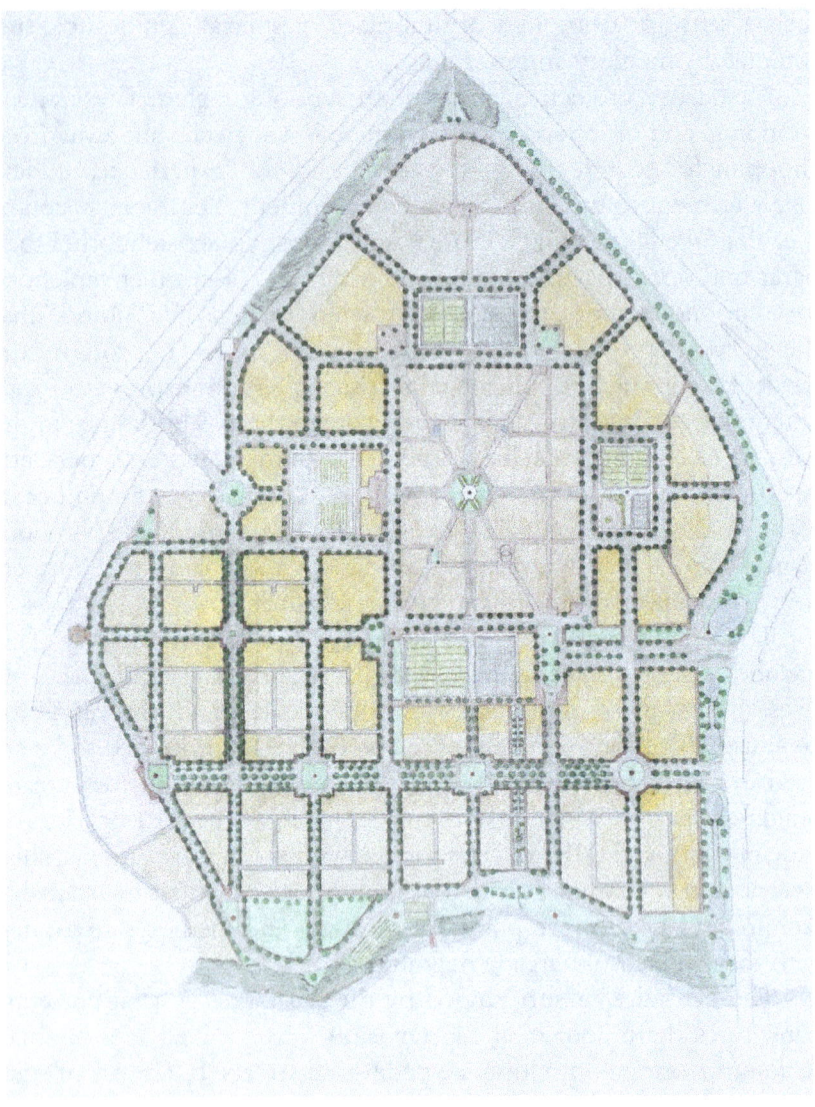

Final site plan for an experimental redevelopment of Park City Center Shopping Center, Lancaster, PA, making use of a process of "symbolic urbanism" to create a mixed-use walkable neighborhood.

There are twenty-three such points on the plan. What might they look like? A few examples include:

- A central tower and plaza placed at the center of the first circle. It constitutes the heart of the community, and functions as the central gathering place and main focal point for the community.
- Two of the points are located within the interior of the reconfigured big box arcades. These might take the form of a sculpture or fountain.
- A children's outdoor stage, similar to the one in the Habersham TND, which might be located in the riverfront linear park.
- The entrance to a community garden, located within the linear park along the Little Conestoga Creek, visible as a terminated vista at the T-intersection of a street children's outdoor stage, which might be located in the riverfront linear park.
- The series of squares along the main boulevard, reminiscent of the various squares of Savannah.
- The northernmost point terminates a street and lies adjacent to the railroad tracks. It might be configured as a water park similar to that found in downtown Lancaster's Steinman Park.
- A point may consist of something as simple as a small sculpture along the sidewalk, perhaps dedicated to a local artist or musician: for this example in Lancaster, Charles Demuth would be appropriate.

While many projects include such features, they are often afterthoughts. Even when quite well done, they may not add up to something greater. This experiment seeks to make these civic elements the primary "skeleton" around which the community is structured. Using sacred geometry to form the urban pattern, as well as to experience the place as a pedestrian, is like the way in which the drawing of a mandala, or walking a labyrinth, acts as a form of reflection and meditation. This not only grounds the place as significant and meaningful in people's everyday lives, but can add value to properties nearby or fronting onto them. It creates places in which people – residents, workers, and shoppers – want to linger. The practical and the aspirational are both enhanced.

The estimated uses for the entire project include:

Residential: 1,500 units (townhouses, condominiums, apartments, retirement "begijnhof")
Commercial: 1,400,000 square feet (retail, office, dining, artisan)
Open Space: 20 acres (parks, gardens, playgrounds, plazas)
Parking: 7,400 spaces (on-street, structured, underground)

Creating lovable places of meaning and memory is the goal, but such a huge undertaking has to be financially viable to the developer. How does this effort fare financially for the property owners and to the city fiscally? A full-blown financial pro forma is beyond the scope of this little experiment, but a quick comparison of appraised value with the properties in the Downtown Investment District (DID), which is approximately of equal size, can give some indication. Park City Center is assessed at $1,602,062 per acre. Properties within the Lancaster DID are assessed at $2,826,373 per acre. The fine-grained, mixed-use pedestrian pattern seen in the DID holds 76% more assessed value than the suburban model of Park City Center on a per-acre basis. Thus, while the costs associated with demolition and redevelopment are enormous, when done incrementally over time, the effort appears very worthwhile.

This plan and its process were presented to the mall owners' on-site management team, Brookfield Properties, in the summer of 2019. While the response was generally positive, this design would involve such an enormous and costly effort that Brookfield was clear that the only way forward is a phased renovation over several years, rather than an all-at-once effort. Even with the increasing number of anchor tenant bankruptcies and vacant storefronts, the mall still creates enough cash flow to warrant continued use for the time being. Lancaster city leadership and county staff were informed of the experimental effort as well. At this writing, Brookfield has approached the City of Lancaster with a request for demolition of one of the empty big box stores, with the intent of developing a series of stand-alone structures. The transition to an unknown future is underway.

CHAPTER XVIII
Back to School

"The future is already here, it's just not evenly distributed"
– William Gibson

In writing this book, I wanted to bring together two threads of my biography. The first thread comes from my professional life, where I'm a New Urbanist land planning consultant and a thirty-year member of the Congress for the New Urbanism. The second thread comes from my personal life, where I'm a life-long spiritual seeker deeply influenced by the traditions of the Episcopal and Mennonite churches, the world of shamanic healing, and Jungian psychology. In bringing these together, I am an evangelical for increasing the spiritual potency of cities. At times I know I've come across as a preacher, but in my more tempered moments, I hope I've come across as a teacher. City life has taught me so much; the city has been my classroom, and I'm also a life-long student. This book compiles everything I've learned from cities, about cities, and I offer it to you, hopefully as a soulful textbook that you can learn from as well. So in this chapter, let's go "back to school." Allow me to summarize the salient points of this book, a conclusion of sorts before the concluding chapter that follows, which offers ways to put these ideas into action.

There are two fundamental assumptions driving this book. First, that the essential task of humanity throughout all of time and cultures is that of spiritual quest. This has both a personal and collective aspect, and is evolutionary in nature; that is, over the centuries, humanity awakens to greater and larger insight. The second assumption is that the built environment has a basic role to play in that process, that the shape and design of our cities and towns can and should support this quest. As spirits embodied in the physical realm, we are blessed with the opportunity to discover the eternal through our experience of the temporal.

As spiritual students, our school is the physical world, and we build cities as repositories of the lessons we have learned. Obviously then, cities can function as sources of spiritual and psychic inspiration just as green nature can – as they have in the past – because they *are* part of nature.

Yet both our spiritual "curriculum" and our urban "classrooms" have become inadequate to the tasks of today and tomorrow. Infusing the design and redevelopment of urban places with meaning and purpose is a critical need. We must no longer simply provide the right elements of community, but put those elements in relation to one another in a *meaningful pattern*. Myth, symbol, and the geometry of metaphor can provide this. In his research and writing, Jung described the context and need; L'Enfant provided us a method and example, with his design of Washington, DC.

The Buddhist teacher Michael Stone has said that when we look at the physical world, all we find are relationships. My sense, too, is that most life lessons have to do with relationship: how to build them, maintain them, repair them. These relationships are not only those of one individual to another, but the individual to the group, and to the environment – including the built environment of the city. Being surrounded by such lessons regarding relationship means that we are all students and by implication, teachers for one another. Life on earth is then for us like attending school. But as any parent today will confirm, the state of our schools is in deep disarray; what repairs are needed for the benefit of our children, regarding both infrastructure and curriculum, is a never-ending controversy.

One of those lessons of relationship involves relationship to the Creator, in whatever manner one conceives of that. In his collected letters, Jung wrote that the real history of the world seems to be the progressive incarnation of the deity. This evolutionary process involves not only our personal spiritual lives but societal institutions and values – again, by implication, the physical places we build. To play its appropriate role in this, our vision of what a city ought to be must also expand. The psychotherapist Keith Hackwood confirms this in his review of philosopher Peter Kingsley's *Catafalque*: "It is plainly the case that certain creations, certain acts of expression, certain bestowals of gift, can only occur in certain *places* and that place itself and the loss of its uniqueness of speech, represents the ground-zero and master symptom of our current devastation." To build a city is to encompass both actually and metaphorically the center of the known and secure world, as opposed to the unknown and threatening world. That is the point at which heaven and earth meet.

The Inadequacy of Sustainability

Climate change and all its associated dangers, disruptions, and losses presents a growing existential threat which must be faced seriously and immediately. This is particularly urgent as an aspect of how we design, and redesign, the places we inhabit. Despite the urgency of climate change, though, there is an equally desperate need for a renewed sense of meaning and purpose in the life of our civilization. Indeed, I would even say that the deepest cause of the negative impact humans have on climate and the environment generally is not related to bad technology, but the lack of embodied values that can direct both the culturally agreed-upon use of technology and the application of policies, and ultimately, the choices of one's personal life habits.

We cannot find technical solutions to non-technical problems of morals and values. Science and technology can describe a situation and present options but cannot themselves determine which solution is most appropriate; that is the role of values and belief systems. The sustainability movement too often tends to seek out technical solutions for the maintenance of a particular standard of living and cultural habits. The question resides, however, in the underlying assumption regarding what we value as worthy of our attention. Sustainability seems to be merely a tool to maintain a lifestyle of convenience, entertainment, and financial gain. As such, it tends to smack of desperation. A more true and lasting approach to urban and environmental sustainability is rooted not in more sustainable technology but in a system of underlying sustainable values and beliefs that can guide our decisions and patterns of living.

Much of life revolves around finding solutions to the myriad problems of mere existence. It has been said that we should never seek the solution of just one problem at a time. Instead, we should seek out an approach to resolve the largest set of problems possible. Solutions that address a multitude of troubles simultaneously tend to have a greater positive, long-lasting impact. Equally, we should never consider ourselves as a "consumer" or a "user" of some product or service, or any such limiting description. At a minimum, we should consider ourselves as citizens of our community and nation. Beyond this, we can know ourselves as including family, community, our local planet earth, and the universe. Taking this perspective into daily awareness is the fundamental shift required of us. Not simply taking on a more sustainable lifestyle, but a new understanding of who we are, of *what* we are, in relation to the largest whole that we can imagine.

Love and Imagination as Practical Values

We cannot "save the planet" from ourselves, nor truly heal anything really, without forging an emotional bond of love. As the biologist Stephen Jay Gould reminds us, we do not fight to save something we do not love. We understand this regarding human relations easily enough. Without love, sustainability and even the process of urban placemaking lose their essence and become a mere mechanical effort of survival. We ought to seek to flourish, not merely survive; the two are not mutually exclusive.

Regarding the design of place, love and imagination provide us with far more motivation and meaning, and in a way that neither a balanced spreadsheet nor more sustainable systems, and certainly the city as entertainment, can conceive of. The most brilliant of scientists, Einstein, reminds us that imagination is more important than knowledge. Everything starts from imagination; working out the details may be a rational, left-brain process, but imagination is the foundation.

Humans have a deep-seated urge to know, understand, and experience the world. There is equally in us a desire for meaning. The discovery and understanding of meaning is unique for each of us. Note that this is distinct from happiness. Happiness comes and goes – it is not a steady-state, nor ought it constitute a primary goal. Rather it is a by-product of a well-balanced relationship between one's ego and higher Self. This meaning can be discovered, as the Jungian psychologist James Hollis puts it, not only from seeking it out but by asking, what is seeking after me? When we seek that out and respond to it, we discover our "why," and to paraphrase Nietzsche, when we acquire a "why" for our lives, we can manage any situation, bear any burden.

Through all of human history, the source of that "why" has consistently been found in works of myth and symbol. Learning our personal and collective history is essential therefore, and yet insufficient. "I've always preferred mythology to history," said French poet and novelist Jean Cocteau. History is truth that becomes illusion, mythology is an illusion that becomes truth." And from the Roman statesman Cicero: "To be ignorant of what occurred before you were born is to remain always a child."

Love and imagination are normally seen as opposed to rationality and logic. Yet they are better understood as complementary polarities, not conflicting opposites. Perhaps the mistake is assuming that order is superior to chaos. They are both manifestations of the same reality and so ought to be valued equally. They can and very often do, however, become unbalanced. Our task is to mediate between them; the physical structure of our brains takes this into account.

No combination of guilt, economics, or scientific evidence will ever change attitudes. Beauty, however, can motivate us because it speaks to love. Beauty, in all its various definitions, has immense value. We can accept this economically by the fact that we are willing to pay for it. More deeply, its value is found in its role as a doorway to the divine. Consider the great cathedrals of medieval Europe, each of which took many decades and multiple generations to build. Enormous financial and organizational resources were concentrated in these awe-inspiring places of spiritual learning. Now and for the future, the whole of a city needs to take on this role of psychic education.

The infusion of meaning in the places we build, through the foundational use of myth and symbol, can be transformative. Symbolic Urbanism as described previously therefore *is* an appropriate response to the urgency of climate change and the re-making of suburban sprawl. Otherwise, our place-making may function merely as a panicked response to an existential crisis, not as an aspect of a larger vision which can last through the coming centuries.

Urbanism as a Tool for Expanding Spiritual Horizons

As I've said numerous times before, we are spirits embodied in the physical realm, here to discover the eternal through our experience of the temporal. This is an evolutionary process of gradual awakening, with various steps or stages involved. As purely instinctual animals deep in our evolutionary past, we acted before we understood why. We then began to create images or symbols which represented those actions. We next began to tell stories about those actions. Only after that did we become aware of the meanings and deeper purposes behind those actions, and only poorly at first. Over the millennia, we began to understand, little by little, what we had experienced. This is the process of coming out of darkness and into the light of conscious awareness. We still, after all these thousands of years, see through a glass darkly.

We have only very recently begun to see the evolution of our species biologically and how that primordial history has acted as a foundation for myth and the narrative of religion. We can now also see the evolution of myth and religion over thousands of years, and how stories build on the past and evolve in their attempt to explain the world and how to act in it. From the early creation stories of the Mesopotamians, to those of the Egyptians, to the Israelites who grew out of their experience during enslavement under those, and then on to the Christian narrative, history reveals a desire to understand our place in the world. Each of these acted as a foundation and teacher for the next, more integrated mythic story of spiritual development. Each new narrative has not so much displaced the previous but incorporated its wisdom and transcended it by providing a larger vision, usually by transcending boundaries of culture. Jung saw the string extending further back into deepest prehistory, and then forward, to include the Gnostics and eventually the alchemists whom he saw as the culmination of the Christian tradition. Thus, what we can anticipate in future generations is not an end to the Christian tradition so much as its transformation and extension into an ever-larger vision with a wholly new yet familiar myth that echoes all the previous – an update not simply in the content of the story but in the language and metaphor.

With all that in mind, how ought our understanding of what a city can provide evolve? Should we ask more of a city than before? Should we ask that it provide not merely shelter and efficient commerce and entertainment, but act as the repository of our highest insights, to assist us in the quest to discover those callings and aspirations, both public and private, and to be designed expressly for that purpose? We are filled with information and knowledge in our unconscious and our souls of which we are not even aware. Our intentional design of cities can be of enormous assistance in bringing this embedded knowledge into the open. Given Jung's understanding of individuation, that our highest calling is the growth and development of our soul, the immersive city of intention can and ought to be an enormous support.

As various mythic traditions tell us, the original sin was to become conscious. This is the Greek story of Prometheus, who stole fire from the gods and gave it to humans; the Mesopotamian drama of Tiamat and Apsu; and most familiar to us, that of Adam and Eve in the Garden of Eden. We have been struggling to manage this horrible gift, which none of us would ever choose to do without, ever since. The subsequent sin is now its opposite; to remain not fully and completely conscious, to remain semi-awake, or even to desire to return to the unconscious womb. We shouldn't have become conscious in the first place, many would say; it is a huge burden of responsibility that we have never been able to live up to. Better to have remained in our pure animal nature, acting purely on instinct, without any conscious intentionality. But the creator of consciousness seems to have wanted it. It is our assigned task to become ever more consciously aware as a service to "the gods." Once awakened, being half-awake is worse. We remain subject to our animal instinct but with no understanding or control, or rather to misunderstand and act out of an inaccurate vision. All in or not at all; there is no stopping or turning back. To a large degree, the task seems to be the integration of opposites; that is, how to deal with and accept both darkness as well as light, good as well as evil, rationality as well as intuition. We appropriately seek out religion in that process, to provide comfort and security. But a spiritual path is precisely *not* secure; it is filled with discomfort and uncertainty. Both have a place in our personal and cultural development, and urbanism provides the setting for each.

For the urbanist and designer of place, a particular responsibility emerges from this. The places we build reflect the values we hold. If we anticipate a continuing evolutionary growth in our consciousness, our conception of urbanism must develop as well. The places we inhabit must be so much more than technically competent and bureaucratically efficient. These are the places which ought to challenge us to rise to our highest visions. From their earliest inception, cities have acted as the physical embodiment of these visions. But for too long, our rationality and analytical science have taught us to look down, reducing our horizons and vision.

As embodied spirits/students, the physical world is our school. We build cities as repositories of the lessons we have learned. The zodiac was developed thousands of years ago as a memory aid, a library filing system where stories and information could be kept available. The zodiac is a collection of symbolic stories by which cultural and spiritual values were maintained. As the centuries have marched on, we have collected many more stories, which we can embed in the physical design of the places we build, as did our ancestors to a greater or lesser extent. One of the enduring tasks of a city is the discovery, creation, storage, and dissemination of our accumulated knowledge.

We are foragers, as psychologist Jordan Peterson reminds us, and have been for most of our evolutionary history. This we share with other species, to forage for food in order to survive, but what distinguishes us is what we forage for. We are foragers not simply for food but for information, which allows us not merely to survive at the moment but to flourish over time by planning for the future. The city, with its vast resources and connections, makes this infinitely more possible, the internet notwithstanding. The city can thus not only contain a library but becomes itself an enormous library and classroom. Walking the streets is akin to browsing all the aisles and bookshelves, filled with cultural and spiritual knowledge. Any space can become sacred, depending on what the visitor carries with them. But space itself can provoke or remind the visitor if designed to do so, if it's shelves have been stocked with the correct books, so to speak.

Since many westerners have given up on traditional mythology and the Christian story, they look to the eastern traditions, particularly Buddhism, as a substitute. But the essential teachings of Judeo-Christian heritage are too deeply embedded, down into our cultural DNA, to walk away from (nor is there really any need to). The coming age may very well focus on the reconciliation/assimilation of opposites. Politics goes only so far, not nearly deeply enough, and cannot supply a viable alternative. The biggest limitation to a developing civilization is the psychological makeup of its individuals. Religious institutions like the church were attempts to psychologically develop the population on a mass scale toward ever-greater psychic maturity. To the extent such institutions fail, it's because they are by their very nature susceptible to being hijacked by the darkest side of our individual natures. In other words, it's not religion that fails us, it's the religious.

We live through story and narrative. We understand the world not merely as a set of discreet objects, but in how we relate to those objects; those objects making up the world are characters in a story and so are we. How do we interact with all we see and experience in the world? What role does this thing, this place, this person, play in my life, and me in theirs? Can we build such questions into a city physically, intentionally? Our ancestors had that ability, and our task is to understand how they did so and make use of it. We must understand the past in order to gain a sense of who we are today, and what we need to create for the future.

A city built only for the purposes of efficiency, security, commerce entertainment, or even happiness will not reach its potential; though these are crucial aspects, they can easily devolve into mere distraction. Much of what passes for urban "placemaking" today revolves around the "Disneyfication" of downtown; witness Times Square in New York City. The design of a deeper urbanism can provoke us to create meaning and purpose, individually and culturally. Entertainment is a distraction for when we have lost a sense of meaning and purpose. As Victor Frankl phrases it, "When a person cannot find a deep sense of meaning, they distract themselves with pleasure." Our culture has reached that point.

The process of psychological growth involves having our self-conceptions and assumptions shattered, so that we can examine the pieces and re-assemble ourselves into a more expansive and intentional Self. We must understand the parts, in other words, in order to approach the Whole. Civilizations throughout history go through that same process. The experience of this shattering and reformation of culture has taken place over the last several hundred years as the rationality of science and technology have come to dominate. We can think of science and technology as a process of the destructive shattering of our unified spiritual sense of the world in order to understand the parts. It has been painful and dangerous, even deeply harmful in numerous ways – the ecological damage we have learned to cause is evidence enough of that. Yet in this way, too, our understanding of reality is expanded. The task collectively is like that of the individual; to weave together the teachings of both spirit and matter, science and soul, into a unified vision. Almost every effort to improve the world begins and ends with a desire to change the thinking, habits, and behaviors of other people. Regard with suspicion any approach at "saving the world" unless it is accompanied by an equal or greater effort to change oneself.

Infusing the design and redevelopment of urban places with meaning is therefore a critical need. When we love and care for a place – just as for a person – we will care for its context and wider setting as well. The natural environment is the context for urbanism. Thus, the repair and healing of urban places is a vital aspect of our care for the earth. In this, the human body is analogous to the city; it is never truly completely "healthy" – there is always some small nick, some infection, some system in need of repair. Urban places too are always going through some process of repair and renovation, and thus are incomplete and in the process of healing. The healing of urbanism requires a renewed infusion of meaning and purpose.

Cities only emerged in the past few thousand years as a manifestation of the rise of complex patriarchal systems. If cities are an embodiment of created order brought forth out of the dangerous unknowns of nature, what form might they need to take on in order to appropriately reflect a new merging of patriarchy and matriarchy?

The design of a city or town involves not simply providing the right parts, but structuring those parts in relation to one another in a meaningful pattern. Geometry, myth, and symbol provide this. Man-made places, such as Stonehenge for instance, often contain meaning and spiritual power because of their location in nature (topography, underlying geology, the presence of water or cave, etc.) but also their power is intentionally created or enhanced through spiritually inspired design. The Dutch sociologist Peter Nas of the University of Leiden has done fascinating research on the ways in which symbolism has been used in cities around the world, described in his book *Cities Full of Symbols*. We can read the city through its symbols in the same manner the medieval world could read stories embedded in church architecture and the Stations of the Cross as inspirational and educational images. The use of symbols in this way is deeply embedded in our unconscious, and they cannot be ignored. We as individuals can even think of ourselves as symbols; the expression of our soul too complex for words. The role of urbanism is to set the stage upon which we act out that evolving mystery. In the setting and furnishing of the stage, the city can also provide something of the script or narrative, like the prompter in a play, reminding us of the story and our roles. Symbolic Urbanism, using the tools of sacred geometry and mythological symbolism, seeks to give voice to the psychic contents into the world so that we can interact with them. The urban pattern is the canvas upon which this work takes place.

The experience we have of urbanism, whether grand city or small town, is largely dependent upon the inner life we bring to the moment. In turn though, urban form and its program impact our inner world.

The two build upon one another. Both benefit when the design of place, and the individual life, are approached with intentionality.

The human brain is the most complex structure in the universe, so far as we know. It represents the highest concentration of consciousness, both intellectual and of spiritual or psychic energy, in the physical universe. A city is the highest concentration of humans, with all their individual and collective aspirations, hopes and weaknesses. What are the implications of this? Our strongest motivations rise from the unconscious, which makes up the vast majority of our being. How do we find out what the unconscious wants? Through images seen in dreams, symbols, visions, and recurring patterns in the stories of mythology and religion over thousands of years. When a city is designed as an immersive environment intended to promote the conversation between ego and soul, we can align ourselves with our larger intentions and manifest these aspirations more fully. "Formlessness seems to be practically the equivalent of unconsciousness," as Jung reminds us. Giving form to our physical environment is thus an essential aspect of coming to consciousness.

Apocalyptic Christianity and New Age thinking aside, we are without doubt entering a new era. Aquarius is slowly emerging, the water-bearer. The coming of this water symbol in the zodiac above coincides with sea level rise, both of which threaten to wash away so much of what we have built over the past centuries, both physically and metaphorically. Water traditionally symbolizes the mysterious and dangerous depths of the human soul. These two together, the metaphorical Aquarius and the existential threat of inundation by rising seawater, comprise a call to us for deeper reflection and new direction. In response to this, I see two new and essential roles for urbanism: to intentionally act as the physical structure in support of private, individual spiritual or psychological growth; and to also act as the physical infrastructure supporting a new and as-yet unformed spiritual cosmology which may act as the foundation of some future cultural myth of expanded and more balanced inclusiveness.

Such an urban design is much like the medieval process of alchemy. The intention of alchemy is not only the redemption and healing of the individual but the release of God, or spirit, from imprisonment in matter. The transformation of matter – the city – and the transformation of soul are equivalent. In this process we are being used as vessels by psychic forces far larger than we, as tools of conscious experience and growth. We have no choice but to rise to the challenge.

"The task of city design involves the vaster task of rebuilding civilization," as we are taught by Louis Mumford in his work *The Culture of Cities*. I would refine the task, that of building a new civilization aligned with the intentions of Spirit – in whatever form or vision we holds of it.

Three Tasks of Life

The angel Damiel, the central character in the wonderful 1987 movie *Wings of Desire*, gives us a sense of the enormous gift of incarnation. Bored from his angelic duty of merely witnessing the lives of the humans around him while roaming the streets of Berlin, he becomes despondent because he cannot participate. He tires of knowing everything yet doing nothing. He aches to *not* know, but to wonder and then discover; to taste blood, to experience the emotions of love and joy, loss, and fear. He asks for and is granted the gift of becoming mortal, and his adventures begin.

Like Damiel, we function in this world as temporarily embodied spirits. This incarnation into physicality is not random or accidental, I am convinced, but intentional, with various tasks and lessons we are to take on. What these tasks are must be discovered by each of us. For our part, this is the process of awakening into ever-greater consciousness, an enormous and difficult responsibility. As far as I can tell, our various tasks in this process fall into three general categories.

The first is our own personal private process of psychospiritual growth and development. This is our primary task and responsibility. It takes any number of forms and may not look overtly "spiritual" at all. It can be prayer and meditation, or the making of art, but it also includes the care and feeding of others, research into the deep workings of biochemistry, the simple act of conversation with others, maintaining the work of our ancestors as custodians, etc. Growth occurs wherever we apply ourselves, even though we may not be aware of it. Jung described life as having two parts. The first half of life is normally devoted to developing a healthy ego, so that we can contribute positively to the maintenance of society and the benefit of others. In the second half, whenever it appears, we learn how to shed the primacy of the ego in an appropriate manner, so that we can begin to rise beyond the limitations of society.

The second task is assisting and supporting others in their project of personal development. This can include so many different elements of daily life – to teach, to heal, to support, to simply witness, and to play various personal and archetypal roles for each other. From feeding the homeless to entertaining children to planting a flower garden, to volunteering for some community or political role, or to smiling to the stranger on the sidewalk, we all contribute to each other in countless unexpected and unnoticed ways. Even those interactions which we find unpleasant – arguments and fights, disagreements, confrontations – have their role to play in supporting the growth of another.

The third task is creating and maintaining some level of civil order and social structure. This establishes the ongoing stable foundation and context upon which our personal work takes place and is a highly complex task. The creation of order involves more than keeping the lights on and making sure the trains run on time. It can easily, and regularly does, veer off into oppressive regulation and misguided policy. Social justice and equity are never-ending goals. Their achievement requires constant re-evaluation as circumstance changes and insight develops. The choices and connections that our civilization provides us with certainly give us freedom, but is there something more important than freedom? If anything, it is perhaps this; what we choose to do with our freedom. Each freedom assumes a corresponding responsibility.

This balancing act of order and chaos brings us into the realm of politics. Participation in democracy then arises as a spiritual act – not in seeking any particular religious or political agenda along the spectrum of left and right, but the informed participation in the process itself, for the care and nurture of each other.

A well-functioning democracy requires an enormous amount of private self-reflection and public participation from its citizens. We cannot merely sit back and enjoy the benefits of the freedoms that democracy can provide; democracy demands informed participation, and fundamentally, that participation requires at its base the intentional effort of self-improvement. Could we therefore say that citizenship is a sort of spiritual undertaking, and democracy with its socially connective tissue, is reflective of a religious undertaking?

While this detour into the realm of politics may seem inappropriate for a book such as this, it must be given at least some minimal attention if a psychologically healthier urbanism is to be considered.

After all, what could be more political than a city?! Here is the connecting string that I see: Myth tells the story of humans awakening to both the world around them and their inner life, from unconscious instinct to conscious awareness. Religion formalizes mythic stories into ritual and culturally organized shared beliefs. Politics then operationalizes the values developed in those beliefs into civic life and mediates the inevitable conflicts. With that in mind, I offer the following five possible elements of successful future democracies: 1. Wide and deep understanding by its citizens of its methods, structures, and processes; 2. Life-long psychological education of self-reflection, self-knowledge, and self-improvement; 3. Empathy for the Other, those unlike oneself; 4. Willingness to compromise and change; 5. Acceptance of connection to something transcendent, beyond the authority of the state.

The introduction of religion and politics to one another is not in any way a part of the American tradition, for a long list of valid reasons including our commitment to the separation of church and state. Yet some sort of neutral territory of mutual acceptance seems necessary. The author Toni Morrison has described herself not as a spiritual person but as "non-secular." Perhaps we can begin to have a vision of a "non-secular" role for the civic commons.

Urban settings, from country hamlet to megalopolis, support these three tasks in ways the natural world cannot. We find both the setting and the tools in urbanism because we are a fundamentally social species. Spiritual development may be a personal journey but by no means is it an isolated one. We are connected to one another with both visible and invisible ties. We act out of evolved instinct just as other species; but we also act out of intention.

Though a social species, our experience of physical incarnation subjects us to a profound fragmentation which cannot be undone. We will experience wholeness on the other side of the veil. Incarnated life is the intentional, or at least unavoidable, experience of limitation and brokenness. All these tasks of humanity are to discover eternal truth by the experience of temporal life. Learning how to repair broken connections is a fundamental and essential lesson of life. Life together in all our urban patterns is the place, and the method we use to work it out.

Faust and His City

One of the great treasures of western literature is Goethe's rich work, *Faust*. The story of Faust goes back much further than Goethe though; the theme of selling one's soul to the devil is an ancient one. Goethe was writing during the late 1700s and early 1800s at a time of rapid decline in faith and religion amidst the rise of science and technology. It seems what Faust did in selling his soul to the devil was to transfer his trust from a vision of spirit to the rational mind of science and technology as his source of salvation. The story of Faust is a critique of this shift of western values.

Part Two of Faust was published in 1832, more than two decades after Part One, and it contains the story that concerns us here. In his adventures with the devil Mephistopheles, Faust is gifted a vast tract of land along the seaside. It is Faust's great desire to build a city, a powerful metropolis. In fact, the land upon which he builds is actually land reclaimed from the sea, which has been pushed back into the far distance. The city is isolated from the sea except for a canal which extends from the harbor to Faust's palace; it is used for pirate ships to bring gold and treasure to Faust.

And yet even with the fulfillment of his desires, he's still deeply unsatisfied. There remains on his land a small hut and temple, the home of the elderly couple Baucis and Philemon, who will not leave. They had been granted their home years earlier by the gods Zeus and Hermes in return for the kind hospitality the couple provided. This frustrates Faust enormously, and he seeks some way of removing them. Plans go awry and the couple are accidently killed. This too angers Faust, who nonetheless heartlessly begins yet another urban development project, which turns out to be the death of him. What he thought was the sound of new wall foundations being constructed was the sound of shovels digging his grave.

It is generally understood that this story in the Faust saga recounts man's desire to control the world through rational means of technology, science, and engineering. Goethe perceived western civilization as having given up on its spiritual foundations, represented by the sea (metaphorically, the unconscious), seeking to rely solely on the conscious ego with all its misguided desires. While the conscious ego arises out of the unconscious (the land Faust reclaimed from the sea), it cannot do without a humble submission to and respect for its source. Faust kept only one small and utterly practical relationship to the sea, the canal used to bring stolen wealth to his urban palace.

What are we urbanists to make of such a story? We can understand the story partially as a critique of the arrogant short-sightedness of the contemporary American cultural experiment with a lifestyle of suburban sprawl. A healthy civilization and its cities must maintain connection to the sea of the unconscious soul, to include it as a partner; and too, not seek to destroy the humanity of kindness and natural relationship as represented by Baucis and Philemon. Perhaps we can instead begin to imagine a city full of metaphorical canals reaching out to the soul of the sea, filled with temples of welcome and relationship.

The Urbanist as Alchemist and Shaman

Western society has become almost completely disconnected from itself, its own foundational history and traditions. An entire civilization has experienced a loss of soul in its choice to replace its spiritual traditions with a new rational, quantitative, and scientific mindset. With the loss of respect for and trust in religion over the past 300 years, our increasingly secular and technocratic civilization relies less on traditional religious leaders and more on poets, musicians, novelists, and artists to communicate the transcendent to society.

I suggest the urban designer be added to that faculty of teachers and seers.

Whenever a culturally approved religion loses its authority, it becomes reviled. Christianity has lost its potency, partially, because it claims to be based on history rather than myth. Whatever cosmological myth eventually takes the place of Christianity will find a way to base itself not only on history, but a balanced vision of history, myth, science, and the personal, individual psyche. From my perspective, a Jungian approach seems to provide the best model for this. Our urbanism too has lost its potency because of its unbalanced reliance on technical engineering and bureaucratic rulemaking. To the earliest pioneers of city life, what they created was enormously inspiring – just like the transition to agriculture was for their ancestors. At one point, the building of a city was revered as reflective of some heavenly form. But after several thousand years, we have come to take things for granted, no longer impressed with such an amazing feat as the creation of a city. Placemaking must regain this, reintegrating a sense of artistic and spiritual aspiration into its vision.

History is filled with advanced spiritual practitioners who reached higher levels of awareness and insight via "abstention from the dirt." But must this be the only way? A Jungian approach includes working with the darkness, not avoiding it, just as this sort of spiritual familiarity with the dark side is fundamental to the ways of the traditional shaman. The city is as "dirty" as life in this world gets. If there is *any* spiritual intention in our incarnation as evolving containers of soul in this physical world, then our goal cannot be to ignore, avoid, or deny the settings in which we find ourselves. We must therefore learn to experience "dirty" urbanism – not only "pure" nature – as sacred space. As the Zen teacher Alan Watts reminds us, "If you can't meditate in a hot noisy boiler room, you don't know how to meditate."

We might think of two approaches to this new role of the urbanist as teacher and healer. As individuals on a personal journey of inward growth and exploration, we can experience the city as an alchemical laboratory, a place of private discovery of our own inner life. In a public and professional role of designer and advocate, the urbanist takes on the role of shaman, bringing together wisdom and esoteric knowledge to the design of place for the healing of both the community of people and the specific physical place.

The built environment becomes the objective place in which we manifest the subjective. That manifestation is a new vision of a deeper "non-secular" civic commons. After all, the places we build reflect the values we hold.

CHAPTER XIX

Attitudes and Actions

"A city must be a place where groups of women and men are seeking and developing the highest things they know" – Margaret Meade

Few people, I imagine, will understand the experience of urban life as an opportunity for spiritual growth and exploration, the very argument I've been making in this book. My hope has been to offer some ideas and insights that will stir my readers' imaginations and inspire their actions, because ideas are only valuable if they are translated into action. Below are some suggestions for putting into action those inspirations that might be found in the preceding pages.

For You the Individual

Almost every effort to improve the world begins and ends with changing the thinking and behavior of other people. It is therefore wise to regard any effort at reforming the world with suspicion unless it is accompanied with an equal emphasis on changing oneself as well. Improving our community begins with changing ourselves.

We are not swayed by information so much as by stories; we are storytellers at our core. We all tell stories in our own way. With this in mind, the suggestions below can act as elements of a personal and collective story.

1. Become a Flaneur

This is a quite simple and straightforward effort in one sense. Make a habit of taking a walk, either on a regular planned route or as random exploration of the new. Wander the streets, randomly or in some pattern, and reflectively observing the built environment and the manner in which people interact with it. This is normally done without any effort at seeking meaning; my sense has always been that meaning or insight will appear of its own accord, perhaps not until long after the walk has ended. In one sense this is walking meditation; on the other hand, we are engaged with our surroundings. That is, we're not seeking to empty the mind as in full meditation, but to engage with the environment in a detached manner.

2. Adopt a Place

Is there a place that holds significance for you? This might be a park, a particular street corner, or some other public place. Spend time in it and observe how it is used by others. Care for it and relate to it as you might to another person. Perform small acts of kindness for the place: pick up trash, weed the flower beds, report anything broken or in need of repair, such as sidewalk pavement, bench, or fountain. Simply spend time with it; learn its history and tell its story.

3. Attend Meetings

This can be exhausting, of course, but it is a fundamental act of caring for and being involved with our community. Council and planning commission meetings are open to the public and an excellent way of informing ourselves and participating in democracy. Other smaller or less known organizational meetings need citizen input as well; does your community have a street tree commission or architectural review board? Neighborhood improvement committees are always in need of volunteers. Attendance and input are improved when citizens educate and inform themselves regarding the public good prior to getting involved. Basic public involvement in democracy at this level can be considered an act of spiritual healing.

4. Learn the History

Who built the town or neighborhood you live in, and when? What is the underlying hydrology and geology? How has the culture changed through the years? Was the place used for other purposes? Who were the native peoples who lived and loved this land before the town was built? All these concerns can have an impact on the life you live today.

5. Go Car-Free

This might be difficult for most of us. We find ourselves living in a culture that has been completely designed for automobile use for the past 100 years. Basic activities of daily life can be impossible without a car in most places in America. With that in mind, start small. If one day a week proves too difficult, dedicate one a day a month to start. Are there any rare or occasional errands that can be done on foot or bike? If this sort of thing can become a routine, the quality of your life can improve significantly. The ability to connect with your surroundings directly, rather than through the windshield of a car, gives a more intimate understanding of place.

6. Buy Local

Farm markets are an excellent first step for this. Quite often there are local craftspeople as well as food offerings in such settings. Forego large corporate chains for shopping as often as possible. Although often more expensive, shopping at locally-owned businesses strengthens the local community and builds stronger ties with neighbors.

7. Paint or Draw

Find a favorite place and interpret it for yourself visually, with your own artistic effort. Perhaps there is a local art school which can provide lessons if this is a new endeavor. Capture the mood of the place, and the emotions it evokes in you.

8. Write a Song or Poem

Like the creation of art though painting or sketching, writing poetry can help us connect to place. This need not be complex; the art of haiku keeps poetry intentionally brief yet allows us to capture depth of feeling. What are the stories and history of the place, what is your experience? Share it publicly, hopefully in the space itself.

9. Become a Developer

This sounds overwhelming but really isn't, and without a doubt your community is in need of more thoughtful and visionary small-scale property developers. In one sense, every homeowner is a developer. Is there an abandoned building nearby that has become an eyesore? Someone should do something about that, and that someone may very well be you. Resources are available for training and support, particularly the Incremental Development Alliance.

10. Advocate

Beyond the idea of simply attending public meetings, attend those meetings with the intention of advocating for change. Some ideas are suggested below for communities; advocate for and promote these or others to your community leaders for the adoption of policies and regulations. Educate yourself and become an invaluable expert.

For the Community

Life can be cruel and unfair. The purpose of civilization though is to make our lives a little less cruel, a little more fair. To repeat a theme from an earlier chapter, a community best serves itself when it promotes the awakening of the distinctive story emerging in the life of each person. Generally, when we consider what a community ought to offer its members, we picture support in terms of basic services, social programming and structures, life-skills training and financial aid to the poor, etc. This can be a useful and appropriate response to everyday needs, but more to the point of this book, we can ask ourselves, what of that more personal story of the soul is asking to be written and lived out? This gets us to the realm of our psychological need for an expanding spiritual depth. This is not an area that any local government can or should attempt to address for an extensive list of reasons. What it can do, though, is provide the means for citizens and private development to give expression to a more poetic approach to policy and the built environment. This comes down to a greater focus on the arts and creativity more generally. Below are some possible actions communities can take to improve the experience of the built environment.

1. Update the Zoning Ordinance

Communities all over the nation are constantly updating and rewriting their comprehensive and master plans, zoning and subdivision ordinances, and other guiding documents. Coordination among these various policy documents is rare; they are often at cross-purposes. A grand vision in a comprehensive plan is often impossible to achieve because of the standards required in the accompanying zoning and subdivision ordinances and building codes. The best guidance available for communities to take when considering policies for development is summed up in the Charter for the New Urbanism. Particularly valuable to consider are the concepts of the urban Transect, "pink tape," and the support of small-scale redevelopment rather than large mega-projects.

2. Adopt "Light-Imprint" Infrastructure Standards

Communities all over the nation are facing an onslaught of broken water and sewer pipes, bridges, and roadways. This is a looming national catastrophe. Light Imprint is an environmentally sensitive approach to stormwater and street infrastructure, implemented in a variety of ways based on location across the urban Transect. Too often, efforts at implementing environmentally sensitive infrastructure result in the "suburbanizing" of the city. With its focus on the Transect, the Light Imprint approach allows the city to remain urban and still respond effectively to environmental needs.

3. Promote "Tactical Urbanism" and "Lean Urbanism"

A variety of innovative approaches to community planning have been developed in recent years. "Tactical urbanism" refers to a grassroots movement, now sometimes adopted by local governments, to focus on small-scale, low-cost, and temporary projects as a way of testing and modeling ideas. This includes pop-up shops and cafés, temporary parklets, and pavement painting. In this way, innovative ideas can be tested without great expense or policy changes.

"Lean urbanism" is a policy and procedural approach in which an area is designated for redevelopment with "red tape" reduced. The specific intent is to promote small-scale incremental rather than large-scale corporate projects.

4. Walkability

Such a simple term as "walkability" turns out to have deeper layers than at first glance. A place that is walkable is defined by more than sidewalks and crosswalks. Even a fine-grained pattern of mixed uses won't quite achieve the goal of walkability. Greater care in the pedestrian experience is needed. There must be a variety of everyday activities within a few minutes' walk; this means purposeful walking, not simply a recreational ramble along a pathway. The adjacent building facades must be pleasant and even entertaining to some degree. And of course, a walkable place is comfortably protected from adjacent street traffic. The street and block pattern must emphasize short blocks and frequent intersections.

5. Dark Sky Ordinance

This is a somewhat obscure policy concern, but one easily implemented. The intent is to reduce light pollution so that we can reconnect with the night sky. This is achieved very simply by requiring that lighting be concentrated in a downward orientation. This includes streetlights as well as signage and building lighting.

6. Water as an Opportunity, Not a Problem

Traditionally, stormwater has been viewed as an engineering problem to be solved by getting rid of it as quickly and efficiently as possible. With flooding in the Midwest and sea level rise in coastal areas both on the increase, water is an increasingly pressing concern. It need not be viewed only as a troublesome aspect of city management, however. When respected and celebrated as a good and not only a problem, innovative management opportunities can arise. Water as an amenity is always an enormous draw for people in the form of fountains, ponds, canals or channels, etc. We can manage and deal with the challenges of water even while celebrating our connection to and reliance on it.

7. Celebrate the Arts and Local History

In programs of public art, celebrate those aspects of culture that have always spoken to us, including poetry and poets, myths and stories, especially those of local significance. This can be implemented in so many ways, from sidewalk design, public statuary, or the naming of streets, schools, and festivals, to name just a few examples. Many zoning ordinances require a 1% set-aside requirement for the budgets of large development projects, specifically for public art. This is a fine start but not nearly sufficient. The dollar amount is not so significant as a set of community values that demand more than sufficient engineering.

8. Municipality as Developer

One final consideration might be the most significant, as well as most difficult undertaking. That is, to revert back to a method of development used by our ancestors, those who created so many of our best-loved places – city as land developer. This might include the creation of a development authority which would then designate an area for development, and masterplan it. It would then improve the area with streets and other infrastructure. Subdivided lots would then be sold to the private sector and local residents with an emphasis on individual and small-scale projects, for construction over time.

AFTERWORD

As I strove to finish this book and bring my thoughts to something approaching a conclusion, I found a nagging question kept appearing in front of me, insisting that I pay attention to it. What is the distinction between spirit and soul?

I tend to use the two interchangeably, as I think many of us do today. Yet in the ancient world, they were distinct, so each of us had a tripartite nature: body (ego), soul, and spirit. Soul played the role of intermediary between the physically embodied conscious ego and the ethereal spirit. However, around the 8th century, a change in understanding apparently occurred within the Christian church so that soul and spirit became more interchangeable. As a result, the tripartite division was reduced to spirit and body.

Perhaps we need to consider a return to the old understanding. Thomas Moore, the spiritual writer and psychologist, speaks to the roles of each: "In the best situations it isn't easy to distinguish spirit from soul because both play important roles in everything we do. But making the distinction gives the deep soul its due. Spirit inspires, while soul delves deep into the complexities of an issue. Spirit likes to have a planning meeting; soul likes to have a long and deep conversation. Spirit sets goals; soul plods along, going deep all the way. Spirit prefers detachment, while soul sinks into its attachment to places, people, and home. The two dimensions are both important and valuable. You don't need to balance them because balance is too perfect, a spirit idea in the first place. It's enough to give each what it wants and needs in the moment."

Perhaps we can think of spirit being at the mountain peak, soul in the valleys; we speak of spiritual enlightenment which takes us away from the earth towards the heavens, but soulfulness is in the here and now. Giving respect to each is essential. A quote from the teacher Toko-pa Turner summarizes this well: "The focus on enlightenment rather than embodiment distances us from the messy business of being human. If you're doing it right, presence, rather than detaching you, sensitizes you to your environment. It puts you smack-dab in the discomfort, the disagreeability, the pain, the awkwardness, and the contradiction – this is where you grow more skilled at meeting life where it's at, rather than how you'd prefer it to be. In other words, allowing the full spectrum of events to be included in your experience, rather than mounting resistance to them."

Perhaps this is the distinction between psychotherapy and spiritual practice. We think of spirit as pure, clean, and pristine. But soul will get dirty with you. Soul can be found sitting in a grubby back alley.

Just as we humans have evolved biologically and psychically – and continue to do so – so must evolve our vision of what a city can be. Much of this involves relearning what the past once knew. The spiritual city is the soulful city. The way of growth is not away from the pain of the world but through the dirt. To reach the pure spirit, our path will take us through the impure soul. This begs the question, is the city more a soulful, rather than spiritual, experience?

Humans spent tens of thousands of years in ancient matriarchal structures; we are now in the seemingly final stages of several thousand years of patriarchal systems. What is the next stage of our awakening, of union and balance? Psychically and culturally but also physically, urbanistically – how will we organize ourselves in response to whatever mythology emerges to represent that union? What impact does that have on our built environment? Cities only emerged during and as a result of patriarchal systems, representing the physical embodiment of a patriarchal order of logic and rationality. And yet the form of the earliest cities was never merely practical in nature. The arrangement of gates and walls and the disposition of various civic and religious buildings always reflected a plan based on some cosmological vision that took into account both the masculine and feminine. The city was often understood as a mother, and its inhabitants her children whom she nurtured. The city acted as a symbol of both its society and its organizing myth.

How must our vision of the city change to reflect a unity including the rational and practical and also a more soulful and intuitive matriarchal perspective? To discover this will be a fundamental task of urbanism in the coming times. Perhaps what we are faced with is not so much the reconciliation of opposites, as Jung phrased it, but of respecting and valuing, delighting in, making use of "complementaries." That feels more soulful.

AFTERWORD

"The task of city design involves the vaster task of rebuilding civilization"
— Louis Mumford

ABOUT THE AUTHOR

Will Selman, CNU-A, is a New Urbanist land planning consultant in Washington DC and founder of the Institute for Symbolic Urbanism. A thirty – year member of the Congress for the New Urbanism, he is professionally focused on issues surrounding land development, zoning and comprehensive planning, the design of traditional walkable and sustainable mixed-use neighborhoods, community visioning and charrettes. He has been involved in the design and planning of dozens of new communities, neighborhoods, and villages. As a lifelong spiritual seeker, he has been deeply influenced by the traditions of the Episcopal and Mennonite churches, the world of shamanic healing, and Jungian psychology.

These two major strands of his life, a love of place in general and of urban living in particular, and spiritual adventure, pose the question; How can the experience of urbanism, its design and development, inspire deeper spiritual understanding and psychological growth?

He holds a degree in religion from Eastern Mennonite University, and a Master's degree in Urban and Environmental Planning from the University of Virginia, and is a Knight Fellow in Community Building at the University of Miami. When not wandering the streets of various cities and towns, he can be found on a bicycle, kayak, or sailboat.

FURTHER READING

Urbanism
~ *Charter of the New Urbanism*, Congress for the New Urbanism
~ *Suburban Nation*, Andres Duany et al.
~ *Death and Life of Great American Cities*, Jane Jacobs
~ *The Timeless Way of Building*, Christopher Alexander
~ *A Pattern Language*, Christopher Alexander
~ *The New Civic Art*, Andres Duany et al.
~ *The Concise Townscape*, Gordon Cullen
~ *The Art of Building Cities*, Camillo Sitte
~ *American Vetruvius*, Werner Hegemann and Elbert Peets
~ *Town Planning in Practice*, Raymond Unwin
~ *The Architecture of Community*, Leon Krier
~ *The Language of Towns and Cities*, Dhiru Thadani
~ *The Light Imprint Handbook*, Tom Low
~ *Design With Nature*, Ian McHarg
~ *The Smart Growth Manual*, Andres Duany et al.
~ *Great Streets*, Allan Jacobs
~ *Original Green*, Steve Mouzon
~ *City*, William Whyte
~ *Sprawl Repair Manual*, Galina Tachieva
~ *Till We Have Built Jerusalem*, Phillip Bess
~ *The Culture of Cities*, Louis Mumford
~ *The City in History*, Louis Mumford
~ *Good City Form*, Kevin Lynch
~ *The Image of the City*, Kevin Lynch
~ *The Spiritual City*, Philip Sheldrake
~ *Re-Shaping Metropolitan America*, Art Nelson
~ *Architecture Without Architects*, Bernard Rudofsky
~ *City Life*, Witold Rybczynski
~ *Beauty, Neuroscience, and Architecture*, Don Ruggles
~*Missing Middle Housing*, Dan Parolek

Spirituality, Psychology, & Myth
~ *Care of the Soul*, Thomas Moore
~ *A Religion of One's Own*, Thomas Moore
~ *The Re-enchantment of Everyday Life*, Thomas Moore
~ *A Short History of Myth*, Karen Armstrong
~ *Myths to Live By*, Joseph Campbell
~ *Creative Mythology*, Joseph Campbell
~ *Thou Art That*, Joseph Campbell
~ *Shamanism*, Mercia Eliade
~ *Maps of Meaning*, Jordan Peterson
~ *Man and His Symbols*, C.G. Jung
~ *Memories Dreams Reflections*, C.G. Jung
~ *The Undiscovered Self*, C.G. Jung
~ *Aion*, C.G. Jung
~ *The Red Book*, C.G. Jung
~ *Psychology and Alchemy*, C.G. Jung
~ *The Origins and History of Consciousness*, Erich Neumann
~ *Jung and Politics*, Volodymyr Odajnyk
~ *The Portable Jung*, Joseph Campbell ed.
~ *Integral Life Practice*, Ken Wilber
~ *City and Soul*, James Hillman
~ *How to Walk*, Thích Nhất Hạnh
~ *Tai Chi Journey*, John Lash
~ *Mythology*, Edith Hamilton
~ *Caretakers of the Cosmos*, Gary Lachman
~ *Fate and Destiny*, Michael Meade
~ *The City is a Labyrinth*, Sarah Kate Istra Winter

Systems and Nonfiction
~ *Nonzero*, Robert Wright
~ *Re-Inventing the Sacred*, Stuart Kauffman
~ *Systems Thinking*, Fritjof Capra
~ *Wilderness and the American Mind*, Roderick Nash
~ *1491*, Charles Mann
~ *Proof*, Amir Alexander
~ *The Sacred Geometry of Washington, DC*, Nicholas Mann
~ *Scale*, Geoffrey West
~ *Second Nature*, Michael Pollan
~ *Small is Beautiful*, E.F. Schumacher

ENDNOTES

~ *Hidden Cities*, Moses Gates
~ *Sacred Geometry*, Stephan Skinner
~ *From Bauhaus to Our House*, Tom Wolfe
~ *The Matter With Things*, Iain McGilchrist

Fiction, Poetry, Essays
~ *Faust*, Johann Wolfgang von Goethe
~ *Brothers Karamazov*, Fyodor Dostoyevsky
~ *All the Light We Cannot See*, Anthony Doerr
~ *Letters to a Young Poet*, Rainer Maria Rilke
~ *Teaching a Stone to Talk*, Annie Dillard
~ *New Seeds of Contemplation*, Thomas Merton
~ *The Lives of a Cell*, Lewis Thomas
~ *Invisible Cities*, Italo Calvino
~ *Thus Spake Zarathustra*, Friedrich Nietzsche
~ *The Republic*, Plato
~ *East of Eden*, William Faulkner

www.ingramcontent.com/pod-product-compliance
Lightning Source LLC
Chambersburg PA
CBHW051110230426
43667CB00014B/2518